TAMING
OBLIVION

D1224189

SUNY series in Japan in Transition
Jerry Eades and Takeo Funabiki, editors

TAMING OBLIVION

Aging Bodies and the Fear of Senility in Japan

JOHN W. TRAPHAGAN

State University
of New York
Press

Published by
State University of New York Press, Albany

© 2000 State University of New York

All rights reserved

Production by Susan Geraghty
Marketing by Anne Valentine

Printed in the United States of America

No part of this book may be used or reproduced in any manner whatsoever
without written permission. No part of this book may be stored in a retrieval
system or transmitted in any form or by any means including electronic,
electrostatic, magnetic tape, mechanical, photocopying, recording, or otherwise
without the prior permission in writing of the publisher.

For information, address State University of New York
Press, State University Plaza, Albany, N.Y., 12246

Library of Congress Cataloging-in-Publication Data

Traphagan, John W.
    Taming oblivion : aging bodies and the fear of senility in Japan /
by John W. Traphagan.
        p.   cm. — (SUNY series in Japan in transition)
    Includes bibliographical references and index.
    ISBN 0-7914-4499-6 (alk. paper). — ISBN 0-7914-4500-3 (pbk. :
alk. paper)
    1. Aged—Japan. 2. Aging—Social aspects—Japan. I. Title.
II. Series.
HQ1064.J3T73 2000
305.26′0952—dc21   99-15653
                                                                CIP

10 9 8 7 6 5 4 3 2 1

For Julian,
who has endured several transpacific trips
so that his parents could do fieldwork.

CONTENTS

LIST OF
FIGURES AND TABLES

FIGURES

TABLES

PREFACE

Many people and organizations to one degree or another contributed to the research projects that produced this book. Perhaps the best place to begin offering my appreciation is by thanking the people of Kanegasaki and Mizusawa, who offered freely of their time and thoughts throughout my research. Their kindness, patience, and generosity will always be warmly remembered. I also wish to thank several colleagues who either commented directly on earlier versions of the book or who have been partners in intellectual conversations that influenced its writing. These scholars include: Barbara Anderson, L. Keith Brown, Brenda Robb Jenike, Akiko Hashimoto, Satsuki Kawano, Susan O. Long, James M. Raymo, J. Thomas Rimer, Richard Scaglion, Andrew J. Strathern, Willis Traphagan, and E. Leslie Williams. The many hours discussing anthropology that Keith Brown and I have spent over good coffee in Pittsburgh and in a particularly elegant coffeehouse in Mizusawa, or riding our bicycles along rice fields, are memories I will always cherish.

Several organizations supported different phases of research. I wish to acknowledge the Asian Studies Program and the Japan Council at the University of Pittsburgh for providing funding to support a pilot study when this project was in its earliest stages. I offer my sincere gratitude to the United States Information Agency and the Japan-United States Educational Commission for providing the Fulbright Dissertation Research Scholarship that supported long-term fieldwork in 1995 and 1996. An additional field trip in 1998 was supported by grants from the Wenner–Gren Foundation for Anthropological Research, the Northeast Asia Council of the Association for Asian Studies, and the Michigan Exploratory Center for the Demography of Aging. The generosity of these organizations is greatly appreciated.

The Population Studies Center of the University of Michigan provided a National Institue on Aging Postdoctoral Fellowship that allowed me the time to complete the manuscript and to make the second field trip to Japan in 1998. The collegial atmosphere of the center formed a superb environment in which to think about many aspects of the book. While conducting fieldwork during 1998, I was very fortunate to have the able research assistance of Hiroko Takahashi, who often provided insightful comments on the work. Mari T. Ellis, Publications Core Head at the Population Studies Center, was also extremely helpful in editing the final version of the manuscript. Portions of chapters 5, 6, and 7 appeared in earlier forms in *Ethnology* and the *Journal of Cross-Cultural Gerontology*, and I wish to thank these journals for allowing me to include those segments in this book (see Traphagan 1998a, 1998b, 1998c). The Japan Gateball Union kindly gave permission to use the drawings that appear in figure 6.5.

I want to offer many thanks to my wife, Tomoko Watanabe Traphagan, for her help with difficult passages of Japanese, insightful thoughts, and stimulating conversation as we both conducted our respective fieldwork, and for her never-ending encouragement throughout the writing of this book. Also, thanks go to my parents, Jeanne and Willis Traphagan, who have supported my various academic endeavors over the years. Finally, I must thank my son, Julian, who was born during the fieldwork in 1995 and who has brought us endless joy.

CHAPTER 1

Introduction:
The Road to Oblivion

"At about noon one day last July, I was outside gardening. I heard an ambulance, but didn't think much of it," recounted Mrs. Nakamura. "A little while later, the old woman who lives next door came over and said that the woman a few houses down had died. At first she only told me she had died, but after we talked, it became clear that there was more to it. The daughter-in-law in the house where the deceased woman lived came home for lunch. When she went into the carriage house in back, she found her mother-in-law hanging from the rafters. They called the ambulance right away, but it was too late."

"It seems that it was because her physical condition was weak," remarked Mr. Nakamura, the local temple priest. "I heard this directly from her, that she was having physical problems. This was probably the reason that she did it. The winter prior to her death, she caught a bad cold and was taken to the hospital. She was in the hospital for quite a while with pneumonia. From the time she came home, she had a lot of physical problems. Her demeanor changed quite a bit from the way she was prior to being in the hospital. Also, they did some blood tests and found she was anemic (hinketsu). And she said she was experiencing side-effects from the drugs she was taking, too.

I spoke with her about a week or so before she committed suicide. She came to participate in the weeding around the grounds of the temple that the old women in the hamlet do once a month. At that time, she was talking a lot about how her body was physically bad and that she wasn't feeling well. But I didn't have any inkling that she might be thinking about suicide. There was nothing in particular that suggested to me that this might be coming. Even though she was sick, she could still do things like weeding, so it wasn't that she was incapacitated. But it seems that she was feeling that she had changed a great deal since becoming sick."

Mrs. Nakamura then said, "Well, she wasn't really able to do much work. She wasn't able to do much work around the house and needed a lot of rest. She seemed to often say warui kedo *(it's bad, but) and then avoid doing things around the house or for the temple and hamlet. For example, when I called her on the phone and said that it is raining a bit today so we won't do the weeding, she just accepted it. She didn't have any of the eagerness after she came back from the hospital that she had had before. She didn't want to do things. She wasn't energetic (genki) and seemed like she wanted to rest all of the time. Rather than wanting to participate in the weeding, she seemed to be doing it more because she felt obligated (giri).*

"*Rumors were that at the time of the suicide, she left a letter,*" said Mr. Nakamura. "*I heard that the letter included an explanation that she killed herself because her physical condition had fallen. She was probably wanting to avoid causing a burden (meiwaku) on her family and was thinking that she didn't want to be a problem if she became physically frail or senile (boke). She was probably thinking about her family. Maybe there were other reasons, too. Her son-in-law was a compulsive gambler and deeply in debt. But my guess is the main thing she was thinking to herself was, 'I don't want to be a burden, so it's best if I am not here at all.' She was around sixty-two at the time she hanged herself.*"

THE FAILING BRAIN IN JAPAN AND NORTH AMERICA

Fear about the onset of physical and mental decline in old age, and of becoming a burden to one's family as a result of that decline, is a theme commonly associated with growing old in industrial societies. In North America, the specter of Alzheimer's disease has become one of the primary cultural themes through which people engage and think about decline in old age. Jokes in early old age or in middle age about forgetfulness, in which people say they are getting "oldtimer's disease," index a more general fear that one's final years might be characterized by a loss of mental or physical function that is painful and burdensome. In Japan, too, fear of functional decline and becoming a burden in old age generates lighthearted joking, or in a few cases, the deep melancholy of the woman from a farming community in northern Japan described in the ethnographic vignette above.

There is a small, but growing, literature in anthropology on the cultural construction of senility or dementia (Henderson and Gutierrez-Mayka 1992; Cohen 1995, 1998; Herskovits 1995; Henderson 1997; Traphagan 1998b). Nonetheless, research on the "failing brain," as dementia has been called, is dominated by biomedical discourses that define it as a "clinical syndrome characterised by persistent impairment of multiple cognitive capacities" (Cummings 1995:1481), giving little attention to the cultural dimensions of senility. In North America, dementia is arranged into two broad categories: Alzheimer's disease (AD) and brain disorders causing cognitive deficits associated with other conditions such as Parkinson's disease, vascular disease, or depression (Cummings 1995:1481–82). The emphasis in this schema is on AD and other dementing disorders of old age as being "caused by specific pathological conditions" and, hence, they fit within the rubric of abnormal cognitive function and pathological aging (Khachaturian and Radebaugh 1996:4). As such, dementia is distinguished from characteristic changes in domains of cognition associated with normal aging that affect memory, abstract reasoning and problem solving, complex attentional processes, and visuospatial abilities—changes that are viewed as not caused by specific diseases, producing little disability, and thus are not pathological (Cummings 1995:1481).

In the North American context, unambiguously differentiating normal and pathological aging has been deemed highly important in helping doctors assess conditions and avoid erroneously attributing normal age-related change to underlying pathologies (Beall, Baumhover, Maxwell, and Pieroni 1996). But when considering dementia as a syndrome of brain dysfunction with various causes, it becomes difficult to define the threshold between cognitive impairment and cognitive changes associated with usual aging processes. Furthermore, physiological and psychological factors such as nutrition or educational attainment tend to blur the lines between what is considered normal and abnormal cognitive function (Morris 1996:76).

The biomedical establishment in Japan follows a similar approach to categorizing cognitive impairment and decline in old age. Alzheimer's disease, known as *arutsuhaimā*, (a direct borrowing from English) and *chihō* (dementia) are causally linked to disease and are placed into the general category of *rōjinsei chihō* or dementias of old age (Kikkawa 1995:188). Unlike North America, however, where senility has become increasingly medicalized and associated primarily with AD as a clinically constructed form of pathology (Cohen 1995) among lay people and medical professionals alike, in Japan *boke* exists as an additional category of senility that is usually distinguished from the pathological conditions of AD and *chihō*.

> With *boke*, there is a feeling of ease, a humorous feeling, an impression of softness, but as a medical term it is unsuitable, I think. For example, if you say dementia (*chihō*), without question there is a sense of disease, an abnormal condition exhibited. (Ikeda 1995:26)

Among many older people, there is also a sense that *boke*, unlike dementia, is a condition that at least potentially can be controlled or even prevented by keeping active in old age. Furthermore, although there is an uncertainty about whether or not the *boke* condition can actually be controlled, most see themselves as having an obligation to do whatever they can to prevent, or at least delay, its onset as they grow older.

My concern in this book is with the culturally constituted category of illness known as *boke* (Good 1994:52). I will argue that *boke* is not only a condition of mental and physical decline that affects older people; it is also a moral concept. The moral content of *boke* is tied to an individual's social responsibility to be an active, contributing member of society by taking care of one's physical and mental health, to avoid situations that burden others, and to return the obligations one incurs through relationships of interdependence with others.

Japanese normative values emphasize social utility as a foundation for generating a sense of self-worth and self-identity (Lebra 1976b). There is a basic assumption in most realms of Japanese society that one should be socially directed and engaged in activities that are aimed not just at self-cultivation, but also at cultivation of the social whole, whether it be household, workplace, hamlet, town, or nation. Those activities that improve or enrich individuals are seen as having the corollary effect of improving the community as a larger entity. One means by which people can contribute to the social whole is through maintenance of mental and physical health. Although important for people of all ages, this becomes particularly significant for the older person, whose ability to participate as a social entity is seen as being threatened by the potential onset of the *boke* condition—a condition that is viewed as fundamentally antisocial in nature.

The social importance of maintaining health in old age, as Akiko Hashimoto notes, is indicated in the Japanese Law for the Welfare of the Aged. This law stipulates that older people are to be "loved and respected as those who have for many years contributed toward the development of society," while they themselves "shall be conscious of their mental and physical changes due to aging, and shall always endeavor to maintain their mental and physical health to participate in society" (in Hashimoto 1996:35).

Implicit in the Law for the Welfare of the Aged is a sense of reciprocal responsibilities or obligations among individuals and between the individual and the community. Members of the community have an obligation to reward with respect those who have built up social and symbolic capital by contributing to the social whole over a lifetime. In turn, elderly individuals have a reciprocal obligation to work to adjust to and manage the physical and mental changes that occur with aging and to participate as social entities throughout the later years of their lives—an activity that, itself, is seen as contributing to the social whole.

In fact, what one chooses to do, as will become evident later in the book, is considerably less important than the doing itself. The very fact of being actively involved in something socially oriented—whether it be sports, games, study, child-rearing, work, or any number of other things—is seen as being inherently good and automatically fulfilling one's responsibility to better the social whole.

This should not be taken as suggesting that people's motivations are always aimed toward the communal good. Individuals are autonomous entities who function within a web of interdependencies that are exchanged in reciprocal form (Lebra 1976a:337). Autonomy and the ability of an individual to function as an autonomous entity are important values in Japanese society. The communal benefit gained through the activity of individuals is largely a by-product of the autonomous actions of those individuals. Although in many cases people may be concerned with the greater good, they are equally likely to be motivated by self-interests that correspond to the interests of their community. Clearly, being recognized by others as one who is oriented toward social good in a cultural milieu that values social utility and harmony is a means by which to maximize the acquisition of social capital.

Because a significant portion of an individual's self-identity is constructed on the basis of social utility and engagement in the web of reciprocal obligations, functional decline in old age presents a serious threat to personhood and, thus, is among the most feared potentialities of old age. Indeed, such decline is sufficiently dreaded for people to believe that an older person, like the woman described in the ethnographic vignette that opened this chapter, would commit suicide rather than burden one's family with the care and embarrassment associated with the condition.

Boke, in particular, is viewed as being antithetical to activity and is equated with inactivity. The *boke* person is one who has failed to maintain mental and physical health by keeping him or herself socially active. As such, the condition indexes a loss of a self-identity built upon social values that stress interdependence among autonomous individuals who exhibit concern for the needs of others (Lebra 1976a). Having lost control over these values, the individual becomes inactive, unidirectionally dependent and, in many cases, a burden on others. In other words, the *boke* condition indexes a shift from a more sociocentric sense of self-identity to a more egocentric one, from social behavior to antisocial behavior. This shift represents the disembodiment of normative values that emphasize sociocentric and, thus, moral behavior. With the onset of *boke*, one embarks upon a road to oblivion, in which one is physically alive but socially dead—a liminal being who has lost control over the values that make one a moral person.

Throughout this book, I will use the term "senility" when referring to the complex of Alzheimer's disease, other forms of senile dementia, and *boke* as they are employed in Japanese society. I use "senility" precisely because of the polysemous and often ambiguous nature of dementia as a cultural construct in Japan. Furthermore, following Cohen's definition of senility as the attribution of difference to an old person or old people in general, particularly when this difference is "embodied behavior" and is to some extent stigmatized, this term is particularly appropriate to the Japanese case (Cohen 1998:33).

DISEMBODYING THE EMBODIED

It is necessary to unpack what I mean by "disembodiment" here, because my use of the term is somewhat idiosyncratic as compared to ways it is more generally employed in anthropology. For the most part, anthropological writings related to disembodiment focus on a juxtaposition of corporeal and noncorporeal aspects of a human being. Anthropologists have reported societies in which there exist myths about spirits of humans that are temporarily disembodied (Barth 1975:128) or rituals in which disembodied spirits can seize or possess the body of living persons, temporarily displacing the human selves that inhabit those bodies (Boddy 1989:132; Bourguignon 1973; Bourguignon 1976). Shaw has used the term in reference to a concept among the Samo people in Papua New Guinea in which there are two aspects of human essence. One is embodied in the living and the other a disembodied aspect that dwells in one's ancestral abode—the living contain embodied aspects of human essence and the dead contain disembodied aspects of human essence (Shaw 1990:133–134).[1]

Another way in which this term has been used more recently is as a heuristic device to assist anthropologists in thinking about the abstract nature of social values. This use of the term suggests that there exist abstract social values that are embodied in individuals, but which can also be thought of, at least from a theoretical viewpoint, as having an existence separate, or disembodied, from the bodies of people living in a particular social context (Strathern 1996). This abstract "something else," as Ots calls it, can either be seen as culture or mind, and from a theoretical point of view "takes possession" of or enters into individual bodies as people internalize social values and behaviors of their society (Ots 1994:117).

My use of the term disembodiment is closer to that of this second idea, but important differences exist in my formulation of the concept. I am following the work of Strathern and Ots in the idea that we can view the "something else," what Bourdieu refers to as the cognitive and motivating structures of a society (Bourdieu 1977; Bourdieu 1990), as being drawn and embodied from one's social environment. These are the abstract features of culture—its rules, values, and ideals—that are reified by actors and treated as having an existence independent of individual actors. These abstract values or ordering principles are embodied as people are socialized to follow patterns of behavior consistent with their own cultural milieu.

Where I am taking a somewhat different turn is in the idea that embodied social values can be lost, or disembodied, when people fail or are unable to function within the framework of the cognitive and motivating structures of their society. In a basic sense, the discussion that follows is concerned with the relationship between the breakdown of internalized patterns of behavior and the decline of bodily and mental control among the elderly. These issues of decline, however, are more than loss of control over physical and mental function; they are also loss of control over basic cultural values that are continually being embodied as individuals interact with others.

In this sense, then, I am using the idea of disembodiment in a way that sets it as a counterpart to Bourdieu's notion of embodiment. For Bourdieu, embodiment is the integration of bodily space and cosmic space, physical and abstract social constructs (Bourdieu 1977). People model their physical gestures and ideas after those they observe in proximate others. Through the practice of modeling, the basic ordering principles of a society become imprinted on the body and form a physicalized memory that stores those principles. Individuals improvise on this stored memory; thus, the nature of the principles is constantly changing. But there remains a core framework of embodied values and motivating structures that Bourdieu terms the habitus, and that he defines as the embodied (cognitive) structures that reflect the ordering principles of a society and regulate the range of improvisational behavior or practice available to members of a given context (Bourdieu 1977; Bourdieu 1990).

In short, embodiment is a process of acquisition of the values that operate in a given social context. The emphasis on the body in this idea is, in part, a means by which Bourdieu and others attempt to move away from dualistic mind/body constructions typical of Euroamerican thinking and toward an idea that the acquisition of culture is a process that holistically affects the person. Bourdieu places emphasis on the "durable" nature of the structures that form the habitus as it takes form within the individual, and this is where I wish to take a somewhat different tack from his work. Disembodiment is a loss of control over or an unlearning of the cognitive and motivating structures that regulate the acceptable range of behavior. In this sense, disembodiment can be understood as a disincorporation of the rules that stipulate what is considered normal (and in the case discussed here, moral) behavior.

There is a basic problem with using the term disembodiment in this way. It can be argued that disembodiment, as I am using it, is, in essence, simply another form of embodiment. To an extent this is true. The disembodiment of social values that I discuss in this book does not leave behind an empty shell. People continue to embody certain aspects of their social milieu and, in some cases, may drift in and out of more or less control over cognitive and motivating structures as the *boke* condition fluctuates. My purpose in using the term is to emphasize the sense of loss of control over one set of values that was embodied and has not simply changed, but has been displaced from the affected person. In other words, it is the loss of the ability to function not only as a social, but as a cultural entity.

CULTURE AND AGING

Culture, as David Plath notes, is the legacy of idioms and values that give direction and purpose to living (Plath 1980:8). From birth we begin an ongoing process of embodying the ideals, patterns of behavior, schedules for life-course events, and values that are normative for a given generation and place (Plath 1980:7–8). This is not a process to which we are passive subjects, but is one for which we are authors, readers, and interpreters. That is, we manipulate and control the themes—the values, norms, and behaviors—that characterize what we call culture at a given time and place.

Aging, at first glance, may seem much more a biological than a cultural process. Indeed, there are biomarkers of aging, age-dependent physical changes that have a correlation to chronological age, and that are evident across the human species. As Turner and Weiss point out, these range from visible phenotypic changes such as the development of pubic hair to subtle changes in biochemical processes (Turner and Weiss 1994:77). In humans, phenotypic markers of the senescent body include features such as loss or thinning of hair, decreased visual and auditory acuity, wrinkling of the skin, muscular weakness, varicose veins, and some loss of short-term memory (Turner and Weiss 1994:77).

While biological manifestations of aging are inescapable, these changes are inevitably interpreted and experienced via the legacy of idioms and values, the web of meanings, that form a given cultural context. One of the central ways in which the aging process is interpreted is through the manner in which people segment the life course into phases or periods such as adolescence or senescence. Meyer Fortes points out that chronological age and the stages of maturation over the individual life course are not necessarily coterminous. Age, as a measure of an individual's time on the earth, may be independent of or neutral in relation to both biological changes and the identification of maturational stages in a given culture (Fortes 1984:101). In other words, age is as much a cultural construct as a biological one. The relationship of age to the changing body over time, like that of gender to sex or kinship to genealogy, is informed by the biological. But age cannot be simply reduced to its biological manifestations; nor can the biological be ignored from the ways in which it is culturally constructed.

The manner in which people in Japan culturally define and manage the transition into senescence forms one of the central threads of ethnological interest that runs through this book. Unlike many other parts of the urban industrial world, Japan is unusual because it exhibits sharply delineated periods of the life course and relatively consistent timing of transitional events such as marriage or retirement. Rural areas are particularly interesting because transitions are often organized around formal age-grading practices that structure the timing of passages between periods in the life course in terms of age group membership.

Age-grading practices related to the transition from middle age to old age highlight an important ethnological contrast with other industrial countries. In most of the industrial world, age is typically downplayed or even legally prohibited as a criterion for differentiating or segregating older people on the grounds that it is discriminatory or ageist (e.g., Littlefield 1997; Frerichs and Naegele 1997). In Japan age is a legitimate criterion for differentiating the elderly from other segments of society (Hashimoto 1996:40). A fundamental element defining the elderly as a distinct age group can be found in the idea that old age is a time when people can legitimately expect to depend upon others for social and economic support—particularly their children, who are viewed as having an obligation to provide that support.

Although one might expect that these social patterns would clear a path for uncomplicated passage into elder status, the transition from middle age to old age in Japan is not necessarily a smooth one. Many people contest a public discourse on aging that defines one as *rōjin* (old person) at the age of sixty-five. Older people often state that there is a discontinuity between how they feel about their own age identities and how they are defined by public discourses that determine when one is considered old. Many believe that with the high longevity of Japanese, one's sixties should be considered a part of middle age rather than old age. At a more subtle level, resistance to assuming the identity of old person is linked to social norms that regulate the degree to which older people engage in dependent behavior. This is expressed in the form of a tension between the idea that the elderly are viewed as being able to legitimately depend upon others and social norms that emphasize avoidance of burdening others at any age. This tension limits the ability or willingness of elderly people to engage in the forms of dependent behavior to which they have a legitimate claim.

In the previous paragraph, I used the word "discourse," referring to public discourses in Japan that define one as old at age sixty-five. The term discourse has become quite popular in anthropological writings, but theoretically its application is not without its problems, largely because it has often been vaguely defined, if defined at all, when used in the social sciences. However, I share the views of Baumann, and others, that there is theoretical work for which the term is appropriately employed (Baumann 1996:10; Lutz and Abu-Lughod 1990:7). Toward later portions of the book, I will frequently use the phrase "public discourse," by which I mean conscious and explicit manipulation of ideational themes in order to foster specific ends at the individual and communal levels (Comaroff 1985:4). Public discourses both regulate and form the basis for improvisational behavior (contestation) as people experience and react to changing contexts and symbolic representations of their worlds. The term discourse implies interaction. In relation to the process of aging, the public discourse that stipulates when one is old, when one can be legitimately dependent, and how much is too much dependency, constantly inserts itself into the lived experience of being old in Japan.

As one of the central symbolic expressions of the public discourse on aging, the concept *boke*, rather than corresponding to senility in the sense implied in North America by conditions such as Alzheimer's disease, indexes a state of being characterized by the disembodiment of basic normative values that operate in Japanese society. There is a wide range of group activities for older people that are intended specifically to help them remain active as social entities and, thus, maintain the ability to control embodied social values. These activities, however, are not simply embraced by people, but are contested as people attempt to delay the transition from middle age to old age and the assumption of a changed self-identity. After people have accepted a self-identity as that of *rōjin* or "old person," such activities become instruments of agency as they attempt to control the process of aging and prevent the onset of the *boke* condition.

The fact of contesting entrance into old age is nothing new. Humans do not passively become old, but either resist or accept self-definition and ascriptive status as old on the basis of self-interest (Counts and Counts 1985a; Counts and Counts 1985b). In this book, I emphasize that in relation to aging, as with other aspects of human behavior, people are agents who manipulate and negotiate the social structures that limit the range of practices in which they can participate. They neither passively embody, nor disembody, the social values and ideas that operate in the social contexts in which they live their lives.

AGING IN JAPAN

A great deal of excellent scholarship has been produced that describes and details the nature of Japan's "aging society" by social scientists in recent years (see, for instance, Kaplan et al. 1998; Jenike 1997; Kinoshita and Kiefer 1992). Thus, I will limit myself here to a few of the more salient statistical and thematic points connected to the aging society.

Results of studies published concerning dementia cases in Japan suggest that the incidence of AD and other biomedical forms of dementia will increase more sharply than in any other developed country over the next twenty years (Ineichen 1969:170). The numbers of people experiencing dementia (*chihō*) are expected to climb from approximately 123,000 in 1995 to a high of 308,000 in 2030 (Ikeda 1995:23; Zenkoku shakai fukushi kyōgikai 1995).

The increase is a consequence of broader demographic trends in which the growth rate of the elderly (65+) population in Japan is predicted to rise from approximately 10 percent of the population in 1985 to slightly under 26 percent by the year 2025 (Zenkoku shakai fukushi kyōgikai 1995:34). In absolute numbers this represents an increase from 12.5 million in 1985 to 31.5 million by 2025 (Martin 1989:7).[2] As of 1999, approximately 17 percent of the Japanese population is sixty-five and above. Perhaps more striking than the large number of people over sixty-five is the expectation that, of the elderly population, slightly more than 15 percent of them will be between seventy-five and eighty-four by the year 2025.

In addition to the growth of the elderly population in Japan, living arrangements for the over-sixty-five population have been changing for some time. Government demographic data indicate that the number of elderly living in multigeneration families has been declining, while the number living alone or as a married couple living separately from children has increased. For example, in 1985 26.9 percent of elderly people lived alone or with a spouse, while 50.1 percent were living in three-generation households. By 1996, these figures had shifted to 42.4 percent and 31.8 percent, respectively (Sōmucho 1998:29).

Interpreting the meaning of these data is difficult, however, because many older Japanese live close to their children, live in separate dwellings on the same property, or even in two-generation houses in which the older and younger generations live in completely independent quarters (N. Brown 1998). Furthermore, many older Japanese continue to live in multigeneration families. In the past, some scholars viewed the high level of co-residence as suggesting a higher quality of life in old age for Japanese than for people in many other industrial nations (Palmore 1975). Recent ethnographic and sociological studies have shown, however, that alienation, loneliness, and the loss of basic sources of meaning can and do contribute to the experience of aging in Japan, regardless of one's living situation (Kinoshita and Kiefer 1992; Kurosu 1991).

Bethel, for example, argues that the legend of Obasuteyama (which translates as the mountain for discarding Grandma) has come to operate, for older people living in nursing homes, as a symbol for feelings of missed expectations and unfulfilled life separated from the context of household and family (Bethel 1992). Kinoshita and Keifer's work in the retirement community of Fuji-no-Sato also suggests the presence of a sense of alienation among some elderly Japanese. The retirement community forms a context that lacks two major institutions the authors deem central to Japanese culture—family and workplace—institutions that help Japanese locate themselves formally within society. Without ready access to family and workplace the residents of Fuji-no-Sato adapt by developing a "routinization of social distance" in which close friendships are rare (Kinoshita and Keifer 1992).

While these works have contributed greatly to our understanding of aging and old age among Japanese who have been dislocated from contexts of household and community, they do not directly address issues related to aging and old age for the large number of elderly who continue to live in multiple-generation families. Nor do they address issues for older people living alone or only with their spouse in the same community to which they have belonged throughout their adult (and often entire) lives, and to which, as in many cases in this study, their households have belonged for several generations. In this book, rather than focusing on older people who have experienced a major discontinuity in the process of growing older as the result of being dislocated from familiar social contexts, I will limit my discussion largely to those who have managed to maintain continuity, at least at the level of community membership, throughout much of their adult lives and whose households have long-term historical continuity in the hamlet where fieldwork was conducted.

ORGANIZATION OF THIS BOOK

The remainder of this book is organized into three sections. Chapters 2 and 3 are devoted to an ethnographic description of the community where research was conducted. My purpose in chapter 2 is to draw a general picture of the town where fieldwork was conducted and also to look at demographic patterns in which many younger people out-migrate to cities leaving behind older people. Much of this chapter is concerned with the meaning of "rural" for both those who leave and those who remain behind, how images of rural life relate to migration and generation, and how the fact of out-migration relates to the experience of old age for those who remain. Chapter 3 focuses on the hamlet of Jōnai that was at the center of fieldwork. Again, I look at the demographic composition of the hamlet and discuss the importance of long-term continuity of household and community for those who live there.

These two chapters are intended to present a picture of my fieldwork site that emphasizes the strong communal bonds that exist within the hamlet, while noting that within families there is often a great deal of social and geographical distance between generations. The central point of this section is that while older people enjoy a considerable degree of integration with age peers, they experience alienation from other age groups. Furthermore, although Confucian ideas that emphasize filial piety have historically meant that if a loss of the ability to function autonomously arose in old age, children (primarily the eldest son) were responsible for maintaining the financial and health needs of their parents, economic and demographic changes in Japanese society have made this pattern increasingly impractical, particularly in rural areas. As a result, interdependency for older people living in rural areas has developed a horizontal character in that, due in part to the out-migration of younger people, people must rely heavily on age peers for social support in times of need, rather than on vertically oriented cross-generational interdependencies within families.

Chapters 4 and 5 focus on age structuring related to both terminologies of age and age-grading practices that operate in the hamlet. My concern in these chapters is to examine the manner in which people think about the aging process and, ultimately, how they contest the transition from middle age to old age by resisting entrance into the elder age grade. I argue that the contestation of entrance into elder status is part of a general contestation of the public discourse that ascribes status as elderly to individuals.

Following this, chapters 6 and 7 look at age-appropriate activities for older people by focusing on a game known as gateball, which is popular among the elderly. I examine how people use gateball in their efforts to control or prevent the onset of the *boke* condition. I suggest that the elements associated with old age that are contested as people move from middle to early old age become instruments of agency as they move from early old age to later old age and attempt to prevent the onset of the *boke* condition. Age appropriate group activities like gateball are often associated with negative stereotypes of old age. But these same activities, because they emphasize social interaction, physical coordination, and strategic thinking, become the primary tools used to delay or prevent the *boke* condition.

Chapter 8 contextualizes the behavior described in chapters 6 and 7 by showing how it functions within an institutionalized system, known as the Center for Lifelong Education, which is designed to provide a framework through which people can endeavor to maintain social and symbolic capital and embodied normative values of Japanese culture. To an extent, this institutionalized framework can be analyzed in terms of Foucaultian notions of the body as reified within the field of political interactions, or power relations, that impose a specific order upon the body. But the same institutionalized framework also forms a collective exercising of power through which townspeople willingly engage public, politicized discourses concerning the healthy old body as they attempt to hold on to the social capital they have acquired over a lifetime and continue functioning as viable social entities in the community.

Finally, chapter 9 provides some concluding observations about the position of this study in the ethnographic literature of aging in Japan and its theoretical implications for examining senility as a cultural construct with symbolic meaning rather than simply as a disease. I will argue that the study complements recent work on aging in Japan among institutionalized elderly by showing that, like those who are institutionalized, older people living in contexts where they have well-established matrices of social interaction experience alienation and social distancing. The primary difference is that the alienation they experience is not with age peers, with whom they experience considerable social integration, but with members of younger age groups from which older people are largely segregated. Just as there is no single setting that characterizes Japan, there is no single setting that characterizes the experience of aging in Japanese society. This book adds another view to important ethnographic studies like Kinoshita and Keifer's work in a retirement community, or Hashimoto's work in an urban setting, by providing a picture of life among the elderly in a rural hamlet.

I will argue that as a cultural construct *boke* functions as a means through which people can engage familiar cultural themes that emphasize doing and self-cultivation as being of central import to being human. As a symbol of decline in old age *boke* mediates between cultural norms that stress effort, doing, and contributing to the social whole as central to being a good person, and feelings of resignation to the possibility that decline and entrance into the oblivion of senility may make it impossible to engage those values.

From a more general, theoretical perspective, I will suggest that this book can be useful to the study of aging because it points out the existence of considerable variation in the ways in which senility and dementia are culturally constructed. The North American tendency to medicalize the aging and dying processes should not be taken as a universal expression of human experience. People in other cultures do not view senility in the same way that it is understood in North America, nor do they necessarily place it into the context of a medicalized or disease-driven state.

PART I

Of Old and New

CHAPTER 2

Inaka

GETTING TO KANEGASAKI

A little less than three hours north by bullet train from Tokyo Station lie two cities, small by Japanese standards, of about 35,000 and 60,000 people called Esashi and Mizusawa, respectively. The bullet train station for these cities seems far removed from the hustle of Tokyo. Set between the centers of the two cities, Mizusawa-Esashi Station is flanked on three sides by rice fields and sits against the backdrop of a mountain range separating inland from coastal Iwate Prefecture. The station contains a small museum dedicated to the crafts of the area, such as furniture-making and, most notably, cast-iron ware, for which Mizusawa is known throughout the region. Directly in front of the station stands a huge cast-iron teapot, more than six feet in height, a testament to the local craft. The station has a small shop that sells cast-iron souvenirs such as teapots, paper weights, and wind bells. In the summer at the local railroad station in downtown Mizusawa, hundreds of these bells are hung, endlessly tintinnabulating in the gentle breezes that cross the platform.

About fifteen minutes by taxi to the north is a much smaller town that sits at the intersection of the Isawa and Kitakami Rivers and is known by the name Kanegasaki (see figures 2.1 and 2.2). The indigenous people who once occupied Kanegasaki were called the Ezo. These people were dislocated with the arrival of the Yamato people from the south (ca. 1700 B.P.). The town's name can be traced back as far as 1051 and was associated with a castle that sat at a point where a weir once diverted the flow of water from the Kitakami River for shipping and docking purposes. The early history of the castle and weir is unclear, but around the turn of the fourteenth century, following a period of civil unrest in the local area, Isawa County, in which Kanegasaki is located, was incorporated into the territory of the Date family located in Sendai (Brown 1979:82–83). In 1644, vassals of the Date family, led by the Ōmachi family, moved to Kanegasaki and occupied the castle and built a community of samurai around it. There they established a gate at the border between the Date territory and the Nanbu territory to the north, controlling the trade that moved along the river.

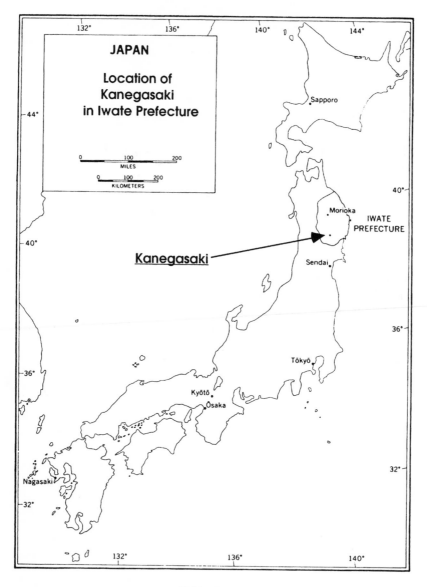

FIGURE 2.1
Location of Kanegasaki in Japan and Iwate Prefecture.

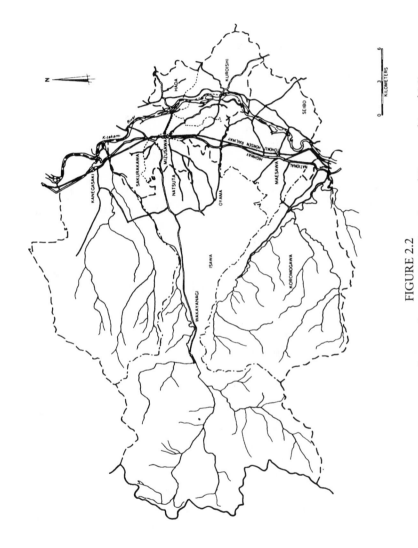

FIGURE 2.2

Isawa County in Iwate Prefecture, showing relative locations of Kanegasaki and Mizusawa.

The Ōmachi family occupied the castle for nine generations until the Meiji Restoration (1868) shortly after which the castle was destroyed. In 1889, the former villages of Nishine and Mikajiri combined to form the village of Kanegasaki, which in 1925 became the town of Kanegasaki. Twenty-nine years later, one year after the Nationwide Town-Village Amalgamation Promotion Act of 1953, the district of Rokuhara to the north separated from Kitakami City and was incorporated into Kanegasaki. Finally, in 1955, the village of Nagaoka to the east was incorporated into the town and the boundaries of the town have remained unchanged since.

Along the way to Kanegasaki, one travels via a bypass segment of National Route 4 (simply known among locals as "the bypass") that avoids the downtown of Mizusawa. Along the bypass are several *pachinko* parlors, with their characteristic flashing neon lights—blazing a multitude of brilliant pinks, greens, blues, and yellows—in which people play a game similar to pinball, with the exception that it is a form of gambling. One can find *pachinko* parlors throughout Japan, as the game is extremely popular, and it is not uncommon for people to spend quite a bit of money at *pachinko*. One informant indicated that he spends around ¥50,000[1] a week on *pachinko* (the amount he loses or wins, of course, varies).

As of 1996, other businesses included a bowling alley (with an attached *pachinko* parlor), Kentucky Fried Chicken, McDonald's, MOS Burger (a Japanese hamburger chain), and several other restaurants. There are two hotels, a hot spring, and a video rental store, which, like most video stores in Japan, is largely devoted to pornographic movies. Numerous car dealers dot the landscape, as well as dealers of farm equipment, a computer store, two large electronics discount stores (that also have personal computers), a supermarket, and four large discount stores that have supplies for home and garden, two of which had gone out of business by 1998. The bypass is always crowded with automobile and truck traffic, so much so that many segments of the pavement have deep ruts worn where the wheels of too many overloaded trucks have trod.

It only takes a few minutes heading north along the bypass before turning off at old Route 4, which runs directly through the center of Kanegasaki, and which was replaced by another bypass about fifteen years ago to take truck traffic out of the center of town. Old Route 4 is very unlike the bypasses that have taken the place of the original road. It is flanked by farmhouses and rice fields. If it were not for the lack of thatched roofs, the ubiquity of aluminum siding, and the pavement, the road would look much like it might have fifty or even one hundred years ago. There are no neon signs, no hotels, and virtually no stores until reaching Kanegasaki.

The road is not without indicators that one is in many ways far removed from the rural Japan of the past. Virtually all of the houses along the way have satellite dishes perched atop their roofs and many have expensive four-wheel-drive vehicles parked in their driveways. Toward the northern end of Mizusawa, just before entering Kanegasaki, there is a new archaeological museum devoted to collecting and displaying the pot shards and other objects that have been dug up in recent years. This is the result of the considerable interest in local history, which has created something of an archaeology boom in the region.

A long bridge over the Isawa River separates Kanegasaki from Mizusawa, and in a sense separates much more; for Mizusawa, even though it has considerable area devoted to agriculture, is a city and carries with it the atmosphere of a city. There are a few French restaurants, numerous bars and karaoke rooms for entertainment, and even a small club devoted to jazz music. The proprietor opens in the evening and plays his large collection of jazz records. At least once-a-month there is live jazz performed by local musicians that sometimes turns into a jam session with other local musicians dropping by to join or to listen. Until recently Mizusawa also had two large department stores in the center of the city, as well as an extensive shopping area (described above) along the bypass. However, one of these department stores closed in the summer of 1998, and several smaller shops have relocated to the bypass area. These changes are in large part a product of the weak economy that Japan has experienced throughout much of the 1990s.

Kanegasaki, in contrast, lacks the amenities associated with city life and seems at first sight to more clearly reflect stereotypical images of rural, agricultural society. The Agricultural Cooperative (JA) dominates a large area of the center of town and farmers' pickup trucks are always in evidence throughout the town. Of the total 179.77 square kilometers, 30.94 is devoted to rice fields, 20.46 is other farmland (particularly dairy farming), 47.82 is mountain and woodlands, 0.95 is marshland, 5.67 is categorized as mixed use, 12.23 open fields, and 5.70 residential.

Nonetheless, even with the prominence of farming, the town is difficult to characterize as purely agricultural in nature. Much as Dore describes in the area surrounding Shinohata, Kanegasaki and its environs exhibit a combination of rural and urban, agricultural and industrial features (Dore 1978). The remaining fifty-two square kilometers of the town's land is classified as "other," which includes a large industrial park with a semiconductor production facility, a pharmaceutical company, and an automobile production plant. These industrial facilities are having an effect on the agricultural character of the town, bringing in new residents who have neither connection to, nor interest in, agriculture. They also provide employment for local young people, thus allowing them to remain in Kanegasaki. Indeed, Kanegasaki is representative of the industrialization of rural areas that can be found throughout Japan and that has been part of an attempt by local governments to stem the exodus of young people in rural areas that accompanied the economic growth that began in the 1950s (Knight 1994a:636).

Regardless of the growing industry in town, Kanegasaki often seems to move at a pace more relaxed and more down-to-earth than that of city Japan. People drop in on neighbors regularly and spend long afternoons chatting over tea and cakes. Farmers normally stop their trucks without pulling over to the side of the road when they head out to work in rice fields. And it is common to see groups of older women sitting at the curbside while chatting, sometimes for hours at a time.

As one moves beyond the bridge, old Route 4 becomes "Main Street" with shops and houses closely packed together for about one kilometer along both sides of the road. Most of the buildings in the center of town are two-story and are covered with white or other light-colored aluminum siding that has become soiled from the exhaust fumes of cars and trucks that pass through, giving the entire area a somewhat shabby appearance. In general, buildings have storefronts at street level and living quarters behind and above the stores for the families that run them. One can see the occasional building with an empty storefront, a shattered window, and old advertising posters that have faded with years of exposure to the sun.

The center of Kanegasaki in many ways looks much as it does in pictures taken during the earlier part of this century. Main Street today is paved and has storm drains, but it is no wider than it was seventy years ago. If one looks carefully, the vestiges of Meiji (1868–1912) and Tiashō era (1912–1926) buildings peek through from under the modern aluminum siding that has covered over their clapboards and wood frames. A few of the old buildings remain virtually unchanged—including the house in which the mayor's mother lives—save the grayed wood and broken latticework that comes with decades of exposure and limited repairs.

Along Main Street there are three bicycle shops, four liquor stores, two electronics and appliance stores, two dry cleaners, two banks, a drug store, a cosmetics store, two clothing stores that primarily have women's clothing, a tailor, a restaurant, a shoe store, and four hairdressers. There are also two private hospitals that cater particularly to the older residents of the center of town who have limited mobility because they do not drive. As one walks around Main Street and the few other streets in town that have businesses, the prevalence of liquor stores and hairdressers is difficult to overlook. At the center of Main Street, two competing hairdressers are separated only by a single building and less than fifty meters down the road there are two more.

Another common store in town is what might best be described as a snack shop or grocerette, although in the United States a grocerette conjures up images of a store considerably larger than the ones described here. These stores usually have a very limited quantity and range of merchandise including chips, candies, drinks, and ice cream. Sometimes they may also have household supplies such as cleaners, shampoo, or even a bag of disposable diapers. In one spot along Main Street, two of these shops sit side-by-side, one of which is also a *sake* store that has been in the family for more than a century. Most of these stores are virtually identical; the following excerpt from fieldnotes gives an example of one such extablishment:

> To enter the store, one goes through a glass sliding door. Inside is not much warmer than the winter cold outside, as there is no heat in the room. The floor is uneven concrete with flecks of paint suggesting that at one time it was painted red. No lights are illuminated, giving the room a very dark appearance. In the center of the room, there are several low tables on which are laid out various merchandise, including chips and candies. Along the wall there are shelves with boxes of laundry soap and a few packages of Pampers, all of which have a thick layer of dust on them. The store is empty, but the sound of a radio playing "*enka*"[2] music is coming from behind a curtain along the back wall of the store. I call out, "*gomen kudasai*," but there is no response.
>
> I call again, but there is still no answer. I move closer to the curtain and can see into the *tatami* mat room in the back. There I notice a pair of feet sticking out from under the *kotatsu* (a low table that has a quilt around the edges and an electric heater attached to the underside of the table top—sometimes a kerosene heater is used sitting in a pit under the table—under which one puts one's legs to keep warm in the winter). I call once more, the feet begin to move, and in a minute or so an old woman, maybe 4.5 feet in height with shoulders hunched over, comes out from behind the drapes. She is wearing several layers of dark clothing, in purples and grays. She smiles, two gold teeth showing in the center of her mouth, and comments on how cold it is today. (Fieldnotes 1/27/96)

Stores like this one usually only have two or three customers a day—more if the few children who live in the area happen to be in school vacation. Invariably, such convenience stores are kept by an elderly man or woman, who spends most of the time in the back room watching the television, listening to the radio, or taking a nap. The proprietor only comes out into the store when necessary, to help a customer, receive a delivery, or if a friend drops by for tea and pickles. Although the lack of customers means only limited supplement to their primary income (from their pension), older shopkeepers like the woman above do not mind because they prefer the slow pace. Many such shopkeepers live in multi-generation families in which at least one younger member works in business or government, bringing in enough money to cover the needs of the household. Thus, the money gleaned from the occasional sale is little more than pocket money for the one who spends his or her days sitting in the back room. In fact, maintenance of such family shops (or rice fields for farm households) is less a matter of income than it is one of maintaining continuity in the household's occupation. Making money often has little relevance to the reasons why such stores are kept operating (see chapter 3).

Along Main Street, large trucks constantly rumble through the center of town, shaking the foundations of the buildings along the street. The force of these trucks is so strong that while chatting in the living room of one informant who lives along Main Street I thought an earthquake had started when, in fact, it was simply a large dump truck. Unlike neighboring Mizusawa, there are no parking meters, no parking garages, no place to put a bicycle or motor scooter, and little room to walk, making shopping difficult, particularly in the winter months when the streets are ice covered. As a result, the parking lot for the bank in the center of town is frequently used by those with other business on Main Street, who ignore signs instructing people not to park there unless they have business in the bank.

A few meters beyond the bank heading north, one finds a large, wide road off to the left that was built, after razing several buildings, during my fieldwork. This road sports iron benches, an international public telephone, and wide granite sidewalks. It was constructed shortly after the opening of the new town hall, to which the new road leads. The town hall is an impressive structure. It replaced an aged and decrepit building that has since been torn down. The building is lavishly appointed inside and dwarfs surrounding construction with its 46-meter tall bell tower (with carillon that plays the Camptown Races every day at noon) that displays the town symbol on all four sides. On the three days that the building was opened to the public before the government workers moved in, about three thousand residents visited it, most commenting favorably upon the grand scale and fine appointments such as dark, wood paneling in many offices.

A hundred meters or so beyond the road to the town hall, Main Street becomes largely residential. There are a few shops in the fronts of people's houses, but they thin out rather quickly. A few more meters brings one to a gas station, beyond which are rice fields. Although most merchants are located along Main Street, the road to the railroad station also has several stores. Dominated by the Agricultural Cooperative, the road's 200 meter length also has a few more hairdressers and the only grocery store in the center of town. Until 1996, there had been another, larger grocery store, but it closed for lack of business. In the area between the town hall and the station, a distance of perhaps three hundred meters, there is another road along which there are a few karaoke bars and a couple of restaurants and, of course, more hairdressers and liquor stores.

As one walks along Main Street or any of the other roads that feed into it, the preponderance of older faces and seeming lack of young adults and children is immediately noticeable—a fact many in town frequently comment on. Men and women who look as though they are from their early sixties to late eighties walk or ride bicycles or motor scooters from one place to another taking care of daily errands. Some wait at bus stops to travel to neighboring cities to shop or to visit hospitals. Some walk along the street carrying a gateball mallet in a pouch slung over their shoulder (gateball is a game that will be discussed later in the book), or they stand outside shops visiting with neighbors. One of the most striking sights of Main Street is the large number of old women, usually in their seventies or above, bent over at a ninety-degree angle at the waist and struggling to hold their heads up so that they can see where they are going. Other older women who are able to stand upright have difficulties walking due to severe bow-leggedness. Local wisdom attributes such conditions to the hard work involved with farming (bending over for hours while tending rice fields or weeding gardens) and to the harsh conditions many experienced after the end of the Pacific War. Local doctors attribute this to arthritis and osteoporosis, caused by nutritional deficiencies that occurred after the war, and back-breaking farm labor.

Sometimes old women push four-wheeled strollers that are quite popular in Japan and are designed specifically for old people who have trouble getting around, although men rarely use them. They have a compartment in which one can put needed supplies or goods bought at the store, and the lid of the compartment serves as a seat on which one can rest.

THE MEANINGS OF "RURAL"

Kanegasaki is a place that for many has not kept pace with modernity. People in neighboring cities sometimes comment that Kanegasaki seems to be in a world of its own, suggesting that the patterns of behavior and even the dialect used there are somewhat different (old and antiquated) than that of, say, Mizusawa or Kitakami. Indeed, to walk along Main Street does give one the feeling of having stepped back in time, and to be seeing a way of life that is beginning to change as a result of factors such as the constant opening of supermarkets and discount chain stores in neighboring cities, which are draining business away from local merchants. But such images are not the only indication of a place that has been in one way or another left behind.

Demographic changes have created a situation in which the prewar and postwar age cohorts in Japan are to an extent geographically divided, with higher percentages of older people living in less urban environments. This is true both across prefectures and within prefectures. In 1990, the percentage of population over the age of sixty-five (hereafter referred to as the elderly population, as it is referred to in Japan) in Iwate Prefecture was 14.52 percent and 15.61 percent in Akita Prefecture. These proportions of elderly are expected to rise to 26.01 and 28.51 percent respectively by the year 2010. This compares with largely urban prefectures such as Chiba, which had an elderly population of 9 percent in 1990 rising to 18.07 percent in 2010, and Tokyo with 10.49 percent in 1990 rising to 21.39 percent in 2010. In 1990, there were some rural prefectures in parts of Japan, which had already passed the 20 percent point in terms of their elderly population, a level that is not expected nationally until around the year 2010 (Zenkoku shakai fukushi kyōgikai 1995:40).

Within prefectures this type of population distribution is evident as well. In Iwate Prefecture, the elderly accounted for 17.8 percent of the population as of 1994. However, the capital city of Morioka's elderly population was 12.3 percent, as compared to outlying villages, towns and cities such as Kanegasaki (18.2 percent) or Esashi (22.5 percent). The largest elderly populations can be found in mountain areas, the highest being a mountain village (Kawai-mura) with a rate of 26.5 percent. Of the sixty-eight cities, towns, and villages that make up Iwate Prefecture, as of 1994 thirty-four had populations of which more than 20 percent were over the age of sixty-five (Iwate Prefecture 1995:106).

The point that these data bring out is that less urbanized areas often have proportionally larger populations of elderly than cities. The reason for this segregation of population is the tendency of younger people to out-migrate from areas associated with ruralness in search of jobs and education.

Japan has a long history of intra- and interprefectural migratory behavior. The most obvious example of this is the *sankin kōtai* system of alternating residence for samurai and their families between Edo (present-day Tokyo) during the Tokugawa period (1600–1867) and their home domains. Movement was not limited to the upper classes, however, although migration was restricted through government policies that made moving, particularly for families, difficult. In the village case studies they present, Hanley and Yamamura found that family migration did not play a significant role in population growth of the specific localities they studied. However, temporary migration of individuals, usually to work in a neighboring village or a major town or city on an annual contract basis, was important in migration patterns (Hanley and Yamamura 1977:254). Temporary migration among unmarried men and women to work in neighboring areas as apprentices was common for people from ages 15 to 30, and household heads also would temporarily move to areas outside of their home villages for economic reasons—a practice known as *dekasegi* (Hanley and Yamamura 1977:254–255). By the eighteenth century, migration out of farming villages in Okayama Prefecture, for example, appears to have been so heavy that domain authorities adopted restrictive measures designed to stem the exodus of population from agricultural areas (Hanley and Yamamura 1977:255). Illegal migration that went unrecorded was common and, thus, makes determination of actual migration patterns difficult for the Tokugawa period.

During the Meiji period, high fertility rates and the patrilineal kinship structure created a situation in which rural out-migration to cities grew as economic opportunities increased with the industrial expansion of the cities (Fukurai 1991:31). Following the Pacific War, legal and political changes, which reduced the power of landlords, further accelerated the movement by freeing tenants who had been tied to the land by debt, thus, increasing the migratory exodus from rural to urban areas (Fukurai 1991:41). The economic expansion of the 1950s and 1960s fueled this migratory pattern. Until the 1970s, rural-to-urban migration, with Tokyo as the centrifugal force pulling people in, was the norm.

In the 1970s there developed the so-called J-turn pattern in which people began moving out of urban centers to the suburbs as economic growth occured in these areas (Fukurai 1991:41). The further development of industrial areas, in part supported by government subsidies aimed at encouraging rural industry (Knight 1994b), created opportunities for companies to locate facilities considerably more removed from the cities. Today, the direction of interprefectural migration is no longer characterized as primarily from rural to urban (Fukurai 1991). Instead, as Fukurai points out, it has become increasingly reciprocal, with people moving between prefectures that are normally considered to be in rural areas (such as Iwate in the Tōhoku region). This is particularly true of unskilled laborers who migrate in search of stable employment (Fukurai 1991:42).

This historical shift in migration patterns is evident in Kanegasaki (see table 2.1). Throughout the 1960s and 1970s, the pattern of migration was such that out-migrants far outnumbered in-migrants. Indeed, the net migration for the years 1960–1970, for example, showed a loss of 3,968 people. By the mid-1970s, this had changed significantly. If we

TABLE 2.1
Out-migration, In-migration, and Net Migration for Kanegasaki, 1955–1995
(Data from Kanegasaki Town Government)

Year	In-migration	Out-migration	Net Gain/Loss
1960	414	792	−378
1961	436	781	−345
1962	466	993	−527
1963	521	912	−391
1964	513	1,022	−509
1965	518	767	−249
1966	639	766	−127
1967	551	821	−270
1968	542	969	−427
1969	643	863	−220
1970	593	869	−276
1971	666	951	−285
1972	632	800	−168
1973	579	910	−331
1974	620	660	−40
1975	678	739	−61
1976	683	654	29
1977	606	706	−100
1978	653	599	54
1979	617	657	−40
1980	679	692	−13
1981	833	746	87
1982	937	870	67
1983	1,030	830	200
1984	1,134	908	226
1985	1,048	904	144
1986	692	938	−246
1987	569	791	−222
1988	712	761	−49
1989	536	698	−162
1990	826	704	122
1991	691	647	44
1992	774	717	57
1993	1,054	742	312
1994	640	676	−36
Totals	23,725	27,855	−4,130

take the years 1975 through 1985 (inclusive), we see that there was a modest net gain in population as a result of in-migration of 593 people. Nonetheless, while in-migration increased considerably beginning in the early 1980s, out-migration has remained fairly constant throughout. From 1960 through 1970 the average annual number of out-migrants was 869 and from 1975 through 1985 it was 755.

In Japan, prefectures with the greatest per capita net loss of population are all located in the northern and southern peripheral areas (Aomori, Iwate, Nagasaki, and Okinawa). Migration tends to be highly selective with respect to age; interprefectural migration is most profound among the 15–19 age group throughout Japan (Liaw 1992:327–331). Peripheral areas such as Iwate are particularly prone to exhibit population loss of younger people who travel to regional growth poles such as Sendai, a city of about one million in the Tōhoku region, or Tokyo in search of education and better employment opportunities.

Kanegasaki follows the pattern in which many out-migrants are younger people, although through examination of the town's population register it appears to be delayed until the period from ages 20–25. Figure 2.3 shows the population pyramid of Kanegasaki at the time of fieldwork in 1995. Immediately evident is the marked drop in population between the ages of about 20 and 35. This is probably somewhat misleading because many people actually out-migrate at the age of 18 or 19 upon graduation from high school, but remain listed on their parents' *koseki* (family register), creating their own *koseki* only after they begin working. In any case, it is clear that the younger age group tends to leave Kanegasaki after high school and usually does not return until later in life, if at all. Men who are the eldest son, in particular, will sometimes return after retirement to succeed to the household headship and ensure the continuity of the family enterprise. In-migration among the 20–25 age group also exists, but this is due largely to individuals coming to work in the industrial areas. These people live in the company dormitories and move elsewhere after a few years.

Those who do not return are unlikely to bring their parents to live with them in the cities. Moreover, for reasons to be discussed later, even in cases where a child wishes for a parent or parents to co-reside in the city, his or her parents generally do not wish to move. The result is a population of older people who are literally left behind.

WHY DO YOUNG PEOPLE LEAVE?

At the time of fieldwork, the town of Kanegasaki had a population of approximately 16,000 people living in 4,800 households. Although pop-

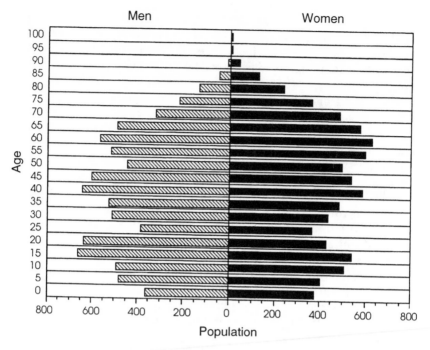

FIGURE 2.3
Kanegasaki Population Pyramid at the time of fieldwork in June of 1995.

ulation density is comparatively low—approximately 89 people per square kilometer, which by Japanese standards makes it rather sparsely populated—Kanegasaki can be characterized by many of the elements normally associated with urban-industrial societies. There is heavy commitment to machinery, high levels of mobility (particularly among the young), growing dependency upon larger governmental institutions and bureaucracy, and increasing numbers of transient residents both from other parts of Japan and from other countries (Anderson 1962; Gmelch and Zenner 1988:3). In 1995, there were more than 150 foreigners living in Kanegasaki, most of whom were transient construction workers from China. Dependence upon large governmental and nongovernmental institutions is particularly evident in the reliance of many part-time and full-time farmers upon multipurpose agricultural cooperatives that operate plural businesses for credit, marketing, purchasing, insurance, machinery banks, grain elevators, and processing (Higuchi and Kawamura 1987:109). Agricultural cooperatives are particularly important in marketing farmers' products, the proceeds from which are directly deposited to farmers' bank accounts with the cooperatives (Higuchi and

Kawamura 1987:107). While full-time farming households exist (primarily among dairy farmers), for most households in Kanegasaki, farming is done only on a part-time basis. Normally, older members of the household carry out farming responsibilities while younger members work in stores or companies either in town or in neighboring cities—a pattern that is common in Japan (Jussaume 1991). This dependence is also evident in the increasing importance of governmental institutions in the provision of health care for older members of the community.

While Kanegasaki displays many characteristics associated with urban-industrial societies, most townspeople perceive of Kanegasaki as rural countryside or *inaka*, an image associated with Iwate Prefecture as a whole by many Japanese. The meaning of this image is complex and tends to vary in relation to age and one's place of residence. For urbanites, *inaka* is often tied to nostalgic imagery of community and belongingness within the context of rural areas exemplified by fishing villages and rice-farming hamlets in which cooperative, subsistence-based work efforts tied people together (Creighton 1997:242). These nostalgic images are associated with another concept, *furusato*, which Creighton appropriately translates as "home village" (because it conjures up pictures of rural life), but can also be understood as hometown more generally. To Japanese, *furusato* evokes images of childhood and peacefulness (Creighton also suggests that motherly love is involved), and rural landscapes regardless of where one actually grew up (Creighton 1997:242). Within these images are notions of a good life and wholesomeness that is connected to stereotyped ideals about Japanese moral values—a point to which I will return shortly.

Inaka can be applied to a region, such as the Tōhoku region, as a whole when compared to, for instance, Tokyo. In such instances, the meaning includes not only agricultural or wooded areas but large cities such as Sendai. It can also be used when referring to a smaller area such as Kanegasaki when compared to a neighboring city like Mizusawa. In fact, people living in the downtown area of Kanegasaki will refer to the farming and mountain areas in town as *inaka*, suggesting that those areas are more *inaka* or rural than their own area. The term also can be used in reference to individuals who may sometimes refer to themselves or others as *inakamono* (*inaka* person). The meaning suggests someone who lacks the sophistication of the city and can be used with a note of pride, embarrassment, humor, or even derision depending upon the person or context in which a particular individual is speaking. But in most cases there is a nuance in the meaning of the word that suggests whether person or place, that which is *inaka* is in some way backward.

This meaning is particularly strong for younger people, for whom the term often carries negative connotations, and the *inaka* image of

Kanegasaki is a significant motivating factor in decisions to leave. Upon graduating high school, younger people are often attracted by the allure of the city, particularly Tokyo, in part to get away from a rural environment many view as backward and boring and in part to gain a college education and find a good job.

In contrast to the image many young people hold of *inaka*, older residents of Kanegasaki, generally those over fifty, typically view *inaka* in a positive light. It is common to hear older residents speak in negative terms about cities, particularly Tokyo, indicating that the pace of life is too stressful, the people are unfriendly or cold (*tsumetai*), and the dangers ubiquitous. This is set in opposition to *inaka*, where life is slower-paced, people are friendly or easy to get along with (*yasashii*), and the streets are safe. Indeed, with incidents in the early 1990s such as the gassing in the Tokyo subway system, comparisons drawing a distinction between the dangerous city and safe *inaka* are both frequent and intense.

In short, a moral discourse underlies local conceptualizations about large cities among young and old alike. But where younger residents often place large cities in a positive light as environments filled with opportunity and excitement, older residents often associate them with danger and ultimately with a way of life that is, if not evil, at least not good. At times, this moral discourse, which pits not only urban against rural, but industrial against agricultural society, is raised to the level of national concern. For example, in an article in the Kahoku Shimpo, the regional newspaper published in Sendai, a seventy-five-year-old man wrote that young farmwomen see farm life as unpleasant and, therefore, want to marry a salaryman (a corporate worker) and live away from the farm. He states that this is a situation that undermines Japanese society because "farming is the foundation of the [Japanese] nation" (Shinohara 1995). The resulting shortage of farmwives in rural areas creates a need to import women from foreign countries to marry farm husbands. To solve this problem, and to preserve Japanese farming (i.e. traditional Japanese values) into the twenty-first century, the author implores farm families to "please teach your daughters from birth to become farm-wives" (Shinohara 1995). The moral discourse operating within this article sets up contrasts between the agricultural and the industrial, *inaka* and urban, older generations and younger generations, and links the agricultural life to "true" Japanese culture and values—specifically, to stereotyped notions about social ties within the Japanese household or *ie*.

This moral discourse is tightly linked to perceptions about the collapse of the traditional *ie* family structure, in which the eldest son or *chōnan*,[3] his spouse, and children co-reside with his parents. Eventually the eldest son takes control of the family business or farm and at the same time succeeds to the headship of the household (Brown 1966; Brown 1968; Dore 1978; Jussaume 1991). In rural parts of Japan, successors often leave home for several years after high school with the expectation that they will eventually return to take over the headship of the family and business or farm.

In some cases, this may involve an exchange between generations. As one eldest son, Nakano-san, in his thirties at the time of our interview, indicated:

> When I was in high school, I wanted very much to go to the city for a college education. My grandfather told me that he would pay for my living and education in Tokyo. But this came with the condition that I attend school to learn to make eye glasses and eventually return to work in the family eye glasses store in Mizusawa.

Nakano-san told me that he had delayed his return to "*inaka*" as long as possible, "because this area is unfashionable and, thus, not an interesting place to sell eyewear. I want to live in a place with young people around, where I can make more money and enjoy the customers." Nakano eventually succumbed to pressures from his parents and grandparents, and to feelings of guilt about not having repaid his debt. However, during his time in Tokyo he had married and had a son. His wife refused to co-reside with his parents, thus a further negotiation occurred in which land held by the family was used to build a separate dwelling so that the Nakanos could live neolocally, on the other side of town from his parents.

Attitudes about the collapse or weakening of the traditional descent ideology is particularly strong among farm families, where people often link the idea of the *ie* to the land itself. In a conversation with an older couple (both in their mid-seventies) whose sons are living in Tokyo, the husband stated:

> Particularly for people who have been doing farming all their lives, there is a strong feeling about the land, even though their current life is quite different from the past. There are more people moving away from agriculture, they no longer farm or live in the way they did in the past. But still, around here, people have an attachment to the land. People who have land that has been passed down from generation to generation have a strong sense of connection to the *ie* in their consciousness. Old people still have a sense that they have their land and their own *ie* of which they are a part because they grew up here, but young people nowadays are encouraged to go out to study and become more educated than their parents. So they know the other world, too. Thus, they are not necessarily attached to their hometown and to their family land. So the concept of the *ie* and its connection to the land is very thin

with young people. When today's elderly were children, *chōnan* were told by their parents that they will be succeeding to the family head-ship—their life was predetermined by their parents. But when they became parents they encouraged their children to do whatever they wanted to do, so as a result people do not come home [from the cities].

The prevalence of this moral discourse is such that when asking why I decided to conduct research and live in Kanegasaki, people often sug-gested it must be because I was interested in studying "true" Japanese culture as it is found in *inaka*, as opposed to the cities, which are less representative of "true" Japanese values and lifestyles. This is quite sim-ilar to Clark's experiences of being told that he had to leave Tokyo in order to find the true Japan (Clark 1994:69).

It is important to note that while there is a distinction between the ways in which many younger and older people view the idea of *inaka*, generalization is difficult. I have encountered several younger to middle-aged (mid-thirties and early forties) residents of Kanegasaki who have very negative images of Tokyo and positive images of *inaka*. Many of these individuals have no desire to live in Tokyo, although they may be willing to move to neighboring cities. In some cases, younger people who returned to live in Kanegasaki after time away did so because they disliked life in Tokyo. One woman, Imada-san, who runs her own busi-ness ordering fashion clothing from designers in Tokyo and brings them back to Iwate, stated the following about her return to Kanegasaki:

I went to Tokyo to school at the strong urging of my father [who is a retired school teacher], who wanted me to become a nurse. I didn't really want to go, but I found that I liked Tokyo and wanted to stay there. After a few years of working, I developed a problem with my kidneys that required surgery. As a result, I returned to Kanegasaki in order to recuperate. I found that I liked the slower pace, the greenery, and the fresh air and now I have no desire at all to return to live in Tokyo, although I do enjoy visiting regularly in connection with my work. Kanegasaki is really well located, right along the bullet train line and the highway and close to two cities. I really like living here now.

Few older people have any desire to live in Tokyo or other cities. Most are content with their lives in *inaka* and frequently comment on the greenery, clean air, and open spaces they enjoy. Throughout all interviews with older informants, only one ever stated that she would like to move to Tokyo. Although she grew up in Kanegasaki, she did not live there for most of her adult life because she moved around as her husband was transferred to different branch offices of the bank for which he worked. She stated that she finds the town boring and that she has little to talk about with her neighbors because they are only interested in talking about gardening and farming, topics about which she knows nothing and has no interest.

Although there is a clear gap in the image of life in Kanegasaki between younger and older residents, migration of younger residents to cities is not necessarily discouraged by older residents. As Cardona and Simmons note, writing about Latin America, the very fact that it is the young who most frequently migrate in many cultural settings is linked to parents' perceptions that their children may find greater opportunity in the cities (Cardona and Simmons 1975:25). This holds for Kanegasaki, as well. Several older informants have told me that they encouraged their children to follow their own paths in life and to move to Tokyo or other cities if necessary for education and work, as was the experience of Imada-san discussed above.

Some who leave eventually return to take over the household headship or to care for elderly parents. However, for those who grew up in Kanegasaki and leave to pursue careers in the city, even if they wish to return it becomes very difficult for them to do so without considerable sacrifice in terms of job satisfaction, income, and access to desired resources such as famous schools, fashionable stores, or entertainment. Several retired couples whom I have interviewed concerning the likelihood that any of their children will return to take over the household and care for them if they become frail in old age have indicated that although they would like their eldest sons (in particular) to return, it is highly unlikely. Most comment similarly to what one man told me while lamenting the fact that neither of his own sons, both of whom are scientists working for companies in Tokyo, will ever return:

> My children are involved with science, and the only work for them is in the area where they are living. If they return home, there will be no work for them. If you graduated from a literature department at a university, you can sometimes find work in Kanegasaki at places such as the town hall, but not if you are working in scientific fields.

Younger people who do return may not do so willingly and are not necessarily happy with their lives in Kanegasaki. For example, Chiba-san, who is thirty-five years old and who moved to Tokyo after attending high school in Kanegasaki to attend a college specialized in training stenographers, recently moved back into his parents' house (now in a neighboring town) having, he said, endured ten years of telephone calls by his parents requesting him to return home, phone calls that over the final five years he described as a weekly event. At the time of his thirtieth birthday, he told me, he began to feel increasingly guilty about not carrying out his responsibilities as the eldest (and only) son and finally returned, giving up his stenography career because there was no work of that sort in or near Kanegasaki. Upon returning to Kanegasaki, due to his age, he had a very difficult time finding work and after several months of job hunting, he finally took a government job as a clerk in a neighboring city. The job paid less than one third of what he was earning in Tokyo and was totally unrelated to his career goals—it was simply the best job he could find in the Kanegasaki area. Many would describe his return as an act of *on* (gratitude) and *oya-kōkō* (filial piety) toward his parents, ideas that carry positive connotations indicating that one's responsibilities toward one's parents have been carried out with genuine gratitude for having been raised by them. Chiba-san, however, sees his return as being the result of *giri*, a term that implies a responsibility that must be carried out, but not necessarily willingly and without any underlying sense of gratitude. In fact, he describes himself as unhappy in his work and bored with his life in "*inaka*," and states rather directly that if his parents were to die tomorrow, he would return to Tokyo as quickly as possible. Two years after our initial formal interview, when I asked him again if he wanted to return, he quickly stated that if he had the chance, he would return to Tokyo as quickly as possible.

Furuhata-san, a twenty-five-year-old woman who had been married for about two years at the time of our conversation and who was originally from a town neighboring Kanegasaki described the situation of her return to the area as follows:

> I met my husband through *omiai* (arranged marriage) in Tokyo. The first year was great and he was easy to get along with. But after a while, he decided to return to Kanegasaki because he is the eldest son. He just said, "I'm the eldest son, so I will return." I was very angry about this because he had not told me anything about returning home prior to our marriage. He had never indicated that he wanted to return. I was working in a good job in Tokyo as an announcer for a radio station and had to give that up with the marriage. He told me that he didn't want me to work after we were married, so I quit. I really prefer to live in Tokyo, but the decision was made without my consent, so I had no choice in the matter and decided to go along. Now I don't know if I can continue in this lifestyle for the remainder of my life.
>
> Japanese men have not changed much. They are the same as they were in the Edo period [1600–1867]. Particularly the eldest son sees himself as *erai* (high status) and as the head of the household who can order around the other members of the household. Men are stubborn and pigheaded and forceful in having things the way they want them. I was handling the money in the family until he said that he wanted to do it. So I let him take over and we started to come up short each month. Rather than letting me work to make up the difference, his solution to the problem was simply to ask for money from his parents.

I don't like living with my in-laws. But when I talked to my parents about this, they told me that I was being selfish (*wagamama*) and that I should just persevere through it (*gaman suru*).

When I spoke with her, Furuhata-san had been living in Kanegasaki for about a year and she was so upset with her situation that she had returned to her natal home in a neighboring city. She was seriously contemplating divorce and a return to Tokyo, where she thought she could reenter the broadcasting industry without difficulty.

Of course, in both examples, there are other issues and themes underlying their unhappiness with returning to Kanegasaki beyond a desire to live in the city as opposed to *inaka*. Both informants returned as the result of pressure from family and would have likely stayed in Tokyo without that pressure. Furthermore, their unhappiness is not connected simply to feelings of boredom, but is connected to a loss of independence and a sense of isolation from friends and a lifestyle that they find attractive. The most common problem younger people cite about living in *inaka* is their lack of privacy. Chiba-san stated:

The style of life is different here [in *inaka*], the way of thinking is different. From 20 to 30 is the most fun time of life. You have your own money and you can live your own lifestyle and do what you want. But when you hit thirty around here, if you live this type of lifestyle you will get comments from others. But in Tokyo this is not a problem. When I came back here, returning to the old style of life (*mukashi no seikatsu*) was very difficult. Relatives and neighbors are constantly bothering you about getting married.

The culture in Tokyo and here is really quite different. The living environment is really quite different. In particular, it is really a problem for people living alone [here]. If you don't have your parents bugging you all of the time, you can really live a free life in Tokyo. It's an incredibly fun way to live, in Tokyo. You have lots and lots of freedom to do what you want.

There are two key points about these examples. First, for some who return, the return is associated with self-sacrifice and frustrated ambitions and is not motivated out of a desire to live in Kanegasaki—the pull of city life remains strong for these people. Second, the ability of older generations to exercise power over their children (and their children's families) can be quite strong—particularly in the case of eldest or only sons who feel at least a responsibility and often a desire to return to their natal home. In Furuhata-san's case, she implies that her husband returned out of a desire to live in an environment where he is indulged and she indicated that upon returning to her in-laws' household, he "began to behave like their child" rather than like a husband. A dependent parent-child relationship formed or was reestablished upon his return to his natal home and this relationship is not what she considers good for her marriage. Her imagery drawn from feudal Japan suggests that her husband's domineering approach to their return is not the kind of spousal relationship she associates with a good marriage; the return to *inaka* was, for Furuhata-san, a return to patterns of family interactions that she associates with an obsolete Japan of the past.

TRADITION AND MODERNITY

These pictures of Iwate as backward are not the only images associated with the prefecture. Iwate, and other places viewed as rural, often produce wistful, nostalgic contemplation of a simpler, more traditional life and a place remote from stresses and dangers of modernity. In fact, it is not unusual to see television shows reporting on businessmen who quit their jobs to head for the countryside to grow strawberries or to do some other type of farming in order to get away from the stresses of urban anomie and industrial society.

But whether positive or negative, for young and old alike the meaning of *inaka* is connected to a juxtaposition of tradition and modernity. The content of how people interpret that juxtaposition varies in relation to age and the degree to which people invest socially in the community in which they live, but Kanegasaki is for both young and old a rural place with values and ideals different from those of urban, modern Japan. As Keith Brown points out, nationally Iwate Prefecture is often portrayed in the Japanese media as a remnant from Japan's past—the "Tibet of Japan," a rather negative term that connotes the prefecture's physical and social distance from the mainstream of Japanese political, economic, and cultural life (Brown 1979).

In much the same way that the prefecture is seen as a holdover from Japan's past, the old people who live there are themselves often viewed as members of a generation out-of-synch with modernity. This perception is not limited to those outside of the older generations; older individuals themselves often comment on feeling out-of-step with modern Japan. As one seventy-nine-year-old retired teacher commented about feeling removed from mainstream Japanese life,

> I enjoy reading the newspaper to keep up on national and world events. But nowadays, the newspaper is filled with words brought in from English and other languages and I usually don't know what these words mean. If I want to read the newspaper in detail, I have to keep a dictionary beside me so that I can look up the words I don't know.

BEING OLD IN KANEGASAKI

The end of the Pacific War is often viewed as a dividing point that separates two distinct age cohorts in Japan. Those educated prior to the end of the war, known as the *senzenha* or "prewar generation" (Plath 1980:50), are seen as being products of a society that placed great emphasis on loyalty to family and to the state. These are the people who Plath points out are sometimes refered to as the "Last Confucians" in the Japanese press (Plath 1980:50). Those educated after the war are seen as being the products of a society that places more emphasis on the individual than it did prior to the war. As a result, people born during the Meiji (1868–1912), Taishō (1912–1926), and early Shōwa (1926–1946) periods are often viewed as having different ways of thinking and acting as compared to those educated after the Pacific War.

Prior to the occupation, education centered around largely Confucian moral themes expressed in the Imperial Rescript on Education (1890). The rescript emphasized filial piety, harmonious relations within the family, and loyalty to the state. Ethics, constructed largely in terms of obligations to parents and to the state (or emperor), formed the symbolic core of the educational curriculum (Rohlen 1983). Embree, who did ethnographic fieldwork in a rural Japanese village during the early 1930s, observed that schools placed considerable emphasis on teaching that focused on the moral rather than the intellectual (Embree 1939:188). Much of this was aimed at producing moral, obedient subjects who, by the sixth grade, had "imbibed a good deal of nationalism and martial Japanese spirit by means of games of war and the watching of young men drilling in the schoolyard four times a month" (Embree 1939:189).

With the Occupation came the import of American educational ideals, and efforts were made to transform the system of education in order to ensure the progress of democratization. Rohlen argues that the primary theme of this reform of the educational system was an emphasis on individualism. This involved the development of an educational system that addresses the needs of individual personalities, and an elimination of the sort of moral training that had been the mainstay of education prior to defeat (Dore 1952; Rohlen 1983:66). It should be noted that this process was not without debate and disagreement. Indeed, after the war there continued to be moves to bring back morality-centered education and the question of what role the schools should play in teaching morality continues to the present.

This should not be taken as suggesting that changes in educational philosophies have been the sole factor contributing to intergenerational tension. As Kaplan and colleagues note, changing fashions, attitudes toward work, and lifestyle preferences all contribute to a generation gap (Kaplan et al. 1998:42). However, people in Kanegasaki, both young and old, overwhelmingly emphasize changes in education as being the primary cause of dramatic differences in the thought and behavioral patterns of older, as opposed to younger, Japanese. People associate the postwar era with democratization and with a much reduced emphasis on the Confucian values that were stressed prior to the war. In other words, people believe that certain elements of the basic logic motivating behavior underwent a reorientation after the war with the import of new educational practices and this created a discontinuity in the way young and old think and act.

This idea is the key theme that shapes perceptions older people have of their relationship to modernity. Modernity, as two women in their early seventies stated when asked if young people today have a different way of thinking from older people, is far removed from the world in which they were raised:

YOSHIYUKI-SAN: Oh, yes, it's completely different, isn't it? They have too much freedom.

MIHARA-SAN: In our day, life was really hard, so it was just seen as normal that you would meet your fate [you have little control over your fate]. If you had a thought or an opinion, you did not let it out. That's the way the people were around here. Maybe the thoughts of young people today were the same as those of our day, but in our day, we did not let out our opinions. For young people nowadays, life is really easy.

YOSHIYUKI-SAN: Young people don't really want to hear the opinions of old people. Nowadays a lot of old people don't say anything [when they disagree with what their children are doing]. In any case, they certainly do not want to hear about the old days. In all of the houses around here there is a lot of history, but the young people are not interested in hearing about it. They do not want to hear about the history of the hamlet or of their households. They are not interested in it.

Both Yoshiyuki-san and Mihara-san used the phrase "*ima no hito*" when talking about younger people (meaning people of their children's and grandchildren's generations), a phrase that literally translates as "people of now" and that they use to distinguish themselves as being different—people of then. Many older people when referring to their own ideas or their ways of life use the term *furui*, which means old, of the past, and can imply a sense that something is obsolete. There is a strong sense among older people that *ima no hito* are not interested in the ideas and ways of acting of old people because those ideas and behavioral patterns are *furui*. Young people have things too easy and they have too much freedom to follow their own desires. This tends to make them selfish and uninterested in the ways and thoughts of older generations.

Images of Iwate Prefecture and old people as remnants of a world apart from that of urban, modern Japan, play an important role in shaping the experience of aging in places such as Kanegasaki. To be old and living in "*inaka*" Japan is to be associated with a way of life that is out-of-step with the modern world, remote from the mainstream of Japanese life. Socialized into different patterns of thinking and behavior because of a different educational emphasis, the older generations of today are seen as being, in fact, generations of yesterday—leftovers from a time that many, both young and old, see as having little in common with a modern, urbanized Japan.

CHAPTER 3

History and Continuity: Household, Community, and Old Age in Jōnai

In the hamlet of Jōnai, virtually all older individuals have experienced the aging process together and have moved through that process in relatively well-defined and congruous stages as a group. They form a good example of what Plath terms a group of consociates or people who have related to each other across time and with some degree of intimacy (Plath 1980:8). Most residents of the community have lived in the hamlet for their entire adult lives. They have common experiences, common life-histories, and well-established matrices of social relationships and patterns of social interaction.

Within Jōnai, older people experience little or no social distancing from members of their own age group. However, even with long-term residence and well-established social matrices, the community of older people is isolated and somewhat alienated from broader contexts of social interaction. This is due to: (1) participation by both younger and older people in activities highly structured around concepts of age appropriateness and a well-defined system of age grading, and (2) strong perceptions among young and old alike of a generation gap deeply rooted in different educational systems that operated prior to and after the Pacific War. This has created a situation in which older residents of Jōnai are at once socially integrated and alienated. Within the framework of the community of their own age group, the young old are highly integrated socially with strong ties of friendship and interdependence. As they become older, they sometimes become less able to operate within these matrices of social interaction, but still often participate in group activities as passive observers (this is a continuum that is related to both physical and mental condition).

However, the elder age group as a whole is socially removed from younger age groups and, in a sense, isolated from broader patterns of Japanese society. Social interactions with members of younger age groups are limited. Aside from the members of their own families, older people rarely interact with younger individuals. In fact, several informants indicate that even within their own multigeneration households, they have little interaction with other members of the family—often eating separately and living in separate sections of the same house.

In chapters 4 and 5, I will return to the issue of life course transitions and the segregation of age groups by examining age-related terms and age-grading practices. In this chapter, I focus on how older people in Jōnai form an integrated community of consociates with well-established ties based upon interdependence and a history of long-term co-residence. Much of how older people experience aging in Jōnai is related to historical continuity of residence and well-established networks of social interaction among individuals and the households of which they are a part.

JŌNAI

Jōnai is a hamlet of approximately 410 people living in 129 households. The hamlet sits atop a hill overlooking the Kitakami River to the east and rice fields and the main railroad line for central, northern Japan to the south. Primarily residential in character, the only stores are three of the small grocerettes of the type mentioned in chapter 2, which are run by older people in the front of their homes. One of these stores has operated since the Taishō era (1912–1926) in a building that looks much the same as it does in pictures from that earlier time.

Most of the hamlet's primary roads are paved, but as recently as ten years ago some of the major roads were still gravel. Only the main road that leads through the hamlet and connects Kanegasaki with Esashi is wide enough for two cars to pass without slowing down. Indeed, the most common forms of transportation in the hamlet are bicycle and foot. Several small footpaths that run behind houses are common routes for daily travel; in winter they are shoveled to keep them easily passable.

Trees line the streets and almost every house has a formal garden, usually behind a stone or cinder-block wall built along the edge of the street and sometimes between properties. These walls make each house look as though it is closed into its own box. Most households also have a vegetable garden somewhere either near the house or on another parcel of family property in the hamlet, and many own rice fields adjacent to the hamlet or in other areas of town.

The most common family composition in Jōnai is two people (see table 3.1). Slightly more than half of the two-person households consist of couples over the age of sixty-five. Among single-person households,

TABLE 3.1
Family Size in Jōnai

Family Size	Frequency	%
1	16	13
2	39	30
3	27	21
4	19	15
5	12	9
6	12	9
7	3	2
8	1	1
Totals	129	100

ten are women. The mean age for single-person households is sixty-four (with a range from 25 to 89, $\sigma = 16$) and the mean age for two-person households is fifty-nine (with a range from 18 to 89, $\sigma = 16.4$).

Jōnai is characteristic of many hamlets in rural areas of Japan in that the population has already aged to the point that more than 25 percent are over the age of sixty-five—a situation that will not obtain throughout Japan until around 2025. Figure 3.1 is a pareto graph of the population distribution of the hamlet. The largest group of people are between sixty and seventy, followed closely by those between fifty and sixty. Interestingly, after the ranges from ninety to one hundred and eighty to ninety, the next smallest group is that of zero to ten years old, reflecting the low birth rate in Japan and the limited number of people in Jōnai of child-bearing years.

If one looks further into the graph, it becomes clear that as of 1995 31 percent of the population was over the age of sixty and 17 percent over the age of seventy. While Jōnai does not exhibit the kind of aged population Jussaume encountered in some parts of Okayama Prefecture (Jussaume 1991:127)—in one village he studied there were no residents under the age of fifty—these data show that Jōnai will experience further significant growth in the number of older people in the near future.

Residents of Jōnai are highly cognizant of the aging character of their community and frequently comment, often with a degree of sadness, that children are few in number as compared to the past. Although three-generation households continue to exist in Jōnai, the majority of households are two- and one-generation. Of 129 households, 46 (35%) are one-generation, 51 (39%) are two-generation, and only 32 (24%) are three-generation. The mean age in Jōnai is 44.9 years (N = 410); 53

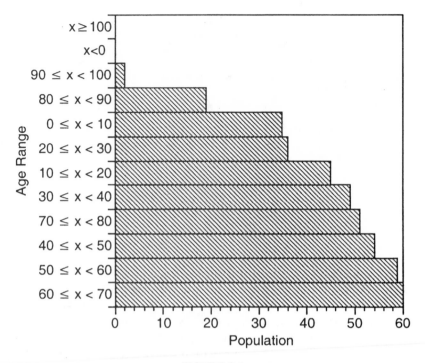

FIGURE 3.1
Pareto graph of age distribution in Jōnai.

percent of the population are over the age of 45 and 47 percent are under. The mean household size is 3.2 people, with a range from one person (sixteen households) to eight people (one household). Taken together, single- and two-person households represent 43 percent (55) of the households in Jōnai. Of these, 71 percent (39) have at least one member over the age of sixty. In other words, about 30 percent of the households in the hamlet are single- or two-person households in which at least one person is over sixty. There are sixty-two people in Jōnai eighteen or younger, representing only 15 percent of the population.

Old age is either directly or indirectly a part of the lives of virtually everyone in the hamlet. Whether one is a young old person in his sixties taking care of a ninety-year-old parent, or a two-year-old child who is looked after by her grandmother, encounters with old age are a part of daily life.

The dominance of older people in the community is not limited to demographics. Older men, particularly those above the age of seventy, dominate all public meetings and hold most positions in the community invested with any significant degree of symbolic capital (Bourdieu 1977).

For example, residents of Jōnai state that the head of the Self-Government Association has always been a male at least over the age of sixty-five (the head at the time of fieldwork was sixty-seven). The two hamlet shrine representatives are men both in their late seventies, and the head of the tax collection association is also a man in his seventies. There is a small group of older men who have the greatest influence in community activities and in the political operations of the hamlet. Women in their fifties and sixties normally occupy positions such as representatives to the town health committee, but the age specificity of positions open to women (those related to health and welfare and education) are considerably less clearly defined.

Older residents state that the main reason older men occupy positions of power is that they are the ones who have time—younger men work at full-time jobs and, thus, have little time to participate in hamlet organization and administration. However, men in their fifties, who have limited political power in the community, comment that they feel excluded from the central decision-making processes of the community. Most of these men have time available during the weekends and in the evenings, but most informal meetings related to operations of the hamlet are scheduled during week days, effectively preventing participation by younger men in the community. Much younger men, such as those in their thirties and forties, have virtually no involvement with hamlet operations, other than those specifically delegated to their age group. Public meetings for planning in the hamlet are usually only attended by one representative from each household, typically the eldest male, following patterns that have historically been the norm throughout rural Japan (Beardsley et al. 1959). Sometimes younger men will participate, however, the younger men who are involved in hamlet activities are those who belong to well-established households, with long histories in the hamlet. There are several families that have moved to the hamlet in the past five years, but they neither generally participate in nor send representatives to hamlet organization and governing activities.

Virtually all community gatherings—such as parties for cherry-blossom watching and the gathering at the local shrine on New Year's Day—are attended largely by older people. The one notable exception to the predominance of older people at community activities is *bon*, the summer festival for the ancestors that occurs in mid-August. *Bon* is attended by people of all ages, including younger family members who return from other parts of Japan for the holidays.

CONTINUITY AND HOUSEHOLD

The Meiji Civil Code, enacted in 1898, extended the family system of the samurai class to the entire population, requiring that everyone be registered as part of an *ie* or household (Lock 1993:87). Although the new Civil Code of 1947 abolished the *ie* as a legal institution, it remains one of the primary social structures in Japanese society. From an ideological perspective, the *ie* is patriarchal and follows patrilineal descent rules, patrilocal residence patterns for newly married couples (at least for eldest sons), and bases inheritance on primogeniture (Hamabata 1990:33). The *ie* represents a group of co-residents, each of whom hold an office (a specified role or position) that carries with it symbolic capital based upon its position within that unit (Lebra 1993:109). A specific *ie* is in many instances associated with a particular occupation, such as farming, shopkeeping, tofu making, and the like. There is a clear distinction between the successor/heir (frequently the eldest son) and other children in the family, who depart from the *ie* upon marriage (Lebra 1993:110). Although varying from household to household, at some point, usually when he is over the age of fifty, the successor/heir will become head of the household and also take control of the family occupation, although his father will likely continue to hold influence over decision making. He receives all or most of the property from his father, in return for which he has primary responsibility for the financial maintenance, housing, and healthcare of his parents as they age.

Households are sometimes linked together into a *dōzoku*, in which either patrilineally or sometimes matrilineally related stem and branch families (*honke* and *bunke*, respectively) are tied together through relationships of reciprocal obligations, and branches are physically situated within the general neighborhood of the stem household (Brown 1966). In such instances, a portion of the family property may be given to a nonsuccessor in order to create a branch family, which may, itself, at some time create further branches.

The *ie* operates as a normative frame of reference that helps Japanese people determine appropriate behavior in relation to family and others (Hamabata 1990:46). However, this ideological frame does not necessarily obtain in sociological practice. There can be considerable variation in who actually takes over the headship, how property is divided, and who actually holds power within a household. Hamabata shows clearly that decisions may be made strategically over who will actually succeed. The abilities or inabilities of a particular son or daughter can influence parents' decisions about who actually succeeds to the headship, as can emotional ties among parents and children. And power may be exercised by a blood-related daughter, for example, while the appearance of patrilineal descent is maintained through bringing in an adoptive husband (Hamabata 1990).

Among some scholars, the *ie* has been viewed as being mainly an economic unit, as opposed to a family unit (Befu 1963; Nakane 1967).

Branch and stem families are viewed as being tied together primarily through economic, rather than genealogical or social, relationships. In this view, concerns over maintaining long-term (multigeneration) economic bonds of interdependence outweigh consanguinity as a basis for relationships between household units. Kinship in this view is primarily seen as a matter of economics, not blood. Some scholars have presented this as one way of explaining the Japanese willingness to adopt nonconsanguineal adults into a household in order to ensure the continuity of the household over time.

The *ie qua* economic-unit position has been called into question on the grounds that *dōzoku* can and do continue to exist, even in the absence of significant economic ties, as a social unit. Brown states that economic transactions in Shinjō (a few miles south of Jōnai) are

> merely coincident to the genealogical and other relationships involved in the branching. They are not essential to *dōzoku* nor do they give it its raison d'être. And the absence of such transactions does not spell the demise of *dōzoku*. (Brown 1968:123)

Dōzoku are rare in Jōnai. This is a consequence of the samurai history of the hamlet in which vassals of the family that occupied the castle (the Ōmachi family), were doled out parcels of land too small to permit branching (between 2,640 m² and 3,300 m²). Of the three *dōzoku* in the hamlet, one is a comparatively new household, which bought land and entered the hamlet around a hundred years ago; the second son and then the second son's second son have both built new houses on family property adjacent to the stem house. The other two are descendants of the original samurai group, but in one case the formation of branch families came in this century after the household bought other land in the hamlet. In the other case, the family is aware of branch family formation in the distant past (at least two hundred years ago), but they do not discuss their relationships with that household as a stem/branch family relationship and, in fact, they are not certain where that branch currently resides. In a few cases, members of the stem household are uncertain of whether or not there has been branching in their own family history and cannot state unequivocally whether their own family is a stem or a branch family.

Of course, there are strong relationships of reciprocal obligations among households in the hamlet, and in some cases newer people can identify a main or branch stem household in a neighboring hamlet, but it would be difficult to describe these as *dōzoku*. Rather, long-term co-residence and intermarriage among the households in the hamlet have created a network of obligational bonds that tie most households together. These obligational bonds are based not on economics, but on blood, friendship, and necessity.

There is a strong emphasis on blood ties in Jōnai that is similar to patterns of interhousehold relationships Lebra found among descendants of the Japanese nobility around Tokyo. In approximately 61 percent of the adoption cases she observed, blood continuity of the household line was maintained. Even in the case of husband adoption (*mukoyōshi*), a practice in which the male takes the wife's family name and is moved from his natal family register (*koseki*) to hers, the daughter would be a temporary household head. The office of household head would be eventually taken over by the adoptee she married and who entered the household. Lebra's detailed analysis makes it clear that, at least among the former nobility, when possible it is preferable "to make adoptions compatible with the preservation of blood" (Lebra 1993:127). The rule of descent through male successors is often ignored, demonstrating the importance of natural kinship (consanguineal relation) in maintaining household continuity across generations.

Lebra's findings correspond well to kinship practices in Jōnai. In Jōnai, households of samurai descent can typically trace back ancestors through between nine and twelve generations. For example, Uemoto Sentaro, an eighty-year-old man who is an adopted husband (nonblood relation to the family), traces his (wife's) ancestry back nine generations (including his and his son's generations) as shown in figure 3.2.

In the kinship diagram in figure 3.2, for conjugal pairs in which the husband was adopted, the males are indicated by solid triangles. In one pair, both were adopted, but the wife was a blood relative (indicated by a dotted line). The first generation of the household, the samurai who originally came to the hamlet, dates back 250 to 300 years. Little is known about these early Uemotos, but it is known that the fourth-generation Uemoto never had a child; the household passed to an adoptive daughter, brought from another part of the family; the exact relation is unknown. It is interesting that the Uemotos assured me that she was a blood relation, even though it seems doubtful that they can be certain of this since they are not certain about the relationship between their own family and her natal family. This is suggestive of how much emphasis is placed on blood relations.

The third generation is of particular interest for our discussion here. Generation two gave birth to a boy and a girl, but the son, who would normally have succeeded to the household headship and inherited the property, died at the age of eighteen before he could marry and have children. As a result, household property passed to the daughter, whose husband was adopted into the family. This point is important for understanding the notion of household continuity.

Five of the total ten generations consist of consanguineal women married to males who have been adopted. Indeed, because the ninth-

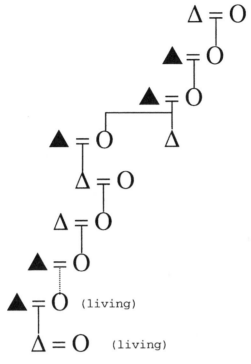

FIGURE 3.2
Adoptions in Uemoto Sentaro's Genealogy.

generation conjugal pair was unable to produce children, both Uemoto Yukiko and her husband are adopted. Uemoto Sentaro did not grow up in Kanegasaki, but in another part of the prefecture and moved there when he married into the Uemoto family. Uemoto Yukiko has always lived in Jōnai, but she was not actually born into her current household.

> I was born on the other side of this hamlet. This household (*ie*) was my grandmother's household. But in this household there were no children, so when I was little, I came over to live here. I came here when I was one year and one month old. I came here to my grandmother's natal household. My grandmother had married out to the household on the other side of the hamlet.

Uemoto-san moved from her natal household to ensure the continuation of her grandmother's natal household line, which was threatened by the failure of her adoptive parents to have children of their own. The pattern of adopting blood relatives from other households was and has continued to be a common practice among the former samurai households of Jōnai. In some cases, consanguineal males who were not themselves eldest sons were also adopted into related families that did not produce children.

Examples such as Uemoto Sentaro, who married into his wife's lineage, are particularly common—approximately one quarter of older males in the hamlet, whether of samurai descent or not, are adopted husbands. This number is higher than what was often found earlier in this century—for example, in 1920 and 1935 the national percentages of marriages in which the male was adopted were 10.0 and 8.5, respectively (Mosk 1983:98). This adheres to patterns evident throughout Japan in which the adoption of successors dropped after the Pacific War, only to begin climbing again in recent years (Ochiai 1997:153–154). Brown has found that in Mizusawa, the incidence of adopted husbands marrying into the wife's natal family and taking her family name has increased in the rural population from 9 percent in 1962 to 16 percent in 1995 (L. K. Brown 1998). The resurgence of such adoptions may be the result of low fertility in the postwar era. This has created demographic patterns similar to those earlier in Japanese history when high infant and child mortality rates meant that adoption of successors was necessary to keeping households without male heirs alive (Ochiai 1997:153).

This sort of adoption emphasizing blood relations is not limited to former samurai families. Kanetaka Owari was the last child born into a family of ten siblings, large even for the time (he was born in 1925). In fact, Kanetaka's birth mother, who had married out to a household in neighboring Mizusawa, was given an award from the government for having a large number of children. Because his mother's sister's daughter (Kanetaka's cousin) had no children, he was adopted into his mother's natal household in order to carry on the household line. Thus, he refers to his cousin, who raised him, as his mother (see figure 3.3).

Another example will be helpful in understanding the importance of consanguineal relations for household continuity. At the edge of the property of all samurai households and some newer households of non-samurai descent in Jōnai one can find a small stone shaped like a Shinto shrine building (see figure 3.4). These stones represent the Shinto god *Myōjin*, whose purpose is to protect the household, including the people and the physical property (house, land, garden, etc.). Many of these shrines have been in place for several hundred years, having been put there when the family originally arrived in Jōnai. In some cases, the shrines have been replaced due to weathering of the original or concern over the placement of the original.

One samurai household, that of Uemoto Noboru (no known relation to Uemoto Sentaro and Yukiko), has a shrine that is, by compari-

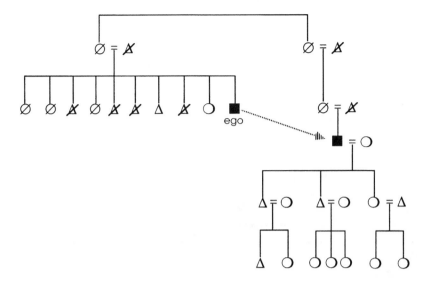

FIGURE 3.3
Kanetaka Owari Adoption.

son to many others in the hamlet, fairly new. There was an older shrine, but it was replaced two generations ago. The ninth-generation conjugal pair were unable to produce children. As a result, they adopted a male and his wife into the family for the purpose of having children and, thus, maintaining the continuity of the household line. Neither the adoptive husband nor the adoptive wife were blood relatives to the adopting household, and it appears that the family decided as a last resort to adopt a husband and wife because no blood relatives were available.

Although household continuity had been maintained, this was not without social cost related to the loss of continuity in bloodlines—a loss that necessitated symbolic recognition. At the time of the adoption, a new shrine was purchased to replace the old one and the old shrine was buried under the spot where the current shrine stands. In other words, at the point where the bloodline was broken, the original shrine, which had been in place since the household arrived in the hamlet, was replaced with a new shrine, symbolically indicating a change in bloodlines even while household continuity was being maintained.

When considering continuity of household in Japan, it is important to recognize the centrality of ancestors. In Jōnai, the ancestors form a bloodline that reflects two hierarchically organized components which structure household continuity. When something such as the inability to produce offspring threatens the continuity of the household over time, a

FIGURE 3.4

A *Myōjin* shrine protects a household in Jōnai.

correction becomes necessary. The best solution to the problem is the adoption of a blood relative; when that fails the household will resort to the adoption of a nonconsanguineal individual or conjugal pair, which is preferable to the death of the household.

Why is this preferable to the death of the household? In short, because of the ancestors. The ancestors are normally an integral part of daily life. Most households in Jōnai have an ancestral altar (*butsudan*) displayed prominently in one room of the house. On the alter one finds daily food offerings to the ancestors (rice, fruit, candies, etc.) and posthumous name tablets (*ihai*) that index the deceased members of the household. In all households in the hamlet, daily offerings are made and people pray at the altar. There is considerable variation in how people think about the ancestors, but most, particularly first sons, feel that there is a responsibility to protect the household they have received from their ancestors and care for the needs of their ancestors. Some informants suggest that the relationship with ancestors is reciprocal; the living care for the ancestors and the ancestors contribute to the protection of the household.

> MORITA HIROSHI: It is important to protect (*mamoru*) the *ie*. It would be unfortunate if my household came to die. Someone needs to protect and care for the house, family, garden, rice fields, *ohaka* (family grave), and ancestors. If you give up the responsibility as successor, everything will come apart—all of those things and the family will expire. I can't imagine anybody who would be happy if their *ie* ended, at least not in this area.

> MORITA YUKIE: The ancestors protect the *ie*. When my husband goes away on trips overseas, as he likes to do, I specifically ask the ancestors to protect him, and they are always protecting the *ie*.

The issue of protecting the household is central to understanding the role of the ancestors in the realm of the living, but it is not an uncontested point among the living. For example, the above conjugal pair strongly disagreed about whether the ancestors can respond to the requests of the living. The wife stated that the ancestors can take an active role in the lives of the living by protecting specific people when asked. And most informants stated that in one way or another the ancestors protect the household, even if they cannot articulate exactly what they do to protect it.

Morita-san, however, after his wife commented that she thinks the ancestors can protect the living, went on to state, "I don't think that if you bring your hands together in front of the family altar and ask for something the ancestors will respond." But when asked why not throw away the family altar, he responded, "Well, although you don't get help, it is good for you from a personal point of view in terms of *kokoro* [spiritual center, mind]. You do *omairi* [prayer] for yourself and your own *kokoro*. But it is useless to ask for things in particular."

Hamabata points out that in some households family gatherings are held in the room in which the family altar is placed. The altar is opened so that the ancestors can be included in the festivities (Hamabata 1990). In other words, the ancestors are a part of the living household. But, perhaps more importantly for our discussion here, the living are also historically defined. They live in relation to the ancestors—as their descendants, the protectors of the property and life that they have received from those ancestors. Particularly among the former samurai households, people indicate that they have an obligation to the ancestors for having received their *zaisan* or fortune from them. The household—as a historically defined center of continuity for and including a lineally descended group of (preferably) blood-related living and dead, their property, and in some cases a specific occupation—requires care and protection by the living. It is the living who have been entrusted with it by their ancestors and who will in turn entrust it to future generations.

This point was particularly clear in a conversation with one seventy-nine-year-old man, Uemoto Kōichi, who is the head of a former samurai household that consists of three generations (Uemoto and his wife, his eldest son and his wife and their children). During the summer of 1995, he worked so hard in his family rice fields that he was forced to spend close to a month convalescing, because he has a bad heart, a condition about which he was well aware when he overworked himself.

UEMOTO-SAN: I have ten rice paddies. That would be about one hectare.

JWT: Throughout a year, about how much time do you spend tending to the rice fields?

UEMOTO-SAN: Well the first thing we do in the year is *tauchi*; this takes about two days. This is done with a tractor. It consists of tilling the paddy field. Next there is *takaki*, which is putting the water into the fields. This takes about 3.5 days. Around this time there is also *tanemaki*, which is sowing the seeds into boxes. I cannot do this alone, but with a machine it takes about one day. It would take longer without a machine.

Following this is *taue*, which is the actual transplanting of the rice. This takes three days. Next there is *josōzai*, the spreading of weed killer. We do this once and it takes two days. At the same time, we also spread chemicals to prevent the rice plants from becoming sick. When the rice is ready, we do *inegari*, which is the cutting and binding of the rice plants and putting them on stakes to dry. This takes four days. Later we spend four days doing *inegoki*, which is rice threshing or the removal of the rice from the stalks. This is also done by machine. In the case that one has a combine, *inegari* and *inegoki* are done at the same time by the combine, but we don't have a combine.[1] Then we carry the rice and put it into storage using a truck.

Finally, there is selling the rice. This year we sold a total of 110 30 kg bags at a cost of ¥9,000 each. After this, about 1,000 kg remained. We have already given away about 200 kg and will probably give away more since we cannot eat all of the rice. We send some to our daughter in Tokyo and to other family members.

JWT: So you get a lot of money from the rice.

UEMOTO-SAN: Well, I wouldn't say that. We get about 100,000 yen from what we sell from ten *are* or one *tan* (or $10,000 from one hectare), which isn't all that much money.

JWT: What do you use that money for?

UEMOTO-SAN: Just normal living expenses.

JWT: What do you do with the leftover rice?

UEMOTO-SAN: Well, I give some to my siblings, some to my children, some to more distant relatives.

JWT: But if you have 800 kg remaining, that's a lot.

UEMOTO-SAN: [laughs] Yes, it's a lot. We can't eat it all. Throughout the year we send some to various people.

JWT: Since you have a lot remaining, and this sort of work is difficult, why don't you produce less? Why not use eight instead of ten of your rice paddies? You would still have enough to give away some to family members.

UEMOTO-SAN: I received the land from my parents. People around here generally received the land from their parents. The most important thing is that people do not want to be disobedient to their parents. This is related to being a good child (*oya kōkō*), one wants to be a good son.

JWT: So, if you did not do the rice planting, you would feel uncomfortable?

UEMOTO-SAN: [laughs]. Indeed, I would. I received this land from my parents and I feel as though I must use it.

JWT: Isn't your heart a bit weak?

UEMOTO-SAN: Yes.

JWT: Then wouldn't it be advisable to quit?

UEMOTO-SAN: Well, I have already indicated that to my eldest son, but he hasn't become involved yet. He is still cunning. He doesn't want to, so he hasn't really done anything yet. He says that since grandpa [Uemoto] is still working, he doesn't need to do it.

Uemoto-san's son works as a teacher and his grandchildren are busy with school, thus they do not have time to help with the farming. Uemoto-san's wife is unable to help with any of the heavy work because of back problems, but she does help by weeding both in the rice fields and in their large garden at their house. Uemoto-san later intimated that his son does help with some of the more difficult work and, in fact, his daughter-in-law takes time off from work during the busiest periods to help with the rice production. However, Uemoto-san does the vast majority either by himself or with the help of his wife.

Robert J. Smith argues that one property of ancestors in Japan is that they are "a category of dead who exercise tutelary powers over some social group" whether it is household, *han*, hamlet, village, or nation (Smith 1974:212). As historical entities, individuals, households, and larger social groups all fall within the framework of the power of the ancestors at times. Older residents of the hamlet, in particular, place great emphasis on their sense of obligation to the ancestors to ensure that the symbols that index those ancestors—photographs, *ihai*, rice fields, the household property, and the hamlet as a whole—are maintained and well cared for. This means that even in poor health, as in the case of Uemoto-san, one must continue not simply to hold the rice fields, but to farm them—to keep them active—much as the ancestors are kept actively a part of the household through the symbolic media of *ihai* and photographs. To let the rice fields go to seed would be to symbolically let the household as an entire historical entity go, and would be an affront to the ancestors from whom one has received life and fortune.

For older people like Uemoto-san, the ancestors can be a heavy weight. A strong sense of responsibility to care for what they have received from their ancestors, combined with children and grandchildren who have either moved away or are unwilling to help with the farming, leaves older people with the burden of caring for farm or garden land that they may not be physically able to handle. But the maintenance of household continuity, that is, keeping the household an active entity, outweighs these concerns. In times of need (usually extreme need) older people who do not have relatives living nearby are particularly burdened by this weight. At such times, rather than family, it is one's neighbors who offer assistance.

CONTINUITY AND COMMUNITY

Jōnai is divided into six subsections, called *han*, which are the smallest social grouping above the household (figure 3.5 shows the six *han* of Jōnai). Each *han* is made up of approximately twenty households. These households are tied together as a social group on the basis of proximity and historically established ties of reciprocal obligations. One's *han* is an important source of friendship and social support, particularly in times of need.

When a person dies, for example, members of the deceased's *han* will be the most actively involved nonfamily members who participate in the funeral. *Han* women prepare food for the various ceremonies

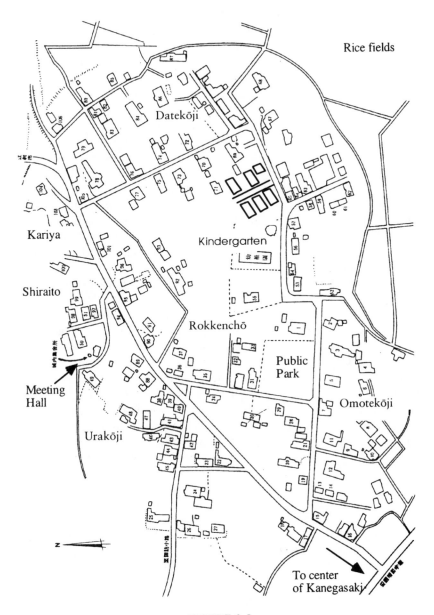

Rice fields

Datekōji

Kariya

Kindergarten

Shiraito

Rokkenchō

Meeting
Hall

Public
Park

Omotekōji

Urakōji

N

To center
of Kanegasaki

FIGURE 3.5
Map of Jōnai.

guests attend, and men participate in an around-the-clock vigil of incense burning in the room of the deceased's house (to cover the odor of the body) and preparation of the body for cremation.

Funerals are attended by the eldest conjugal pair from each household in the *han* and one representative from each household in neighboring *han*. The most intimate activities in the funeral process, which lasts between three and five days, occur in the house of the deceased or a relative and at the crematorium. These activities are attended by family and *kinjo no hito*, those people living in one's *han*.

Elements of the funeral ceremonies that occur at the temple are attended by representatives from all of the households in the hamlet, unless mitigating circumstances prevent a household from sending a representative (such as sickness). Ceremonies that occur in the house, however, are normally attended only by family, kin, and *han* people (which may include family, as well). One of the most important ceremonies associated with the funeral is the *nembutsu*, which takes place on the night of the "sending-off ceremony" (*kokubetsu shiki*) that occurs at the local Buddhist temple.

In Jōnai there are two associations (*nembutsu kō*) that conduct the ritual. Although both are led by the same man (because the leader of one of the organizations died and no one was interested in taking on the leadership of the group), there is some variation in the performance of the ritual depending upon which association one is considering. These two associations are geographically oriented, one being limited to residents of the *han* called Datekōji, the other incorporating all other *han* in the hamlet, which are commonly referred to collectively as Omotekōji even though that is the name of one *han* (the largest) in the group.

In both associations the ritual is similar; members of the *han* come to the house the evening of the sending-off ceremony and chant "*namu amida butsu*"[2] repeatedly for about twenty minutes while the leader rings a bell and chants the words, after which the participants repeat his chanting. The major difference between the two associations is that in Datekōji, participants sit in a circle around the edges of the room and pass a huge set of wooden Buddhist rosary (*juzu*) beads—consisting of 851 beads strung together with a rope—through their hands while chanting. According to residents, the beads have been in the *han* for approximately three hundred years. The Omotekōji association does not have a set of such rosary beads, thus each member of the association holds his or her own beads during the chanting. According to participants, the purpose of this ritual is for the *han* residents to assist the deceased in gaining entrance into heaven or to help him or her along in his or her journey.

Failure to attend the ceremony appropriate for one's social and geographical location in the hamlet relative to the deceased is considered to be impolite. At one funeral, for instance, two of the *han*'s households failed to send representatives to the *nembutsu* ritual. This generated a certain amount of quiet gossip among those who were in attendance as to why the households sent no representative and some indicated that the failure to attend was rude.

Perhaps the most powerful evidence for the closeness of the *han* as a social group can be seen in the ritual for cremation of the dead body. Throughout much of Japan, cremation is followed by a ritual in which kin, handling ceremonial chopsticks with their left hands, pick the bones out of the ashes and place them into a box. The use of the left hand is common in funeral practices because it is the opposite of what is considered normal, right-handedness, symbolizing the opposition of life and death. What is unusual about this ritual in Jōnai is that not only do kin participate, but residents of the *han* also participate in the bone picking. When asked about this, one informant indicated that

> since we [our households] have been living here so long we are all probably related anyway, but there is a sense that, whether related or not, the *han* is like a family. So everyone in the *han* participates.

Although by no means having a festive atmosphere, the entire cremation process, which takes about two hours, is a time during which family and *han* residents socialize and men drink beer or *sake* while waiting for the process to be completed.

Han membership, although largely defined geographically, is not entirely a matter of where one lives. In addition to geographical locality, there is a social orientation to *han* membership that is constructed in terms of historical household bonds. For example, in Datekōji, there are several newer families that entered in the past twenty to thirty years. At the lower corner of the *han* there is a religious monument that is devoted to Fudō and Yama-no-kami. Fudō is a *hotoke* or Buddhist god that, according to residents, is for the purpose of protecting the *kami*, the Shinto entities usually translated as gods or deities, although this translation does not sufficiently convey the full meaning of the term (Nelson 1996). Yama-no-kami is intended for women and is related to fertility. There is an association of women in the hamlet devoted to Yama-no-kami, but they rarely meet due to the advanced age of the women.

On the 28th of April some residents of Datekōji participate in a ritual with the priest from Kanegasaki Shrine. This is only done by the people in Datekōji who are members of samurai-descent families. In other words, it is only done by those families who have been in the hamlet for between 200 and 400 years. New families who enter the community are not allowed to participate in the ritual, nor in the association that manages the ritual performance and maintains the shrine. The explanation given for this is that the land on which the shrine is placed is jointly owned by the older households. New members, because they are not part of the joint ownership group, cannot participate, although their children participate in the cleaning of the shrine as part of the hamlet's Children's Association work responsibilities (see chapter 5) and anyone can pray at the shrine if they so desire.

Following the ritual there is a meeting of the Fudō Association during which members discuss the finances of the organization and any work that needs to be done to the shrine. During the meeting in 1996, there was also a long discussion of what to do about those households whose successors were unlikely to return to Jōnai. The leaders of the association had contacted all of the association's member families who had moved away from the *han*, but retained property in the *han*, to determine who was planning to return or not return. Membership in the association is by household, and individuals in a given household lack the power to have their household's name removed from the list of members. Annual dues are required, but many of those who have moved out of the hamlet no longer pay their dues, which presents a problem for keeping them as members of the association. Some members suggested that nonpaying households that have moved away should be removed from the association, but others objected stating that participants did not have the power to remove any of the members because the charter of the association did not permit such a change. Some also suggested that perhaps those who said they would not return might change their minds as they grew older. No decision was achieved.

These examples suggest that membership in the *han*, at least for older households, should be understood not only as geographical, but also as social and historical. The older households are tied together via their mutual samurai past. In particular, their relationship to the Ōmachi family, to which many still indicate gratitude for having received their property, is seen as binding them together. The historical circumstances that brought together the original group of households still has some degree of power over those who have remained in the hamlet and the dissolution of that original group is seen as something to be avoided, even if some of the original households have left the hamlet.

In addition to the formal division of the hamlet into *han*, Jōnai can be roughly divided into three distinct areas that correspond approximately to the geographical areas of the *han*. In referring to figure 3.5, one can see the different *han* in the hamlet. The areas called Urakōji, Shirai, and Kanaya are largely newer development, consisting of households that have been in the hamlet for between 20 and 100 years.

Datekōji and Omotekōji largely consist of much older households that have been in the hamlet for between 200 and 400 years. In-migration, when it has occurred, has largely resulted from the subdivision and sale of property of former samurai households, including the property that was connected to the Ōmachi family—part of which was turned into a park and the remainder into housing.

These subdivisions are not always under the best of circumstances. The most recent development has been the result of the subdivision of one household's property, which brought five new households into the hamlet over the last five years. At the corner of the area of new development sits a two-room house that is occupied by the eldest son of the family that originally owned the property, Chida Ichiro. According to neighbors, the Chida household once occupied one of the largest lots in the hamlet. But several years ago Chida-san's mother died and his father remarried to a woman who had designs on the family fortune. When the father died, she sold off all of the property, leaving nothing for the children. After a court battle, the eldest son won a small piece of land on which his little house now sits and in which he lives alone. The remainder of the property is occupied by five large, modern houses owned by families of men working at one of the companies in the town's industrial park. Had this situation not developed, it is unlikely that the recent group of in-migrants would have come.

The point I wish to emphasize here is the considerable historical continuity of household composition of the hamlet; in-migration has occurred in groupings and there have been extended periods in which there has been very little change. Several parts of the hamlet are occupied by the same households that have been there for as much as four hundred years. By comparing historical maps with modern maps one can see that thirty-three of the families currently in the hamlet occupy the same land that their direct ancestors occupied in 1688, while a few other families have moved to different parts of the hamlet.

The long history of common occupation of the hamlet by a core group of former samurai families, and the presence of several other families that have been in the hamlet for at least fifty years means that there is an extensive network of social ties between and among households in the hamlet. Reciprocal obligations are not only formed on the basis of kinship—common residence itself is one source from which households draw obligations.

This network is an important part of the lives of older people living in Jōnai. Older women and men in the hamlet are constantly visiting at one another's houses to chat and gossip over the customary tea and homemade pickles that are offered to guests. Neighbors also look out for those who are in need. The following is an excerpt from fieldnotes that describes the living situation of one older resident of Urakōji, Fukai Uta. The interview on which this excerpt is based took place in mid-winter, with the temperature outside around 20°F.

Fukai-san lives in a very small, single-story house at the corner of the main road and the road leading into Urakōji. The house is in poor condition. There are broken windows that have been patched with plastic. Inside, the woodwork is old and, Fukai-san told me, stained from years of smoking and use of the kerosene stove. She said that the ceiling was originally a white wood, but now it is a very dark brown. The sliding doors that separate rooms are stained with brown spots that look as though they came from water. The paper in the other sliding walls is brown with age and many of the wooden panels are broken or have holes. The *tatami* mats on the floor are very old and soiled and the walls are a bit dirty. There is scant furniture in the living room: a stool, a *kotatsu* (a heated table with a quilt attached to it), a TV, a telephone, a small shelf on which she keeps knives and tea and some food, and another shelf. There are four calendars hanging on one wall and an old clock on another wall.

From the living room you can hear the road noises very clearly; it sounds almost as though one of the windows is open. There is a bit of a draft in the room and it is fairly cold. When I arrived, Fukai-san was only using the *kotatsu* to keep warm, she did not have the kerosene stove lit even though the outside temperature was below freezing, and only lit it after a while when it became cold enough to see our breath as we spoke.

Fukai-san is dressed in a sort of casual kimono type of outfit with a shawl over her shoulders. Her hair is still largely black, but she has some gray and has a bald spot in back. She walks around easily inside the house, but she uses a cane when she goes outside. She tells me that she is ninety years old. She is very short, perhaps about 4'10" and is a bit hunched over, but not as seriously as some of the women in the area. She smiles constantly, exposing a single tooth in front. She served some apples and she had to slice them rather small, at which time she commented that it was a problem having only one tooth.

Fukai-san's husband was in the military and went to Manchuria during the war. After he returned, he worked at a bank in Mizusawa. After a major fire that destroyed much of the area in Urakōji, they bought land and built the current house. That was between thirty-five and forty years ago. Her husband died in a railroad accident shortly after they moved in. From that point onward, she and her only son lived in the current house until he died when he was forty, about twenty years after his father. She has lived alone (for more than twenty years) in the house since that time.

After her husband died, she had to support herself so she worked in her home making kimono (Japanese traditional clothing). She was able to make a living through sewing and continued making kimono until about three years ago, when her eyes began to give her too much trouble to see well enough to sew. She also said that the amount of orders dropped considerably over the years because people came to wear Western clothing. Early on, she said, everyone wore kimono and business was good.

Fukai-san lives only on her government pension (*kokumin nenkin*). She receives ¥67,000 per month. She said that for basics such as kerosene, electricity, telephone, etc. it costs her about ¥50,000 per month, after which she has to buy food. She said that she goes to the doctor every ten days. She goes to the local hospital in downtown Kanegasaki, less than a mile away, by taxi. But the taxi ride costs about ¥570 each way. Thus, it is expensive given her budget. Her income is insufficient to meet her needs. In order to make up the difference, Fukai-san draws from her savings, which she expects to last her about another five years, after which she does not know what she will do, but expects that she will receive help from the town.

For food, because she cannot get to a grocery store easily, she relies on the food truck that comes selling groceries each week. For raw things, such as fish, people in the neighborhood buy them and bring them to her. She also relies heavily upon the small vegetable garden next to her house, which she cares for as much as she can physically handle. She grew vegetables on her own there until a few years ago, but now it is too difficult. For the past few years, Yamazato-san across the street has been doing the gardening and giving a portion of the vegetables to Fukai-san. She needs the garden in order to have enough food, because her pension is so small. (Fieldnotes, 12/29/95)

Fukai-san's neighbors regularly check in on her, and Yamazato-san, who lives across the street, takes care of Fukai-san's garden. There is no formal arrangement between them concerning how the food is divided up. Fukai-san works in the garden when she can, but usually Yamazato-san is out at 5:00 a.m. daily weeding and taking care of the vegetables. Fukai-san is able to take as much of the vegetables as she needs and Yamazato-san takes what she wants. This practice is common. When another hamlet resident was hospitalized during the spring of 1995, neighbors took care of planting her vegetables and weeding as needed until she was able to work in the garden on her own.

EXPERIENCING OLD AGE IN JŌNAI

Older people living in Jōnai, whether of samurai or nonsamurai descent, experience old age within the context of a matrix of interdependencies and reciprocal obligations that is grounded in history and provides a primary source of continuity in life. At the level of the household, relationships have existed across decades or centuries. The people who reside in

FIGURE 3.6

Woman (68) tends her garden in the center of Jōnai.

the hamlet today interact with the descendants of ancestors who interacted with and in many cases intermarried with their own ancestors. Blood is important in maintaining household continuity, but even more important is the continuity of the household because it is the living who care for the needs of the dead. The ancestors provide historical continuity to the household and older people experience a sense of obligation to maintain that continuity because they have received what they have, including their lives, from their ancestors.

At the level of community, this matrix of interdependencies between and among households forms a basic source of support that people can depend upon in times of need. Although most households rely on this matrix from time to time, it is particularly important for older people living alone or older couples who do not have immediate family members living with them and upon whom they can rely in times of need.

As a result of these factors, unlike older people who are institutionalized, even those who are separated from their children are not necessarily dislocated or alienated from established contexts of social interaction. They find continuity in their social interactions and they function within the framework of obligations that limit or even prevent social distancing. In general, only those who are unable to participate in group activities fail to do so. And those who experience difficulties in independently handling the needs of daily life, like Fukai-san, receive informal assistance through the matrix of social connections operating in the hamlet.

This, however, does not mean that older people do not experience alienation or social distancing. As noted at the beginning of this chapter, the system of age-grading practices, the emphasis on age appropriateness in behavior and social interaction, and perceptions about a generation gap isolate older people within the context of broader social structures. In the next chapter, I will turn my attention to the manner in which older people are distanced socially from other parts of Japanese society.

PART II

Age-Structuring Practices

CHAPTER 4

Talking about Age

This and the following chapter focus on the question, how do people in Jōnai and surrounding areas categorize relative age and organize the aging process? Emphasis on this question is important for understanding the experience of aging, because, as will become evident below, people in Jōnai, as in other cultural settings, think about and reckon age in several different ways. When we speak about age or the aging process in Western societies, we typically are concerned with chronological age, reckoned on the basis of a dating system such as years, or in the case of infants, months (Fortes 1984:99). In many of the preindustrial and pre-literate societies anthropologists have studied, chronological age is not necessarily a relevant criterion for differentiating age or may not have a significant function in daily life (see Keith et al. 1994:20). Indeed, in some societies people may not know their age in calendar years (Counts and Counts 1985:137).

Age in most societies is simultaneously measured on the basis of a variety of social categories including calendar years, birth order, social status, membership in age-related groups that are only loosely tied to one's chronological age, and so on. The importance of chronological age as a measuring scheme appears largely tied to the rise of bureaucracies and the administrative and record-keeping functions that develop as societies become more complex (Marshal 1985:260; Thomas 1976)

In Jōnai, although individuals are well aware of their age in calendar years, chronological age is of less significance than one's position in the life course relative to others, particularly in reference to birth order and social status. In fact, reckoning of age in terms of calendar years can become difficult as one grows older because the Japanese calendar is not based on a continuous progression of years, rather it renews with the ascension of each new emperor. It is normal for an older person, when asked the age of children or grandchildren, to take a moment to calculate the age of the child. For example, a person born in the year 1961 of the Gregorian calendar would be born in the year Shōwa 36 (the 36th year of the reign of the Shōwa Emperor) in the Japanese dating system. Because the Shōwa Emperor died in 1989, the year recycled to 1 in 1989 with the ascension of the Heisei Emperor. Thus, in 1996 to determine the above person's age on the basis of birth year, it is necessary to do the following calculation (63 − 36) + 8 = 35. Sixty-three represents the last full year of the Shōwa Period, thirty-six is the person's birth year, and Heisei 8 is the Japanese year for 1996.

Most people in Jōnai think about age on the basis of a combination of one's stage in the life course, relative age in terms of birth order and generation, and calendar years. This adheres to patterns common throughout Japan, where the prevailing ideological framework depends upon a high level of age incongruity in determining how people move through the life course. As Mary Brinton points out, "the timing of life course transitions in Japan is more *irreversible* than temporary, exhibits little *variance* or *spread* across individuals, and is *age-incongruous* (exhibiting very little overlap between the spreads of two or more transitions)" (Brinton 1992:83). There is a well-defined schedule of transitions from one role to another in the course of aging, and many people within Japanese society follow closely, or aspire to follow closely, that schedule. The relative stage of people within this scheme contributes greatly to how they interact and communicate and forms one of the criteria through which Japanese ascribe social status.

Many of the passages of life are connected to contexts such as work. Work-related forms of partitioning the life course have been well studied by anthropologists (Noguchi 1983; Noguchi 1990; Plath 1983; Vogel 1971), as have rituals of the life course (Edwards 1989; Kumagai 1984; Long 1987; Plath 1989). Although these issues are important for our understanding of age and aging in Japan, I will not directly address work and ritual transitions here. Instead, I will consider two other less studied factors that contribute to how Japanese think about age—the terminology of age and age-grading practices.

Although the focus of this book is old age, it is necessary to think about the life course more generally before looking at age-structuring practices in later life. There are two reasons for this. First, age-structuring practices represent an integrated framework in relation to which people think about age and through which they organize the life course. One period cannot be taken as independent from others, because each transition and each new period builds upon and may be interpreted in relation to both past and future periods. The transitional points often form liminal periods in life during which the meaning of a given age or phase is negotiated and contested (see, for example, Kawano 1996). Second, a broad examination of age structuring is ethnographically interesting in Japan, because early and later periods of life show similarities in how they are culturally constructed.

AGE TERMS

One of the theoretical dimensions of aging that has received limited attention in anthropological literature is the use of age terms in different cultural settings. Age terms, like kinship terms, are one of the primary ways in which people situate themselves and others in society. Indeed, age and kinship as principles of social organization often intersect. Age structures may form bases of social organization that cross-cut or reinforce kinship ties within a community, or form alternate frames of social interaction that can complement or conflict with the sphere of kinship (Keith 1989:30). Much like kinship terms, age terms index ways in which people think about their social position relative to others.

In Japanese, a wide variety of terms apply to different points or periods in the life course. Calendar age is often a component of meaning in age terms, but many of these terms do not designate specific years in life. Rather, they designate periods of time punctuated by significant changes or transitions in the life course or relations of seniority between people.

In order to understand how the life course is partitioned, it will be useful to develop a lexicon of terms that are commonly used by people in Jōnai to describe different periods of life. The data for this lexicon are drawn from fifteen interviews in which individuals were asked to list the terms they would use to describe different periods in life, beginning from birth, and then identify the conditions under which use of one term stops and another begins. The terms presented are only some of those available in the Japanese language. Hence, this should not be taken as an exhaustive treatment of age terms. Rather, this lexicon is intended to represent those terms used on a regular basis by people in Jōnai.

The words that emerged from the interviews tend to fall into two broad categories: relational and periodic age terms. However, there are elements of periodicity within the relational terms and elements of relationality within the periodic terms. Thus, although I will employ these categories throughout the chapter, they should be seen as analytic devices rather than as emic frameworks used by Japanese to categorize the terminology of aging.

RELATIONAL AGE TERMS

Identification of seniority is one of the major themes in some of the most generally used age terms. Three terms divide people into categories based upon relative rank: *senpai* (senior), *kōhai* (junior), and *dōryō* (colleague) (Nakane 1970). In school, for example, a fourth-grader will be referred to as a third-grader's *senpai* and a fifth-grader's *kōhai*. Her classmates are *dōkyūsei*, which uses the same character 同 as found in *dōryō*, which means "same." These terms can be used throughout life simply to identify people's relative ages or relative positions within an institutional setting such as school or work, without reference to their specific age in calendar years. They also play a role in determining one's position within hierarchies of power both in school and in the working world. One's *senpai* in a school club, for example, may well be in a position to make demands such as performing menial tasks.

Kinship terms that connote relative age also carry this emphasis on identifying seniority in terms of birth order. Anyone who has spent time learning the Japanese language is likely to be struck by the absence of generic terms for sister and brother (although there is a generic term for sibling). Japanese categorize siblings on the basis of relative age; one has an older brother or younger brother, older sister or younger sister.[1] In fact, the generic term for sibling (*kyōdai*) refers to the number of siblings in a household, inclusive of the speaker, in contrast to the English pattern of identifying one's siblings exclusive of oneself. When referring to a specific brother or sister, a distinction is always made on the basis of age relative to the speaker.

The importance of acknowledging relative birth order is not limited to kin. Japanese people frequently invoke kinship terms to encourage or symbolize relationships of closeness between individuals who are not otherwise defined as related within the framework of Japanese kinship patterns. Use of kinship terms in this manner sometimes falls under the rubric of fictive or ritual kinship (Parkin 1997:124). Here, I will refrain from placing the terms discussed within this rubric, because it superimposes a theoretical category from anthropology upon the context in which people act. By labeling these terms as ritual or fictive kin terms, one inevitably privileges the kinship and genealogical meanings of the terms. Although words drawn from the lexicon of kinship are employed and manipulated in nonkinship contexts, this does not suggest that the content of the relationships to which they are applied are thought of as reflecting the closeness of kin ties, although in some cases they may. In the case of Japanese, kin terms can be used to encourage kin-like closeness, but also to insult, ingratiate, or joke with others.

In Japanese, terms such as those for older brother and older sister, aunt and uncle, and grandmother and grandfather not only identify kin, but are also used in reference to nonkin as a means of differentiating age on the basis of birth order. Use of these terms for nonkin is based not on chronological age, but on relative age, although this takes into account difference in chronological age. For example, when a mother refers to her neighbor's eighteen-year-old son while talking to her own five-year-old daughter, she will call him *onii-san*, older brother. However, when she refers to the eighteen-year-old's thirty-year-old brother or fifty-five-year-old father, she may use the term *oji-san*, uncle. When the twenty-five-year-old is speaking to a person who is twenty, he might be called *onii-san* or have no age-related referent at all, and when he refers to a forty-year-old man or woman, he is likely to use the terms *oji-san* and *oba-san*. Thus, the same person can be "older brother/sister" and "uncle/aunt" depending upon that individual's birth order relative to the person with whom he/she is speaking or to whom he/she is referring.

Uncle and aunt (*oji-san* and *oba-san*) are generally used for people who are older, but not dramatically older, than the person who is relating her- or himself to them. To some extent they have specific referents in the life course in that marriage or childbirth can indicate that one has entered into uncle- or aunt-hood, but during the period of one's thirties it may be unclear as to whether or not these terms apply. Children will often refer to their parents' friends as given name plus uncle or aunt (e.g., Hirohsi *oji-san* or Keiko *oba-san*) in much the same way that American children often refer to their parents' friends as aunt and uncle, even though there is no blood relationship. In these instances, use of aunt or uncle, although tied to relative age, is also functioning as a means of indicating social closeness that indicates familial emotional bonds.

Although the terms are often used to indicate social closeness, people in their thirties, particularly women, may resist being called aunt or uncle because the terms carry negative connotations that are ascribed on the basis of how others perceive the agedness of the referent. As one informant put it, the term *oji-san* refers to a man "who no longer understands what it is to be young" and *oba-san* refers to a woman "who thinks that she is getting older." *Oji-san*, in particular, can have a very negative meaning and a man who is "*oji-san kusai*" is one who has given in to middle-agedness and behaves in an unattractive manner. He wears unfashionable business suits that may not fit all that well, picks his nose in public, makes sucking noises as he attempts to clean matter from between his teeth, and has become quite set in his ways. *Oba-san* is, perhaps, a less negative image, but indicates a woman who has also given into the aging process and no longer perceives of herself as young. When women in their thirties first meet the young child of a friend, it is not uncommon for a brief discussion to ensue concerning whether the child should refer to her as older sister or aunt. Women who do not themselves have children are very likely to resist being referred to as aunt, preferring the child to call them older sister. The birth of a child seems to some extent to resign women to the idea that they have entered the stage of life in which they are to be called aunt.

While these terms are negotiated during the thirties, by the age of forty there is little question that one has entered into the phase of life associated with aunt- or uncle-hood. At this point, people usually will not hesitate to refer to themselves this way (some do not hesitate in their thirties either) and others will not hesitate in using these terms to refer to them. There is some variation in this on the basis of having not married nor had children. For some, it may seem odd to describe a single woman, for example, who has no children at age forty-five as aunt. Part of what identifies one with these terms is having experienced both marriage and child-bearing. However, to people who do not know her personally, such a woman will likely be referred to as aunt.

The terms for grandmother and grandfather (*ojii-san* and *obaa-san*) also can be used for nonkin (please note the distinction of these terms from *oji-san* and *oba-san*, which both have short vowel sounds). Any older person can be referred to by these terms or the more familiar (diminutive) *ojii-chan* and *obaa-chan*. Use of these terms is also relational and has a connection to both one's age in calendar years and one's physical appearance. At the most basic level, when one has a grandchild, within the family the grandparent will be referred to as either *ojii-chan* or *obaa-chan*. However, if there are still great-grandparents in the household, use of these terms for grandparents may be delayed in order to avoid confusion.

As with other kin terms, the terms for grandma and grandpa index more than simply having had grandchildren. They also are related to appearing old, both in terms of one's physical body and behaviorally, and to one's social status in the community. For example, when asked about a particular seventy-year-old man, Takeshita-san, no nonrelative stated that they would call him *ojii-san* (or *ojii-chan*). This was true even when they were informed that he has several grandchildren. Takeshita-san, a retired high school teacher, was the head of the town's board of education, organized and directed his hamlet's participation in one of the major rituals in town, took various classes, and was in good physical condition. Informants stated that his active social life and apparent good physical condition meant that it would be inappropriate to call him grandpa. Additionally, his position as a community leader and retired high school teacher gave him high social status that would further limit the appropriateness of using such a familiar term.

However, when another man of seventy was described who is slightly hunched over and walks with difficulty, or when a woman of the same age who has a severe case of osteoporosis was described, informants stated that they would use these terms for such people. They might, in some cases, describe the person as a *kawaii* (cute) *obaa-chan* or *ojii-chan*. For such individuals, having grandchildren is unrelated to the use of these terms (nonkin would, in fact, often have no idea if the person did or did not have grandchildren). Instead, these are indicators of the referent's age and generational affiliation relative to the person using the term. They imply a kind of familial closeness and respect for older people. As one twenty-three-year-old woman stated, *ojii-san* means a man who knows everything, somebody who has attained wisdom (*subete ga wakatte iru hito*). *Obaa-san* means a woman who has become kind in everything, who is in a stage of life in which kindness characterizes her behavior (*subete ni yasashiku naru, sō iu jiki no hito*). For this informant, these terms, when referring to outsiders, have absolutely nothing to do with having grandchildren.

Ambiguity, of course, pervades the usage of these terms and, as evident in the case of Takeshita-san, the social status of an individual may play a significant role in whether or not kinship terms are used. The above terms identify relations of seniority that are age-based, but most age terms are not specifically connected to seniority. Rather, they identify periods of the life course through which people travel as they grow older.

PERIODIC AGE TERMS

Birth is a starting point through which people in all cultures begin a process of moving through various phases of life, the transitions of which are often punctuated by ritual activities and the periods of which often have specific names like adolescence, middle age, and old age.

In Japan, there is a wide array of terms, many of which overlap in meaning, with which people talk about the phases of the life course. From an ethnographic perspective, identifying the points at which usage of periodic age terms changes as people age is daunting because the transitions themselves are vague. At what point does a child stop being a baby and start being a toddler? Collecting data related to the use of periodic age terms presents problems to the researcher because of the ambiguous nature of their usage. In the following discussion, I am drawing from fifteen interviews with people of varying ages. Informants were asked to begin with birth and indicate the words they would use to describe a person as he or she ages. They were asked to identify the points at which they would begin using a different term and why they would change. The basis for shifting to a new term varied among informants; some people based the change on chronological age, some focused more on changes in life such as entrance into school or the workforce, and some used a combination of the two.

Although there is variation in how people use periodic age terms, patterns do emerge. As people talk about a new arrival, the most frequently used term is *aka-chan* (baby). Some people also use the term *akambo* (equivalent to *aka-chan*) in reference to the child or *nyūji*, which most people define as being limited to the first year of life, while *aka-chan* and *akambo* may be used for a longer period of time. People also refer to the child by his or her name, usually with the diminutive *-chan* added to the end of the name (or sometimes *-kun*, if the child is a boy).

The point at which a child is no longer in the *aka-chan* stage of life is ambiguous. When the child begins to walk, or is weaned from breast-feeding, or is about one year old, some people will no longer use these terms to describe the child. Others may use these terms as late as three years old. The size and behavior of the child come into play in determining when to end use of terms for baby. A child of two who is big for his age is not likely to be referred to as a baby.

There is a considerable degree of overlap in the terms used for infancy and the next stage of life, which we think of in America as the toddler stage. From around the age of one, people refer to boys as *bōya*, *bot-chan*, or *bō-cha* and girls as *jō-cha* or *jō-chan*. These terms can be used up until entrance into elementary school, as can another term, *yōji* (the period is called *yōnen*), which carries no reference to gender. It is also during this time in life that people begin using the general term *kodomo* (child) to refer to both boys and girls. Although the exact timing at which people stop using terms like *aka-chan* and begin using terms like *bōya* is not precisely defined, it is during the toddler years that some terms for children become differentiated on the basis of gender, although many age referents do not carry gender-based connotations.

With entrance into school, children are referred to on the basis of their grade level. Elementary school students are called *shōgakusei*, middle-school students *chūgakusei*, and high school students *kōkōsei*. Each term represents the level of school plus the term for student, thus *shōgakō* plus *sei* becomes *shōgakusei* and refers to all elementary school students. When asked the age of a schoolchild, a parent will normally not respond with the child's age in calendar years. Instead, the response will be something like "he's middle-school, second year" or "she's elementary school, first year." The age of school children is rarely referred to in terms of calendar years and it is not unusual for a parent or grandparent to find it much easier to give the school year rather than the chronological, calendar age of his or her child. The chronology of grade takes precedence over the chronology of calendar years for school children.

There are also more inclusive terms covering school years—*jidō*, *seito*, and *gakusei*—although there is some variation in how these terms are applied. *Jidō* refers to the period of elementary school, thus it corresponds to *shōgakusei*. The other terms are less clearly defined. Some people state that *seito* applies to middle school and high school students, while others state that *gakusei* applies to high school and college students. It seems fairly clear that middle school students are not *gakusei*, but *seito*; however opinions about where *seito* ends and *gakusei* begins vary. Some informants indicate that *gakusei* is only for college students, but others apply it to high school students as well.

Graduation from high school brings entrance into a new phase of life, but how one should think about that stage is complicated by the fact that the life-course trajectories of people after high school vary. At this point, an individual can enter the working world and become a *shakaijin* (public person, see Roberson 1995), but some go on to college, which delays entrance into public personhood; as long as one is a student, he or she is not yet *shakaijin*. A problem that occurs is that at the age of high school graduation (eighteen years old), one has not yet participated in the ritual called *seijinshiki*, which is a nationally practiced coming-of-age ceremony that ushers in adulthood. Most informants state that entrance into adulthood corresponds to *seijinshiki*, but at the same time it is difficult to call someone working at the age of eighteen anything other than an adult. Furthermore, for college students *seijinshiki* occurs during one's college years. This means that college students have a period of overlap between studenthood and adulthood; most older informants hesitate in granting full status as an adult until graduation from all formal schooling.

The period between high school graduation and adulthood represents what Van Gennep and Turner would describe as a liminal period. In this case, rather than occurring within the context of a ritual performance, as Van Gennep and Turner indicate, the liminal period occurs in relation to the transition from one phase of life to the next and its associated ritual. People at this stage of life fit well with what Turner describes as having "liminal *personae*" (Turner 1977:95; Van Gennep 1960). They are threshold people or liminal entities perched between childhood and adulthood. Those who enter the working world immediately after high school have acquired the social status as worker that allows for them to be called adult, but they have yet to carry out the appropriate ritual performance that punctuates the transition from one age status to the next. Those who are still college students have usually carried out the ritual, but lack the appropriate social status to be definitively termed adults. Regardless of one's choice, graduation from high school initiates an extended period of liminality that is not resolved until *seijinshiki* or college graduation, depending upon the path chosen. And for women the liminal state may continue until marriage or family formation (Kawano 1996).

Emergence from this liminal period brings with it status as a young adult and a new term that identifies that status. From this point onward, a person can be called *otona* or adult and young adults are usually referred to as being in the period of life called *seinen*, meaning "full age." The word "*seinen*" is problematic for translation into English because there are three different combinations of *kanji* (Chinese characters used in Japanese) that are pronounced in this way, all three having to do with age. The first means "full age" (成年) and describes the age at which one becomes an adult (twenty years old) and experiences *seijinshiki* (成人式). The second means "youth" or young adulthood (青年) and describes the early years of adulthood, particularly for men. The third (盛年) also describes a period of life, one's "prime of life." This term is not regularly used by people living in Jōnai when referring to periods of life, thus, I will not deal with it here.

While the year of *seinen* (full age) is clearly defined at twenty, there is some uncertainty as to whether the period of *seinen* (young adulthood) actually starts at age eighteen or twenty because of the fact that *seijinshiki* does not correspond to the age from which one can become a public, working person. The period of *seinen* continues until sometime between the ages of thirty and forty, but no informants were certain as to what constitutes the end of *seinen*. Some indicated that either at marriage or the birth of one's first child one was no longer in *seinen*. Nonetheless, a fifty-year-old man who is unmarried and has no children will not be considered still in *seinen*.

Following *seinen*, men enter a period of life called *sōnen*, which translates as "prime of manhood." This period lasts from around forty to around sixty, or the point of retirement from work. It corresponds to the period in one's working life when one has achieved higher levels of responsibility, has a wife and children, and is at one's peak abilities.

There is no definitive similar term for women, although some informants suggested *chūnen*, which means middle age and can be applied to either males or females, or *jukunen*, which appears to be a recently created word that means coming into maturity or ripening. However, application of this word is somewhat unclear among informants. Suggestions about its meaning were that it applies to both men and women between forty and fifty, fifty and sixty, or to only women between forty and sixty. Another term that informants suggested is a new word for women in this period of life is *jitsunen*, which implies a period of sincerity, kindness, and fidelity. This was described as occurring between thirty-five and fifty, fifty and sixty-five, and a few variations in between. These terms are not commonly used in daily conversation and appear to be attempts promulgated through popular media to fill a void in the aging lexicon for women. By far the most common term for women from marriage until entrance into the *rōjin kurabu* or Old Persons Club[2] is *fujin*. The term simply translates as "woman," but employs the Chinese character for a housewife or married woman and is not generally used for young, unmarried women; although widows and women in their forties who have not married would be referred to using this term.

Age terms for later years of life, although clearly defined, are often highly contested. Many older people do not like the commonly used terms to identify their stage in life, thus there are occasionally new terms that arise, but many older people find these unsatisfactory, as well. The two most common terms for older people are *rōjin* ("old person") and *otoshiyori* ("upper years") or simply *toshiyori*, the "o" adds a feeling of respect to the term. These two terms are generally seen as beginning at the age of either sixty or sixty-five and the term that applies to this period of life is *rōnen*, which lasts until death. The term *rōjin* is the official term used by the government to identify people over the age of sixty-five. In order for an institution to be classified properly and receive government money as a nursing home or other facility for older people it must include this term in its name. Nonetheless, the term is not generally considered politically correct. Older people often do not like the term because it carries with it a strong image of oldness and to some extent failing health. Most older people prefer the more familiar *ojii-san* and *obaa-san*, which mean grandpa and grandma, respectively, a point to which I will return in the next chapter.

In addition to these terms, several newer terms have arisen in recent years. Like some of the newer terms used for women, these terms have been developed and encouraged through the popular media as a way of providing less negative terms for old age. The most common of these is *kōreisha*. There is a great deal of variation in how people perceive this term. Some informants stated that it is the same as *rōjin* and *otoshiyori*, but some indicated that it is reserved for later old age. For example, one informant stated that use of this term corresponds to one's first participation in Respect for the Aged Day (a national holiday that occurs on September 15th). In many towns the age at which one can begin participating in the annual ceremony for the aged is stipulated by the town government. In the case of Kanegasaki, one can participate from one's seventy-third birthday onward. Thus, for this informant, the term *kōreisha* can be used from the age of seventy-three, but it would vary depending upon the town. Other informants indicated sometime between seventy and eighty years of age as the point where this term is used. These informants suggest a strong sense of later old age associated with the term. In addition to *kōreisha*, one older informant indicated that the term *jukunen* (mature years), mentioned above, is used for early old age by people who "are old, but do not want to be called *rōjin*, because they do not yet see themselves as old."

TALKING ABOUT OLD AGE

Understanding the terminology associated with periods in the life course and age-based relations among people helps to clarify the manner in which the life course is structured in Japanese society. As the above stated explanation for the use of the term *jukunen* suggests, terms related to old age, in particular, are contested. Indeed, as will become evident in the next chapter, entrance into elder status and the definition of old age as a period in the life course, is highly contested among older residents of Jōnai.

CHAPTER 5

Age Grading around Jōnai

Anthropologists and gerontologists have shown that most societies exhibit some form of age stratification, by which particular social roles and statuses are associated with specific age strata (Foner 1984; Kertzer and Schaie 1989; Riley 1976). However, highly formalized age-set and age-grade systems observed by anthropologists in East Africa and some other parts of the world (Sangree 1989; Stewart 1977; Evans-Pritchard 1940; Suenari 1996) are rare, particularly in urban industrial societies.

As noted in the previous chapter, Japan is one urban industrial locale that exhibits very clearly delineated periods of the life course and limited variation in the timing of transitions from one period to the next. In rural parts of the country, entrance into elder status is often formally structured around a system of age grading that provides a more linear framework for defining different periods in the life course than the age terms we explored in the previous chapter. This framework not only defines the point in life that one makes the transition from middle age to old age, it also symbolically represents the public discourse on aging and, thus, can be used as a basis upon which to resist engaging that discourse. Rather than move smoothly into old age, people negotiation the transition from middle to old age by resisting entrance into the elder age grade and identification with terms that directly index being old.

AGE-GRADING PRACTICES

The term "age grade" has been used in a variety of ways, sometimes referring simply to different age strata in a society or in some instances being applied to specific structures such as career ladders that are segmented on the basis of age (Featherman et al. 1989:56). It is necessary to precisely define the term for the purposes of this book, because I am using it in the narrow sense typically employed by anthropologists. By age-grading practices, I simply mean the institutionalized ordering of people on the basis of age, by which membership in one graded age group precludes membership in any other and is a basis for social differentiation by virtue of membership in that group (Traphagan 1998a). Age grades are distinguished from age sets, another form of age structuring that has been identified by anthropologists. As Evans-Pritchard points out, age sets are characterized by permanent membership (Evans-Pritchard 1940:6). Once an individual has been initiated into an age set, he or she remains a member until death. By contrast, age grades are social structures through which individuals or the members of a specific age set pass as they grow older (Radcliffe-Brown 1929; Sangree 1989; Stewart 1977).

In rural Japan a formal system of age stratification operates that approximates the age-set and age-grade systems that have been observed in less complex societies in East Africa. Much like Evens-Pritchard's observations among the Neur, in rural Japan this system of age stratification, and use of the age terms discussed in the previous chapter, structurally defines every member of the community in relation to every other member on the basis of seniority, equality, or juniority (Evans-Pritchard 1940:257). Formalized age stratification is a key feature of Japanese social organization that distinguishes it from other urban industrial societies that, although clearly exhibiting age strata, do not base age-related social differentiation on institutionalized age-grading practices.

The presence of age-grading practices in Japanese society has been observed by anthropologists since the earliest ethnographic studies in rural areas. Embree, working in 1930s rural Japan, noted the importance of age-related associations for allocating community work among different members of the village:

> Most hard work is performed by men between the ages of eighteen and forty, termed collectively *seinen*. . . . Men from forty to sixty, while doing plenty of work, act as advisers to the *seinen*. It is this older group which decides and directs all *buraku* [hamlet] affairs. (Embree 1939:87)

In the 1950s both Norbeck and Beardsley noted again the presence of age grades (Beardsley et al. 1959; Norbeck 1953). For these scholars the remaining formalized age grades seemed to be vestiges of a past that was losing relevance as Japan modernized and urbanized. More recent Western literature concerned with the segmentation of the life course in Japan has focused upon the relatively low degree of variation in the timing of life-course transitions among Japanese and the high degree of distinction between different periods in life (Noguchi 1983; Noguchi 1990; Plath 1983). Although there is no formal age-set system operating in Japan, the timing of life-course transitions exhibits little variance across individuals and shows very little overlap between the spreads of two or more transitions (Brinton 1992:83). Japanese tend to form tightly bound age cohorts, reminiscent of age sets, that are formed in relation to school, entrance into the workforce, or childbirth.

In urban areas, the uniformity of age transitions is less directly attached to age-grading practices than in rural areas, because few of the former age-grading structures remain in urban settings. This point has been noted by several Japanese scholars who have conducted studies of age-grading practices in recent years (Emori 1976; Fukuda 1982; Kurusawa and Akimoto 1990; Suenari 1981a; Suenari 1981b). In rural, agricultural areas, age-grading practices persist as what I call "age-grade associations"—formalized local groups whose composition is based upon membership in a particular age category (Traphagan 1998a). Modern age-grade associations, like age grades of the past,

> involve people who live in the same village, often work in close proximity and even bathe together nightly. They not only grow up together, they grow old together too. Apart from close family, they are probably the people one knows best, yet relations between them are institutionalised in quite definite ways. (Hendry 1981:44)

Today people in age-grade associations are less likely to bathe together on a nightly basis (they do bathe together occasionally when members of an association take trips to hot springs). Still Hendry's description of such groups in Kyūshū rings true in other rural regions of Japan.

Age-grade practices are important for understanding the experience of aging for older people in Jōnai, because age-grade associations form contexts in which older individuals can insulate themselves from changing patterns of social behavior. The age-grade system provides a framework for older individuals to participate in activities that are limited to the broadly defined over-sixty-five age cohort. These are people who generally perceive of themselves, and are perceived by others, as sharing common life experiences and patterns of social behavior that are different from those of younger Japanese. As an age stratum in Japanese society, it is viewed as having its worldview shaped largely by the events surrounding the Pacific War and, as noted in chapter 2, the educational system that operated prior to the Occupation.

In Jōnai, an institutionalized system of age grading operates through five different associations whose membership is based upon one's stage in the life course and gender. These five age grades are the Women's Association (*fujinbu*), Young Men's Association (*seinenbu*),[1] Children's Association (*kodomokai*), Upbringing Association (*ikuseikai*), and the Old Persons Club (*rōjin kurabu*). In some neighboring hamlets two further associations exist, the Middle-Aged Men's Association (*sōnenbu*) and the Young Married Women's Association (*wakatsumakai*). Much like what Embree describes, these associations have specific work responsibilities within the community.

Before moving into a discussion of each age-grade association, two points are important. First, age-grade associations are split on the basis of gender throughout much of the life course. The exceptions to this are grades that occur at the early and later years of the life course—the Children's Association, Upbringing Association, and Old Persons Club. The fact that associations only at the beginning and later stages of life are mixed-gender suggests that there is a common element in how Japanese people think about these two periods of life, a point to which I will return later. Second, all of the associations are part of the administrative organization of the hamlet. In general, age-grade associations fall within the scope of the hamlet Self-Government Association (SGA, *jichikai*), which is the political body responsible for managing the hamlet. It organizes community work groups such as park cleaning and sewer cleaning, delegates work to different associations within the hamlet, and collects fines levied against households who fail to carry out their responsibilities for a given activity (such as ¥500 for failing to attend park cleaning). The SGA is also the body through which most hamletwide social activities are organized. For example, the SGA organizes hamlet New Year celebrations, the summer *bon* festival for the ancestors, and manages the election for the offices in the hamlet.

There are forty-six hamlets (*chiku* or *buraku*) and six larger districts (*ku*) in Kanegasaki. Each of these *chiku* has its own SGA and, thus, its own set of age-grade associations. The SGAs for the section of the town in which Jōnai is located are organizationally structured under the district of Machichiku, and the heads of each respective SGA have regular meetings, but there is no direct connection of the SGA to the town government. Each hamlet's SGA operates as an independent entity. There is a standard organizational structure for hamlet Self-Government Associations that is presented as a guide in a town-produced book on plans for the twenty-first century (Tsukamoto et al. 1985) and the chart presented in the book is similar to what is found in most of the hamlets in Kanegasaki. But hamlets are free to improvise on this plan or organize the SGA in any way they see fit.

In Jōnai the organizational structure of the SGA is similar to the model proposed by the town, with the exception that some suggested offices are not included. Also, according to the head of the Jōnai SGA, other hamlet SGAs are not normally administrative organizations; hamlet administration is handled by the *gyōseikai* (Administration Association), which has a separate structure. In Jōnai the administrative functions are merged into the SGA, and, in fact, the head of the SGA is also the head of the hamlet administratively (*kuchō*).

The SGA in Jōnai consists of the following sections or departments (*bu*): general affairs section (*sōmubu*), preservation of physical health section (*hoken taiikubu*), welfare section (*fukushibu*), and education section (*bunkyōbu*). Each section has a head who does most of the daily work and a vice-head who stands in when the head is unable to take care of his or her duties. According to the current SGA head, these four sections organizationally fall under the direct control of the SGA. The hamlet's age-grade associations are not directly under the SGA. In organizational charts showing the SGA, the age-grade associations are connected by dotted lines and, thus, are not directly under the SGA umbrella. This is a subtle point that others in the hamlet do not generally recognize. Residents of the hamlet simply view the age-grade associations as being a part of the SGA, and in neighboring hamlets the age-grade associations are clearly presented as subsections of the SGA in materials produced by those hamlets.

Figure 5.1 shows a fully elaborated age-grade structure as it would fall under the framework of the SGA in a given hamlet. There are few hamlets that have developed a complete system of age-grade associations and many have one or more association in the process of formation. Membership in each age-grade association excludes membership in any other hamlet-based age-grade association, although it does not preclude membership in outside age-grade associations and other age-related groups.

Of course, membership in the Women's Association and Young Men's Association is exclusive due to the fact that these are gender- as well as age-segregated associations. Furthermore, although one usually cannot become a member of the Old Persons Club while still a member of one of the other age-grade associations, in some cases exceptions are made to allow a woman to belong to both associations at the same time. In one instance, a woman who was 59 wanted to join the gateball team in the hamlet. Gateball, however, is organized and run by the Old Persons Club and is limited to members of that club. An exception was made so that the woman could be a member of both associations at the same time. She has stated that when she is sixty-five she will quit the Women's Association. I know of no similar instance for men and the large separation in age between membership in the Young Men's Association and the Old Persons Club makes this highly unlikely.

In addition to these hamlet associations, residents may also belong to other age-grade associations related to their work. Both the Agricultural Cooperative and the business association in town have Young Men's Associations and the Agricultural Cooperative also has a Women's Association (mentioned above). These are townwide organizations, although they do have subdivisions that are related to sections of the town. Furthermore, there are associations known as *fujinkai* (Women's Association) and *seinenkai* (Young Adult Association) that operate across hamlet lines. In the town where Jōnai is located, there are six *fujinkai* and six *seinenkai* (open to both men and women), which are linked to prefectural and national women's and young adult associa-

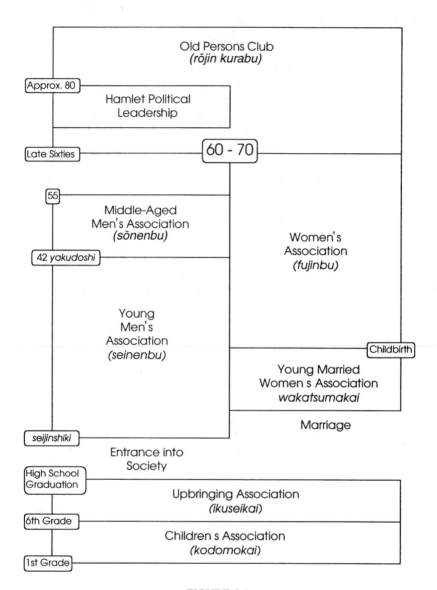

FIGURE 5.1
Fully articulated age grade structure. Few hamlets have all components of this structure.

tions. In Kanegasaki, however, participation in these associations is weak because many of the activities with which they are concerned—such as fire-prevention awareness—are duplicated at the hamlet-level *seinenbu* and *fujinbu*.

THE CHILDREN'S ASSOCIATION

The first age-grade association that one enters is the *kodomokai* or Children's Association, which includes children who are in elementary school (grades one through six). Activities of the Children's Association include both recreation and work. As of 1996, there were twenty-three children in the Children's Association in Jōnai. All children in the hamlet of the appropriate age are automatically enrolled in the association and children do not have the option to quit the association. As a result of the uniform enrollment, these children approximate an age set in that, provided they remain in Kanegasaki, they form an age cohort that will move through the following age grades together throughout the remainder of their lives.

In summer and winter breaks from school, the group has an outing for lighting fireworks and a barbecue. In the winter they go to a hot spring that has a pool in which the children can swim. Plans for the future include a summer camping trip and a winter ski trip, both of which have been requested by the children. Activities vary from one year to the next depending, in part, upon which adults are involved and the desires of the children.

Other activities of the association are related to work responsibilities within the hamlet. In Omotekōji, on the second Saturday of each month from May to November, the children in the Children's Association do cleaning of garbage along the streets and also clean the rain gutters that run along the edge of all streets in the hamlet. In Datekōji, the children clean the Fudō-san and Yama-no-kami shrines on the second Saturday of each month (children are not required to attend school on the second and fourth Saturdays of each month).

Furthermore, the Children's Association plays a significant role in environmentally oriented recycling activities in the hamlet. Three times per year, the association collects bottles and newspapers and receives money for turning these in at a recycling center. This money is then used to help support other activities of the association. Usually, they manage to bring in around ¥15,000 or ¥16,000 for each collection, thus making around ¥50,000 per year. They also receive an additional ¥10,000 or so from the town government for recycling activities. Altogether, they bring in about ¥70,000 to ¥80,000 for an average year's recycling efforts.

Finally, during the summer vacation the association meets in the hamlet park at 6:30 a.m. for *rajio taisō*, an exercise class held in conjunction with the morning exercise program broadcast by the Japanese national broadcasting organization NHK. Some of the children do not like the early hours of the exercise meeting, but, as the mother of the current association head stated, "children cannot refuse to participate."

The organizational structure of the Children's Association follows that of other age-grade associations in the hamlet. The association has a head, who is always a sixth-grader, and two vice-heads who are also sixth-graders if there are enough sixth-graders to take the job. Otherwise, the position is given to fifth-graders. As of 1996, the association head was a boy and the two vice-heads were girls, these three accounting for all of the sixth-graders in the association. Girls do at times take the position of head, but this happens only in the absence of a sixth-grade boy. The mothers of the association head and vice-heads become the primary adults involved with guiding the association, although the regular operations are run by the children.

THE UPBRINGING ASSOCIATION

The Upbringing Association is intended for children in middle school and high school. Adults in the hamlet describe this as an association on paper only, because all children of the appropriate ages belong by default of living in the hamlet and it virtually has no meetings or events. The only activity in which it is routinely involved is the annual Children's Association softball meet in which the Upbringing Association members coach the younger children. The lack of activity is attributed to the high levels of involvement in school club activities that begin in middle school and the importance of high school and college entrance examinations, which limit the participation of children in this age group in community activities.

THE YOUNG MEN'S ASSOCIATION

For men, the first adult, hamlet-oriented age-grade association that one enters is the Young Men's Association or *seinenbu*. Membership in the Young Men's Association is connected to the early years of a man's working life. Membership is open to men from the time they begin working, usually from around the age of eighteen or nineteen if one does not go to college (later for college graduates), and continues until the age of forty-five. In neighboring hamlets, the age at which one leaves the *seinenbu* is usually forty-two. This age is known as *yakudoshi*, considered an inauspicious year particularly for men in Japan. In Jōnai, because there are few men between the ages of twenty and forty-two, the age has been gradually pushed upward in order to keep the membership of the *seinenbu* sufficient to carry out the association's activities.

Young Men's Association activities include softball outings, a father-son bowling day, a New Year gathering, participation with the Minamimachi (the immediately neighboring hamlet) Young Men's Association's "beer garden," which takes place on the main street of Kanegasaki, and meetings on the third Saturday of each month for conversation and drinking. The only hamlet work responsibility delegated to the Young Men's Association is the running of the annual *bon* festival for the ancestors held in August. This entails decorating the park where the festival is held, ordering beer and food, and setting up tables for children's games. The association also builds a large, elevated platform on which a drum is placed. This drum is used for beating the time for dancing and is played by members of the association while recorded music is played over a speaker system.

THE WOMEN'S ASSOCIATION

For women, the first adult, hamlet-oriented age-grade association one enters is the Women's Association (*fujinbu*). Entrance in the Women's Association is later than entrance into the Young Men's Association, and membership is connected not to work, but to marriage. Women are eligible to belong to the association from the time they are married, although they usually enter sometime between the ages of thirty-five and forty, the early years of marriage being devoted more to activities associated with child rearing. Membership in the Women's Association continues until a woman enters the Old Persons Club at the age of sixty-five.

The Women's Association also has regular social gatherings and outings throughout the year. The primary work responsibility for the association is assistance in the work of the Health, Welfare, and Culture sections of the Self-Government Association. The association also is responsible for promoting fire awareness in the hamlet. Although not formally charged with the responsibility, members of the Women's Association invariably handle food preparation for most hamlet social or administrative gatherings.

THE OLD PERSONS CLUB

Sometime between their early sixties and early seventies, most people in Jōnai become members of the *rōjin kurabu* or Old Persons Club.[2] As of

1996, there were seventy-eight members of the club, which included most of the people in the hamlet over the age of seventy. Unlike the other age-grade associations in the hamlet, the Old Persons Club is connected to larger organizations of Old Persons Clubs at town, county, and prefectural levels. Heads of the Old Persons Clubs in town have meetings and the head of the town-level group meets annually with heads from other parts of the prefecture. Old Persons Clubs throughout the town receive some financial support from the town's Health and Welfare Center (*Fukushi Sentā*). The Jōnai club, for example, received ¥57,600 from the town in 1995.

As with other hamlet age-grade associations, members pay dues (annual dues are ¥2,400 per person) and there are occasional fees for special events that can be as much as ¥10,000 per person depending upon the kind of event. In 1995, these fees were for the New Year meeting (a party), the spring trip (an overnight trip to the ocean), and a potato-roasting gathering. There are also other events such as trips to hot springs for which people pay if they participate. The club's expenses include money for the annual Old Persons' Sports Meet, various parties throughout the year, dues to the townwide Old Persons Club organization, a Social Communication Meeting in the town, and various recreational activities.

Throughout 1996, there were fifty-six different activities, events, or meetings in which some or all members of the club were involved. These activities included regular meetings of the club or of the club's leadership and meetings of the heads of Old Persons Clubs throughout the town. Those activities in which several members of the club participated included nine gateball tournaments, five athletic tournaments, two visits to bed-ridden individuals living at the local nursing home, and several town- or county-sponsored classes or meetings on health. Additionally, there was a "tea gathering for thinking about human rights," a "traffic safety tea gathering," and a meeting for younger people to come and talk with older people.

There are no formal work responsibilities in the hamlet assigned to the Old Persons Club. However, as is indicated in figure 5.1 (and also in chapter 3), much of the power in the hamlet is in the hands of men who are members of the Old Persons Club and whose ages range from the late sixties to the early eighties. Virtually all high-level offices in the hamlet Self-Government Association are occupied by men who are also members of the Old Persons Club. The exceptions to this are those offices related to health and child rearing (education) and the hamlet treasurer. These offices are normally occupied by women, and age plays a less significant role in determining which women occupy a particular position. Women in the Women's Association are actively involved in hamlet operations, and frequently hold those offices available to women. This point seems to correspond to the fact that the woman's side of the age-grade structure is less elaborated than the men's.

The head of the Old Persons Club is an important office that carries considerable symbolic capital in the hamlet. The head is always a prominent, respected man who is asked by other prominent men to fill the position when a sitting head resigns. The head has a great deal of influence over the general affairs of the hamlet. He can be seen at all important hamlet functions, such as elections for the town assembly or any of the hamlet gatherings that include all ages. At such gatherings, he is always seated in a position of honor with the other important men in the hamlet, and is asked to give a speech (*aisatsu*). Consultations about important hamlet business always include the head of the Self-Government Association, the head of the Old Persons Club, and a few other prominent males. Typically, those older men who once held hamlet offices, and those who have held important offices in the town, such as assemblymen, belong to the circle of elders who manage the hamlet.

In Jōnai, a considerable amount of hamlet business is conducted informally among a small group of men who include the head of the Self-Government Association, the representative to the Town Assembly, three older men who have held important positions in the past, and the head of the Old Persons Club. Men who do not participate in the Old Persons Club are rarely involved in hamlet decision making.

CONTESTING THE TRANSITION TO OLD AGE

In Jōnai the Old Persons Club allows membership by both men and women who are aged sixty and above. One might imagine that with Japanese concerns about age-appropriate behavior and the uniform timing of life-course transitions in Japan, people would smoothly transfer into the Old Persons Club when they become eligible. But one's sixties is a time of often contested transition from ascribed and self identification as middle-aged to identification with the elder portion of the population. Membership in the Old Persons Club symbolizes having completed this transition, and having succumbed to and accepted an identity as old.

> At sixty-six, I don't feel at all like I am an old person (*toshiyori*). It used to be when I was younger that if you made it to fifty, you were really an old person, but it is totally different now because the life expectancy has gone up so much. It feels strange to be in the Old Persons Club [OPC], and I didn't want to join it at all. The reason I joined is because I love playing *go* (a Japanese boardgame similar to chess or checkers)

and the OPC has three meetings a month for playing *go*. Throughout the year there are gatherings for *go* playing in different towns and I can only participate if I am in the OPC. It's probably insulting, but I wouldn't have enterred the OPC if I had not wanted to play *go*. I don't want to do things characteristic of old people (*rōjinteki*), but I love *go* and it was the only way I could arrange to play a lot.

Indeed, people do not usually enter the club when, on the basis of having become sixty, they are eligible. A comparison of the club roster in Jōnai and the town's population register shows that there is a tendency to delay entrance until approximately the age of seventy (see table 5.1). If entrance into the OPC corresponded at least roughly to eligibility, one would expect to find membership patterns largely matching the age distribution of the hamlet; mean ages between the two groups would not likely vary significantly.[3] By looking at the frequency distributions of age in the hamlet and Old Persons Club (see table 5.1), it is evident that OPC membership corresponds to hamlet age distribution only after the age of sixty-nine.

Of a total sixty people between the ages of sixty and sixty-nine who are eligible for membership in the OPC, only eight actually belong. However, from the age of seventy and above, all eligible individuals, save one, belong to the club. The one individual who does not belong is a man of seventy-nine who states that he has no intention of joining the club in the future and who generally does not involve himself in any hamlet activities, either recreational or political. Simply looking at the data suggests that the variation in the age distributions of the OPC and hamlet is unlikely to be due to chance and, indeed, statistical analysis supports this. Bivariate analysis using the chi-square statistic indicates that the probability that the variation is due to chance is negligible at p = .0001.

TABLE 5.1
Bivariate Table Showing Old Persons Club (OPC) Members
and Hamlet Residents by Age Group
(Expected Values in Parenthesis)

	60–69	70+	Totals
In OPC	8 (35.73)	70 (42.27)	78
Not in OPC	52 (24.27)	1 (28.73)	53
Totals	60	71	131

Jōnai is by no means unique in this pattern of delaying entrance into the OPC. In the neighboring city of Mizusawa, in a neighborhood of 552 people in which 112 were over the age of 65 as of 1998, only 56 belonged to the OPC. The mean age for members was 74 (σ = 6.57) with a median age of 72.5. There were no members under 64, and only six under 68. As with Jōnai, membership appears to be delayed until around the age of 69 or 70.

Like the sixty-six-year-old resident of Mizusawa quoted above, people living in Jōnai and its surrounding areas often indicate that they delayed entrance into the OPC as long as possible. As one farmer living in Jōnai commented:

> I didn't enter the *rōjin kurabu* (OPC) until I was seventy, which I guess was late. I don't like the name "*rōjin*." I think they should call the club the *seinenkai* [Youth Association] or something like that [laughs]. The reason I didn't enter the club is because I really don't like the name, but people kept asking me to join so I finally gave up and accepted that I am *rōjin*. But I put it off as long as possible. If you call the club something like that you will end up coming to the feeling that you are *toshiyori* or *rōjin*. I think older people should live with a way of thinking that is more like what people have in *seinen*. You should come to think that you are a *rōjin* on your own. This is something you should come to think about on your own and not in relation to group membership.

The above informant stated that he did not like the name of the OPC because he dislikes the term *rōjin*, a term that to him symbolizes being old and contributes to the asciprtion of an identity upon him as an "old person." He does not want to be identified with elder status on the basis of his age or group membership, but would prefer to decide or control the point at which he is identified as *rōjin*. Thus, he delayed entrance into the OPC (and the assumption of an identity associated with old age) as long as possible.

Along a similar vein, a sixty-five-year-old woman, Futagawa-san, spoke about leaving the Women's Association and entering the OPC as follows:

> FUTAGAWA-SAN: I am in the Women's Association, but I am thinking about entering the Old Persons Club now that I am sixty-five. But I still have things that I want to do. We have been taking a tea class in the Women's Association over at the community center and I have been thinking that I might want to continue at that. The Old Persons Club doesn't really do anything like that.

> JWT: If you leave the Women's Association can you still participate in that sort of class? Will you be excluded from participating in the activities like tea?

FUTAGAWA-SAN: No, I don't think so. But, you know, I don't really feel like I want to enter the Old Persons Club. I think I want to wait another five years before I go into the Old Persons Club. Now that I am sixty-five, I've been thinking that maybe I should switch over, but I don't really feel like I am a *rōjin* yet. Not until I am seventy, then I guess I will be a *rōjin*. I just feel like I am not ready to go into the *rōjin kurabu* yet.

Part of Futagawa-san's desire to stay in the Women's Association is related to having a circle of friends with whom she participates in activities at the local community center. Undoubtedly as her friends begin to move into the OPC, she will do so as well, and, in fact, several informants stated that there is a tendency for groups of women to move together from the Women's Association to the OPC. Because of the large gap in age between the Young Men's Association (which one leaves at forty-five) and the OPC, men are more likely to join on an individual basis.

But there is another important point here. Associated with entering the Old Persons Club is a sense that she would basically stop doing things like the tea ceremony, because that is not what old people do. This points to an emphasis on age-appropriate behavior that shapes decisions about the kinds of things people do at different points in life. Of course, there is nothing stopping Futagawa-san from participating in these activities if she is in the OPC, but the two do not seem to go together for her. Since she does not yet view herself as *rōjin*, she does not want to be in a social framework and to have assumed an identity that reflects oldness, nor does she want to give up activities she associates with being *fujin* or a middle-aged woman. She realizes that it will come soon, but she wants to delay it for another five years or so, when it is more clear that she will fit the category of *rōjin*.

The sentiments of this man and woman are echoed by many in their sixties. In part this is connected to a general resistance to being defined as an "old person" (*rōjin*). Some in their sixties, when talking about entering the OPC, joke that when they reach seventy, perhaps seventy-five will seem like a good time to join. People in their sixties, like the man quoted earlier, state frequently that they do not feel like they are *rōjin*—they do not feel that they are old—even if society tells them that as of age sixty or sixty-five they have officially reached that stage of life and that they are now officially termed *rōjin* and can belong to the OPC. In short, people contest entrance into elder status by delaying or resisting entrance into the OPC.

In fact, as noted in the previous chapter, the term *rōjin* itself is strongly disliked by many older people in the hamlet, as are other terms that directly index being old. In order to develop a better understanding of people's reaction to age terms, I administered a forced-choice questionnaire to all residents of the hamlet over the age of sixty who were able to respond. The sampling universe for the questionnaire was the hamlet; thus my intention was to gain as close to a 100 percent sample as possible. Some residents were physically or mentally unable to respond; the response rate was approximately 73 percent. Of ninety-three returned questionnaires, seventy-two contained usable responses to the question discussed here.

Informants were asked to indicate which of nine terms they prefer to be called by people outside of their own families. Informants responded with "negative," "positive," or "neutral" depending upon their reaction to the listed term. The reason for specifying people outside one's family is connected to the fact that some kin terms, as noted in the previous chapter, can be used in reference to nonkin as well. The list includes commonly used terms to refer to older people as well as a few less common terms. This should not be taken as an exhaustive list of terms that reference old age; rather it is a sample based upon terms commonly used by people living in the speech community. The terms are as follows (see table 5.2 for distribution of responses):

chōrō 長老
An elder or senior, such as in the village elders or a council of elders.

kōreisha 高齢者
The aged or a person of advanced age. In terms of common use, this is a relatively recent word intended to replace *rōjin*.

nenchōsha 年長者
A superior in age, an elder.

nenpai 年配
A person of many years.

ojii/obaa-chan おじい/おばあちゃん
Grandpa/grandma, can be used either for kin or nonkin.

rōjin 老人
An old person; old folks; the aged.

rōreisha 老齢者
A person who is old or advanced in age; from *rōrei* (老齢), meaning old age.

shirubā シルバー
Silver (from English). A recent term used in reference to older people such as in "silver seat," a reserved space for older people on public transportation, or "silver center," a senior citizen's center.

TABLE 5.2
Frequency breakdown of negative and positive responses to terms for old age

Score	Count
Chōrō 長老	
Positive reaction	13
Negative reaction	48
Uncertain	11
Kōreisha 高齢者	
Positive reaction	29
Negative reaction	37
Uncertain	6
Nenchōsha 年長者	
Positive reaction	32
Negative reaction	32
Uncertain	8
Nenpai 年配	
Positive reaction	38
Negative reaction	24
Uncertain	10
Ojii/obaa-chan おじい / おばあちゃん	
Positive reaction	62
Negative reaction	9
Uncertain	1
Rōjin 老人	
Positive reaction	15
Negative reaction	53
Uncertain	4
Rōreisha 老齢者	
Positive reaction	9
Negative reaction	59
Uncertain	4
Shirubā シルバー	
Positive reaction	23
Negative reaction	39
Uncertain	10
Toshiyori 年寄り	
Positive reaction	19
Negative reaction	49
Uncertain	4

toshiyori 年寄り
An old person; an oldster; an aged person. Sometimes this term is equated with *rōjin*. Both *toshiyori* and *rōjin* can carry a connotation of being out-of-date.

Less commonly used terms on the list are *chōrō, nenchōsha,* and *rōreisha.* These terms were included because the hypothesis of the question was that terms weighted in meaning toward oldness should have a more negative connotation than other terms. The terms *chōrō* and *rōreisha* both directly index oldness because they include the character *rō* (老), which literally means old. *Nenchōsha* does not directly index oldness, rather pointing simply to a senior in years.

The responses to these questions were compared by generating a score for each term that weighted terms on a scale of positive and negative connotation. The data were coded so that –1 represents a negative response, 1 represents a positive response, and 0 represents a neutral response. Table 5.3 shows the resulting mean scores for each age term. The term *ojii-chan/obaa-chan* receives, by far, the highest score (0.74) with the lowest standard deviation, suggesting that this term has the highest level of agreement among respondents. The most negative score is for *rōreisha*; again this term has a comparatively low standard deviation suggesting general agreement in the connotation of the term. Other highly negative terms are *toshiyori* (–0.42) and *rōjin* (–0.53) and *chōrō* (–0.49). Interestingly, the fairly recent terms *kōreisha* and *shirubā* receive moderately negative scores, but the high standard deviations (0.96, highest in the group, and 0.91, respectively) suggest a degree of uncertainty in how people respond to these terms. *Nenchōsha* and *nen-*

TABLE 5.3
Mean Favorability Scores and Standard Deviations for Old Age Terms

Age Term	Mean Score	σ
chōrō	–0.49	0.79
kōreisha	–0.11	0.96
nenchōsha	0.00	0.95
nenpai	0.19	0.91
ojii/obaa-chan	0.74	0.67
rōjin	–0.53	0.82
rōreisha	–0.69	0.68
shirubā	–0.22	0.91
toshiyori	–0.42	0.88

pai receive neutral and positive scores (0.00 and 0.19 respectively), but again both have high standard deviations, suggesting some degree of ambivalence.

Analyzing the data, it becomes immediately obvious that terms that include the character *rō* (old) receive very negative responses. Terms without this character receive responses that range from positive (*ojii/obaa-chan, nenpai*) to neutral (*nenchōsha*) to mildly negative (*kōreisha*). In short, terms that apply to later years (*ojii/obaa-chan, nenpai, nenchōsha*) but do not directly index oldness receive less negative reaction.

The emphasis of meaning in terms such as *rōjin* and *toshiyori* is oldness itself, while the emphasis in terms such as *obaa-chan, ojii-chan,* and *nenpai,* less directly indexes oldness and, instead, points to experience, wisdom, pleasantness, and relative age. As noted in the previous chapter, although these terms certainly can and do indicate a person who is in the later years of life, more importantly, they imply a kind of familial closeness and respect for older people.

Of course use of more positively connoted terms too early in life also can be problematic, as one eighty-year-old woman, Fujimori-san, indicated:

> I was a bit off-schedule in my life because I became a grandmother at the age of forty-three. I found this very embarrassing at the time. It was particularly embarrassing when the neighborhood kids would come and ask "*obaa-chan*" for money, like my own grandchildren would do. At the time I still felt that I was middle-aged, but because I had a grandchild, from the perspective of others I had entered into the *obaa-chan* stage in terms of name and that embarrassed me. From fifty it might have been o.k., but the forties is too early for that and it was embarrassing.

The terms *ojii-chan* and *obaa-chan* are particularly important because they indicate two ways in which old age is both defined and negotiated. When grandchildren arrive, one can move from middle age to old age. But this transition is not only related to having grandchildren, as Fujimori-san's case indicates. Fujimori-san states that she became a grandmother far earlier than was appropriate for her to be called by the name *obaa-chan*. As a result, she found herself embarrassed when neighborhood children used the term because she did not feel that she was ready to depart the stage of *obasan*-hood. The presence of grandchildren at an early age, and the ensuing use of the term *obaa-chan*, meant that her life situation was incongruent with what is considered normal and natural for a woman of forty-three.

OLD AGE IS DIFFERENT

Although writing about the issue of age discrimination in Japan and the United States, Akiko Hashimoto makes a point about age that is relevant to the discussion here. "In Japan old age *is* different. Age remains a legitimate criterion for differentiating social participation" (Hashimoto 1996:40). The movement from middle to old age in the Japanese context is ethnologically intriguing because it contrasts with other industrial countries, where, as noted in chapter 1, age is typically downplayed or even legally prohibited as a criterion for differentiating older people on the basis of antidiscriminatory or anti-ageist sentiment (e.g., Littlefield 1997; Frerichs and Naegele 1997; Campbell 1991). The public discourse that represents the characteristic divisions of the life course in Japan defines old age as beginning in one's early to mid-sixties and identifies that as a time at which people can be legitimately differentiated from other groups on the basis of their having become old people or *rōjin*.

The ages of sixty and sixty-five, in particular, are important years that identify entrance into old age. The age of sixty, in particular, has long been viewed by Japanese as a point of transition into old age. Beardsley noted in the 1950s that at sixty people participated in a ritual called *kanreki*, a gathering of family and friends at which the newly-turned-sixty person receives a red hat and sweater, symbolizing a rebirth into a second childhood. The color red is associated with newborn babies, which in Japanese are called *aka-chan*, *aka* being the Chinese character for the color red (Beardsley et al. 1959). This ritual continues to be observed throughout Japan, and even among those older people who do not observe *kanreki*, the ritual is well known and its meaning thoroughly understood.

Some of the most powerful examples of the public discourse on old age can be found in the administrative programs that are available to the elderly. The Employee Pension System (*kōsei nenkin*), which covers employees in most companies, pays benefits from the age of sixty, while other pension systems such as the National Pension System (*kokumin nenkin*) (for farmers, shopkeepers, etc.) and those through Mutual Assistance Associations (*kyōsai kumiai*) vary anywhere from fifty-five to seventy, in terms of ages at which people become pensionable (Campbell 1992). Age sixty or sixty-five, depending upon one's local rules, is the point at which people become formally eligible to join their local Old Persons Club. For purposes of defining public policy related to the elderly, the Japanese government uses age sixty-five as the point at which one is officially classified as an old person or *rōjin*. Hospitals, for example, in which 70 percent of the beds are occupied by people sixty-five or above are termed "old-people hospitals" (Campbell 1992).

The public discourse that contributes to the ascription of agedness through nationally practiced administrative policies and programs are important in how people in Jōnai define the beginning of old age. The local government adheres to national policies that identify when an individual becomes officially old, and people living in Jōnai often comment on their dislike for the naming of public nursing homes as *rōjin hōmu*, because of their distaste for the term *rōjin*. While these widely articulated symbolic identifiers of agedness are important, the proximity of the age-grade system means that entrance into the elder age grade stands as one of the most potent symbols of having become old. By symbolically representing this public discourse, however, the age grades not only reinforce it, but also can be used as a basis upon which to resist engaging that discourse. Rather than move smoothly into old age, people contest the transition from middle to old age by resisting entrance into the elder age grade and identification with terms that directly index being old (Traphagan 1998a).

Part of this contesting behavior may have to do not only with taking on the ascriptive status of old age, but also with the meanings of agedness in Japan. Analysis of the age-grade system suggests that while old age is different, it also has similarities to another period of life—childhood. The Old Persons Club is the only adult age-grade association that is not differentiated on the basis of gender. Like the Children's Association, the Old Persons Club includes both males and females, and like childhood, old age is a time in which group activities are participated in by both women and men together. Throughout most of the middle years of their lives, men and women participate in activities, at least within the hamlet, largely divided on the basis of gender. But when they enter old age, they return to patterns of participation that were common in childhood—a return symbolized by the *kanreki* ritual.

People often speak to older people in much the same way they speak to small children, slowing their speech and using a higher pitch to their voice. This is particularly evident in hospital waiting rooms where, for example, older people waiting to see the doctor are often called by their given names, rather than the usual use of family names when speaking to outsiders. This also occurs in banks when people are waiting to be served. And, as noted above, when using the terms for grandmother and grandfather, outsiders will typically use the diminutive ending *-chan* rather than the more formal *-san* (thus, *obaa-chan* or *ojii-chan*). It is highly unlikely that one would ever hear the same diminutive used for someone in middle age. An outsider would not refer to a person who is forty-five as *oji-chan* or *oba-chan*.

This type of adjustment in speech style when talking to older people—referred to as "speech accommodation" in language studies and not limited to speech with older people—is not unique to Japan. Although studies of this phenomenon are limited in the gerontological literature, Ryan and colleagues found similar speech accommodation used with thirty-three elderly women living alone in England. In this case, Home Care Assistants frequently used what the authors describe as a form of "baby talk" in their interactions with elderly women. In many cases, the speech accommodation was responded to favorably by the elderly, "signaling affection, warmth, nurturance and liking" (Coupland et al. 1988; Ryan et al. 1986:7). In Jōnai, people who have made the transition from middle to old age respond to questions about the use of this type of speech in a positive way, stating that it makes them feel as though they are being treated pleasantly and warmly. People in their sixties, however, are usually uncomfortable with being spoken to in this way.

Deconstructing the commonalities between old age and childhood is difficult. But perhaps the most telling characteristic of childhood and old age is that both children and the elderly are often seen as being cute (*kawaii*). There is an innocence and feeling of warm closeness and kindness associated with those who are, in one way or another, dependent or potentially dependent upon others. While feelings of closeness and kindness are by no means rejected by older people, the association of old age with dependence is contested when they react negatively to terms that index oldness or when they resist entrance into the Old Persons Club. This is important because people are not necessarily contesting the fact of growing older itself—I have never witnessed older people attempting to dress younger than their age as is sometimes the case in America. Nor has any informant ever indicated a desire to spend a great deal of time with younger people other than their own grandchildren; outside of family the preference is clearly to spend time with one's age peers. Of course, older people often comment that they would prefer not to experience the physical and mental decline associated with old age, but this is connected to a desire to avoid becoming dependent, as will become clear in the next two chapters.

The main reason that informants state for resistance to entering elder status is that they do not yet feel as though they are old. Most people in their sixties state that they feel as though they are still in middle age and that they desire to continue participating in activities that are appropriate for middle-aged life. As noted above, one of the youngest members of the Old Persons Club joined not because she was ready to identify herself as a *rōjin*—in interviews she stated directly that she is not a *rōjin*—but because she wanted to participate on the hamlet gateball team, which requires membership in the OPC. Indeed, as with the man of sixty-six quoted at the beginning of this chapter who joined the OPC because he wanted to play *go*, early entrance into the OPC usually is associated with a desire to participate in an activity only available through that venue.

Informants attribute the discontinuity between how they feel about their own age identities and how they are defined by broader discourses that determine when one is considered old to the dramatic mortality decline that has occurred in Japan since the end of the Pacific War. In 1950, average life expectancy at birth for women was 63 years and for men 59 years; by 1994 these figures had increased to 83 years and 79 years, respectively. Older people today comment that with extended life expectancy, the sixties should be considered a part of middle age rather than old age. In terms of both physical and mental characteristics of their identities, people state that while in their sixties they do not feel as though they have changed greatly from their fifties; any significant onset of functional decline is not expected to develop until one has entered into one's seventies or eighties. In other words, older people argue that there is a discontinuity in the discourse or the fabric of meaning that defines old age as a period of life and the demographic changes that have greatly altered the characteristics of old age for most Japanese over the past fifty years.

Of course, people lived into their eighties and nineties fifty years ago, as well. Although the demographic changes in Japan clearly play a major role in people's perceptions of how the life course should be divided up, there is a further theme underlying this resistance. The role that dependency plays in Japanese discourses about the meaning of the experience of old age contributes to the desire of older people to resist entrance into elder status. Older people can to some extent legitimately expect to depend on children for social support in old age (Hashimoto 1996). However, this social norm rests in opposition to another social norm central to Japanese culture—avoidance of burdening others—and this opposition contributes significantly to the way in which people negotiate the transition from middle to old age.

This dependency/burden relationship forms the basis of contesting behavior related to the transition to old age. In short, to be old is like being a young child. It is to be identified with dependence, an identity for the elderly, because of the association of agedness with illness, that also carries with it the potential for significantly burdening others. I will return to this point later in the book. The important aspect of our discussion here is that institutions such as the Old Persons Club symbolize entrance into a state of being characterized by physical and mental decline, reduced self-sufficiency, and a correlated growing dependence upon others. Older people contest the fabric of meaning that underlies the institutionalized system of age structuring, both in relation to the age-grade system and the terms that people use to define others and themselves as having entered old age.

Definition as old is not limited to the terms of old age or membership in the elder age grade. There is a strong correlation between one's level of activity and the manner in which others react to the person as an elder identity and potentially dependent. An active body and mind are important indicators of one's level of independence. As discussed in chapter 4, when informants responded that Takeshita-san did not seem like an *ojii-chan*, even though he has grandchildren and is seventy, they were in part referring to his body. He does not *look* like an *ojii-chan*. He stands upright, walks briskly, and is busy with work and a variety of activities. While he is *ojii-chan* to his grandchildren, he is not *ojii-chan* to outsiders and certainly not a *kawaii ojii-chan* (cute grandpa). He has yet to take on an appearance both physically and behaviorally that indexes old age and a condition of dependency.

When Fujimori-san indicated that her entrance into *obaa-san*-hood was too early, the key defining factor was that she did not yet feel as though she was at that point of life. She still felt like an *oba-san* (middle-aged woman), she still felt as though she were in middle age, regardless of the fact that she had grandchildren. And Futagawa-san, although at age sixty-five was old enough to enter the Old Persons Club, stated that she did not yet feel like a *rōjin*; she had not yet reached the proper bodily and mental state to classify herself as such and, thus, thought that she would wait at least five years before entering the Old Persons Club. Those five years represent a prediction of when she will arrive at that stage or, at least, an expectation about when she will no longer be able to stave off the opinions of others about her stage in the life course.

What will become clear in the following chapters is that control over mind and body is the symbolic medium through which people attempt to negotiate old age (Strathern 1996:21). The social construction of one's self-identity as old is linked to a range of powerful symbolic meanings that associate old age with dependence and burdensomeness.

PART III

Aging, Activity, and the Body

CHAPTER 6

Being a Rōjin:
Activity and Camaraderie
in the Elder Age Grade

In the previous chapter, I noted that when looking at the age-grade system operating in Jōnai, the only group that does not have a formalized work responsibility in the hamlet is the Old Persons Club. In a sense, as I will return to at the end of the book, the work of the Old Persons Club is to keep people involved socially and, thus, to provide a context in which they can make efforts to prevent the onset of *boke* and control the aging process. In this chapter, I will begin to look at the specific group activities, many of which are organized around the Old Persons Club, that people use as they try to control the process of aging and the meaning of old age by enacting age identities associated with independence and good health.

Much of the transition from middle age to old age is concerned with the point in life at which both self and others define an individual as *rōjin* or old person. The processes of negotiation and contesting are largely external processes related to maintenance of status and role relationships, social environments, and activities (Atchley 1989; Atchley 1993:12). In essence, what people are contesting and negotiating is entrance into a new status, that of old person, which brings with it different relationships vis-à-vis others within the community.

This change in roles and statuses is particularly important in Japanese society, where emphasis on age-appropriate behavior means that many people make a clear shift in behavior when they enter into *rōjin*-hood. For men in business and government, within the course of a few years, they will retire, perhaps work at a part-time job similar to what they were doing prior to retirement, leave that job, begin spending a great deal of time at home, and enter the Old Persons Club. In places like Jōnai, of course, age-grading practices mean that people continue to associate, at least within their residence community, with the same group as they grow older and move from one age-grade association to the next. In chapter 5, I noted that one function of these associations is to provide a context for participation in group activities like softball games or sewing groups. In fact, the decision about what type of activity one pursues is limited by the age group to which one belongs. Ideas about age-appropriate behavior play a major role in determining the types of group activities selected for participation.

As people begin to clearly identify with the elder age grade, their behavior becomes differentiated from younger age groups. Although age-appropriate behavior changes throughout the life course, it is particularly pronounced as people enter old age. For example, there is a distinctive style of clothing that older people, particularly women, wear. Women in middle age may often wear skirts and, if not necessarily bright, more colorful outfits than they wear later in life. As they move into old age they begin to wear dark purple, gray, or blue patterned pants and somewhat lighter patterned tops. Skirts are rarely worn, usually only for formal occasions such as funerals (in which case they are black). So common is this outfit among older women that it often seems like a uniform of old age. It would be very odd to see a woman at any age under sixty wearing such clothing, just as it would be odd to see a woman in her seventies wearing a light-blue skirt with matching jacket and a white blouse. For men, the primary change comes around the time of retirement. The blue or gray business suits that men wear throughout their working life often are replaced with tweed jackets, gray slacks, and a dark pullover shirt. Again, it is unusual to see a younger man wearing this sort of outfit. Of course, there is variation in terms of occupation in the style of dress worn by women, in particular. Farmwomen are more likely to wear the patterned outfit described above, while women who have been employed in other businesses such as banking or nursing, or who have been housewives in which the husband is employed as a teacher or in government, are more likely to wear skirts in solid, dark colors. In either case, the color of clothing darkens as women enter old age.

Strathern has suggested that articles of clothing can be viewed as metonyms for the person that reflect something about the inner state of that person (Strathern 1996). In Jōnai, the clothing metonym points not simply to the person in a general sense, but to the person as fitting into a particular age category. As people begin to clearly identify with the elder age grade, they start wearing clothing appropriate for that station in life.

Such changes in body adornment are one example of how the body is an index of social and cultural forms (Bourdieu 1977:94). In Jōnai we can find another kind of age-linked, body-centered metonym for the person-as-*rōjin*. The group activities in which people participate, which are usually closely connected with the age-grade association to which they belong, form important metonyms for the person because they represent specific types of behavior that are age appropriate for members of their own age grade. This is particularly evident in relation to the activities of the Old Persons Club. In many cases, the activities associated with Old Persons Club membership symbolically represent or index old age; participation in such activities is a clear indicator that one has begun to view oneself as *rōjin* and that others have done so as well.

While these activities index entrance into old age and, thus, are often contested as people move from middle age to early old age, they also become an instrument of agency as people negotiate the aging process. The external manifestations of person-as-*rōjin*, evident through behavioral patterns associated with the elder age grade, not only index membership in the elder age grade, but also index attempts on the part of the individual to control changes in self-identity manifested in the form of physical and mental decline.

ACTIVITIES OF OLD AGE

Although few studies have been conducted (Tinsley et al. 1977; Tinsley et al. 1985; Tinsley 1984), research in gerontology suggests that, at least in some cultural contexts, people often attempt to maintain the meaning of leisure activities (motivational factors) as they move from middle to old age (Lawton 1993:37). Research has shown that older people often attempt to draw on preexisting domains of activities, using established skills and interests, when pursuing new activities in old age or activities that they have pursued earlier in life (Atchley 1989; Atchley 1993).

Although to some extent older people do draw on preestablished domains of activity when pursuing hobbies and leisure activities, in general these studies do not obtain in Jōnai, particularly among men. The presence of age-grading practices and the emphasis on age appropriateness in terms of behavior tend to generate a situation in which old age is a beginning for a new phase of life with a new set of age-appropriate activities. Furthermore, the motivations behind these activities are directly connected to one of the most pressing concerns specifically of old age—control over physical and mental decline.

One of the key differences in activities associated with age-grading practices for older people is that, unlike those in middle age, many are mixed-gender. Although throughout life people may participate in group activities that include both men and women, those activities connected with hamlet age-grade associations are separated on the basis of gender throughout much of the life course. Only in childhood and old age are these activities mixed-gender. Games associated with old age, such as ground golf[1] or gateball (discussed extensively in this chapter), or hobbies like calligraphy include both men and women. Other activities are separated on the basis of gender. For example, men are likely to play *go* or *shōgi* (games similar to checkers and chess), while women are more inclined toward sewing, paper box making, or music lessons. Among both men and women, virtually all such activities are performed in groups of people who are over the age of sixty-five. Here I will present a detailed description of one of the most popular activities in which older Japanese participate, a game known as gateball.

Gateball is one of the most pervasive images associated with old age in Japan. According to the Japan Gateball Union, which organizes and promotes gateball nationally, over six million Japanese play gateball. Precise data on the ages of participants are unavailable, but the Japan Gateball Union estimates that 75 to 80 percent are over the age of sixty-five (Traphagan 1998c). The game is sufficiently popular that one can find gateball magazines, books, and a television show on a cable channel that broadcasts gateball competitions.

The popularity of the game can be largely attributed to active support by local governments, which often provide facilities for playing gateball. Community centers and parks throughout Japan have gateball courts permanently laid out for regular use, and in northern areas town gymnasiums are often reserved for indoor gateball throughout the winter months. Gateball teams compete in local, regional, prefectural, and national gateball tournaments. In Kanegasaki, the mayor is normally present at townwide tournaments (such as the Agricultural Cooperative Tournament); he opens these events with a few words of encouragement. Sporting equipment companies such as Asics and Sunshine Sports have been instrumental in encouraging the game's popularity. Equipment produced by the Sunshine Sports company, for example, carries a stamp of approval from the Japan Gateball Union. Even in smaller cities like Mizusawa, one usually can find a gateball specialty shop that sells books, equipment, and even do-it-yourself gateball court kits.

The business and economic elements of gateball are inescapable. Sporting goods companies such as Asics and Sunshine have identified older people as a market interested in participating in athletically oriented games. In response to this, there is an effort by sporting goods companies to create new games that will be attractive to older people. Ground golf is one example of a new game that requires equipment that needs to be purchased by older people. The cost for such equipment can be quite high. For example, when one tallies up the cost of equipment needed for gateball, a group interested in playing can easily spend more than ¥100,000 ($1,000) simply to get set up, not including the cost for grading or surfacing of a new court.

THE GAME OF GATEBALL

In order to understand the role gateball plays in the lives of older people in Jōnai, it is necessary to discuss the rules and strategies involved with the game. From a purely ethnographic perspective, it is useful to present a thorough description of gateball, because the game has been discussed extensively neither in the ethnographic literature on Japan, nor in gerontological works related to Japan (see Kalab 1992 and Traphagan 1998c). My purpose in going into detail in this chapter, however, stems less from the ethnographic value than from the importance of the game's complicated rules and strategies in motivating participation. At the core of gateball participation is a theme that will frame the remainder of the book—the exercising of one's brain and body.

Gateball is perhaps most easily described as team croquet. It employs balls (7.5 cm in diameter) and mallets (a minimum 50 cm in length with a head 18–24 cm in length and 3.5–5.0 cm in diameter) similar to those used in croquet (Nihon Gētobōru Rengō 1995:6). Excluding the least expensive, all wooden mallets, gateball sticks, as they are called in Japanese, are collapsible instruments made with high-tech materials. The head of the stick, which is made of either wood, brass, or an alloy, can be removed from the shaft, which is normally made of an alloy metal or graphite and can be adjusted in length. Sticks are the most expensive investment in gateball equipment. On average sticks cost approximately ¥15,000, but can cost as much as ¥40,000; most players buy their own stick, spending somewhere between ¥10,000 and ¥20,000 depending upon how seriously they are involved. It is not unusual for more serious players to have more than one stick, and under regular use sticks wear out after a few years. Thus, a stick is not a one-time expense.

The manner of play is also similar to croquet. Players attempt to hit their own balls through three wickets, or gates (*gēto*) as they are called in gateball, with the ultimate goal of hitting their ball against a post, while preventing other players from doing the same. A gateball match is played by two teams, each with five players. The teams are represented by white balls with red numbers and red balls with white numbers. Ball colors are alternated so that ball number-one is red with a white number, ball number-two is white with a red number, ball number-three is red with a white number, and so on. Players for the two teams wear bibs that are alternately numbered to match the numbers of the balls which they are using; the red team consists of players using balls and wearing bibs numbered 1, 3, 5, 7, and 9 and the white team consists of players using balls and wearing bibs numbered 2, 4, 6, 8, and 10. In tournament play, each team also has a team captain who calls strategies and who may or may not be a playing member of the team.

The game is played on a rectangular gravel court that measures between 20 and 25 meters on one side and 15 and 20 meters on the other. The court has three gates through which balls are directed and one post at the center of the court (see figure 6.1). Gates (20 cm high by 22 cm wide) are placed at appropriate positions proportionate to the size of the court. The court is surrounded by a warning zone that is one meter in width. During tournament play, this zone can only be entered by each team's captain, the person taking his or her turn, and by the referees. Inside the warning zone, there is a batter's box from which each player puts his or her ball into play at the beginning of a match.

The object of the game is quite simple. Each team attempts to get all of its balls through the three gates, after which it then attempts to hit its balls against the post at center court. When a player sends her ball or a teammate's ball through a gate, the team scores one point. For each of its balls that touches the post at center court, only after having passed all three gates, the team receives two points. However, because a match is timed (thirty minutes), there is pressure for the players to get their balls through the gates as quickly as possible, and the opposing team will do what it can to block the other team's progression through the gates.

A match begins with each player, in numerical order, attempting to hit her ball out of the batter's box and through the first gate (see figure 6.1). If the ball goes through the gate, then the player gets another shot. However, if the ball does not go through the first gate, or if it passes through the first gate but goes out-of-bounds, the umpire removes the ball from the court and that player must wait until her next turn to get the ball through the first gate. A player cannot progress beyond this point until she gets the ball through the first gate without going out-of-bounds. This rule does not apply to the other gates. After passing the first gate a player can send her ball to any part of the court, although she cannot receive a point for sending her ball through the third gate until she has passed through the second gate.

After a player passes the first gate, she will hit her ball either in the direction of the second gate or to some other part of the court. The decision about where to go after passing the first gate depends largely upon what player number-one has done. The red team has the advantage (much like the white pieces in chess) in that it goes first, because the number-one ball is red. If the number-one player succeeds in passing the first gate, then she normally will hit her ball in the direction of the second gate. This forces the number-two player, white team, to hit his ball to some other section of the court in order to avoid number-three, who will come through the first gate next—the usual strategy is to hit in the direction of the third gate.

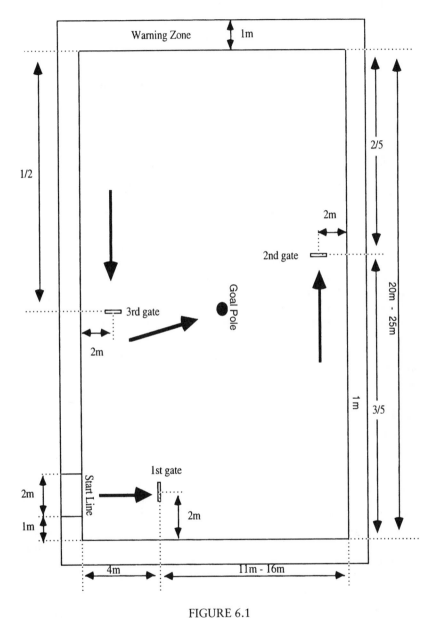

FIGURE 6.1

Diagram of gateball court. Large arrows indicate the direction of movement of balls during a gateball match (see Nihon Gētobōru Rengō 1995:4 for a similar diagram).

Like in croquet, when a player touches another player's ball with his own ball, he picks up that ball, places it next to his ball while holding his own in place with his foot, and sends the other person's ball away by striking his own ball with his stick. But because gateball is a team game, when a player touches one of his teammate's balls, he will send that ball in a direction that is advantageous to the team—for example, toward the gate or through it if the ball is close enough (which scores one point for his team). Touching another ball also gives the player another turn. If a player manages to touch two balls with one shot, called a "double touch," he gets two additional shots.

However, if a player touches a ball belonging to the opposing team, she will in most cases send that ball out-of-bounds, a tactic that is employed as a defensive strategy by which a team blocks the opposing team's progression through the gates. Thus, if the number-two player in the above example hits his ball in the direction of the first gate, he risks becoming an "out-ball" because the number-three (red) player will have an opportunity to touch the number-two ball if the number-three player succeeds in passing the first gate. Becoming an "out-ball" is a serious problem because players are prohibited from either passing through a gate or touching another ball when they inbound-shoot on their next turn. Thus, they cannot extend their turn beyond a single shot, nor can they aid their teammates in progressing through the gates. If a player's ball either passes through a gate or touches another ball during an inbound shot, her ball is removed from the court and returned to out-ball status until the next turn.

The turn of the tenth player often represents a key point in the progression of a match. Because the tenth player will not be followed through the first gate, he has the opportunity to take the advantage away from the red team. Usually, the tenth player will pass the first gate and then attempt to touch one of the red balls clustered around the second gate. If he succeeds, and if the balls are clustered fairly close together, he will have the opportunity to send all of the red balls into out-ball status, taking the advantage away from the red team. One cannot touch the same ball more than once in a single turn. When this occurs, the touched ball is returned to the position where it rested before the second time it was touched and the ball of the player who was playing out his turn is placed out of bounds at the point closest to where the second touch occurred.

In order to fully understand the complexity of strategies involved in a gateball match, it will be helpful to give an example of actual play. The reader is encouraged to work through the following example, because understanding the detail allows for a full appreciation of the complexity of the game. This example includes three turns played during one set of

FIGURE 6.2

Gateball player directs teammate's ball through second gate.

ten turns, five for each team, which occurred during a practice session that I observed a few days prior to a summer tournament. The turns occur about fifteen minutes into the match, after all of the players have passed the first gate and the white team has entirely cleared the second gate. Figures 6.3 and 6.4 accompany this description. Figure 6.3 shows the progression of balls through the three turns. The solid arrows indicate the progression of the player taking his or her turn, and the lined arrows show the direction in which touched balls are sent after they have been touched. Figure 6.4 shows the final resting places of all balls after the turns of players one, two, and three have been completed.

Player number-one, who was hit out-of-bounds in the previous set of turns, inbounds in the direction of number-three. Because balls three, five, and nine are clustered fairly close together, he sends his ball somewhat behind number-three in order to avoid touching any balls on his inbound shot (a penalty situation that would result in a return to out-ball status). Next, number-two touches ball number-four and proceeds to send it gently in the direction of the edge of the court, somewhat lower than the line between number-six and the gate, being very careful not to accidentally send the ball over the boundary line, which would result in out-ball status. She then touches ball number-six and sends it toward gate-three. Finally, she hits her own ball so that it rests between balls four and six. Her purpose in selecting these shots is to set up for the turn of number-four.

Her selection of positions in which to send the balls has arranged the court so that number-four, the next white-team player to shoot, can direct all three balls through gate three. Had balls two, four, and six been closer to the gate, she would have attempted to send them through herself. However, because there is sufficient time left in the match (about ten minutes) she simply moves the balls closer to the gates to prepare for the turn of number-four. Indeed, had there been only one or two minutes left in the match, she might well have chosen to take a chance at sending the balls through the gate herself, thus increasing her team's score before the game ends and also increasing the chances that number-four would have time to send her ball and number-six's into the post at center court, gaining two points for each touch of the post.

The next turn, that of number-three, is more complicated. She begins by touching ball number nine and sending it through gate two. Following that, she touches ball number-five and sends it through gate two. Because of the position of number-ten, she has a good chance of scoring what is called a *tsūka tachi* or pass-through touch. When a player succeeds in touching a ball on the other side of a gate while sending her own ball through the gate, she receives two additional shots— one for passing the gate and one for touching another ball. Being care-

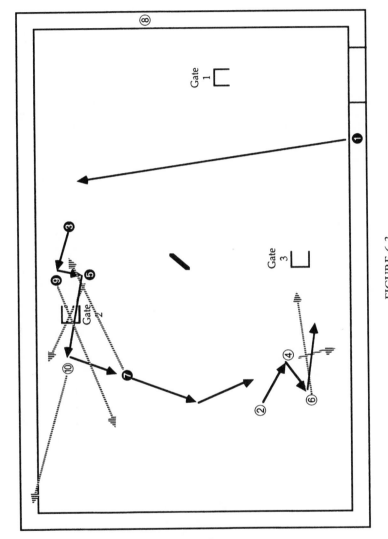

FIGURE 6.3

Progression through three turns of a gateball match.

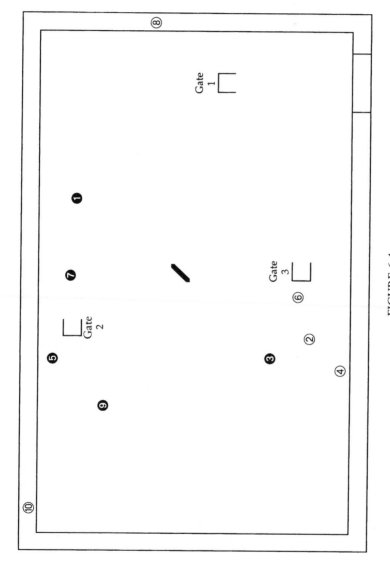

FIGURE 6.4

Positions of balls after turns in Figure 6.3 have been completed.

ful to avoid number-five, which, because she has already touched it once, would lead to a penalty and out-ball status for her ball should she touch it, she sends her ball through the gate and touches ball number-ten. She then sends ball number-ten out-of-bounds, removing it to out-ball status. Next, although number-seven has already passed gate two, she sends it to the other side of gate two in order to aid number-one in passing gate two because number-one is too far away to be confident of getting his ball through gate two in a single shot. By placing the number-seven between ball number-one and gate-two, number-three has created a situation in which number-one can use number-seven to progress toward gate two, increasing the probability that he will succeed in passing the gate.

Finally, because she has two shots remaining (having scored a pass-through touch), she decides to attempt to touch one of the white balls on the other side of the court, in hopes of being able to send them into out-ball status. On her first shot, she goes a little over half the distance toward ball number-two. This puts her in a good situation to touch number-two, but on her second shot she does not hit her ball hard enough and it falls short of ball number-two, ending her turn. Although number-three did not manage to block the passage of balls two, four, and six through gate three (on the next turn of number-four that follows), she did succeed in scoring three points for the red team by sending three of her team's balls through gate two (balls three, five, and nine). She also sent number-ten into out-ball status, thus blocking number-ten's progression toward gate three, and sent ball seven back in the direction of gate two, improving the chances of number-one passing the second gate.

If we were to follow the example further, ball number-four would likely touch balls two and six and send them through gate three, and follow through the gate himself. He would then touch ball three and send it out-of-bounds, removing it to out-ball status. Another possibility would be to send ball number-six close to ball number-seven on the other side of the court. Number-six will shoot before number-seven, thus number-six would have the possibility of blocking the passage of number seven through gate two by touching number-seven and sending it out-of-bounds. She might also be able to block number-one in the same manner after sending number-seven out-of-bounds. Finally, in either case, number-four would send his own ball through gate three and on his final shot would probably hit his ball in the direction of the post at center court. This would prepare for either number-six's or number-two's next turn (depending upon what he chose to do with number-six on his previous shot), which would probably be aimed at sending balls two, four, and six (if it is in the area) into the post, scoring two points each.

In addition to planning strategies, players must take care to avoid rule infractions that result in penalties. For example, if a player picks up a ball he has touched with his ball before both his ball and the touched ball completely stop moving, the touched ball is returned to its original position and his ball is removed to out-ball status and his turn ends. As noted above, when attempting to send off another ball, the player places her foot on her own ball and then carefully places the touched ball next to her own ball. If she accidentally hits her own ball with her stick, or if she misses her own ball and hits her foot instead, her ball is removed to out-ball status and her turn ends.

Obviously, this is only one example of turns and strategies followed in a gateball match; an infinite range of possibilities can occur depending upon missed shots, accidental touches, or gambles that fail or pay off. What should be clear from this example is that a fairly sophisticated level of strategic thinking occurs in a gateball match. Teams must continually adjust their strategies on the basis of the course of events in the match and all of these adjustments are done under the pressure of a time clock.

WHO PLAYS GATEBALL?

In 1986, the Japanese public television network, NHK, aired a month-long, nine-part special series on gateball that described the rules of the game and gave instruction on both form, such as proper posture and use of equipment, and strategies. Accompanying this television series was a magazine that people could use to follow the progression of the series and to study the information presented in each installment. Interestingly, the front cover of the magazine shows a woman who looks as though she is in her twenties playing gateball. Along side her are what appear to be an early teenage girl, a middle-aged man, a middle-aged woman, and an older-looking man, all of whom, save the middle-aged man, are holding gateball sticks. Participants in the televised program included several young women in addition to a group of older people, and the magazine contained several advertisements throughout the book showing young people holding gateball sticks, playing gateball, or families playing gateball together. The imagery of young people playing gateball is common in literature devoted to the game (Endō 1997), and many involved with organizing gateball are interested in presenting the game as being appropriate for people of all ages. I have been told on several occasions by workers in community centers that they encourage family participation in gateball and want to have people of all ages, particularly children, involved. And in some cases, this actually occurs; in the summer of 1995, a gateball tournament reported in the television

FIGURE 6.5

Instructional drawings from the Japan Gateball Union book, *Formal Gateball Contest Rules 1995*, showing two young women and a young man playing the game. These images show the presentation of gateball by the Japan Gateball Union as attractive to young people, in contrast to the common image of the game as being only for older people (Nihon Gētobōru Rengō 1995:42–43). Illustrations: Courtesy of the Japan Gateball Union.

news included participants aged from middle school into their mid-eighties. In fact, according to the Japan Gateball Union, at present there are gateball clubs in some elementary schools (personal communication, July 27, 1995).

Nonetheless, as noted above, most people who participate in gateball are over the age of sixty-five. In the gateball groups to which I belonged, all players were over the age of sixty, the majority being between the ages of seventy and eighty. The reason for this is connected to both the tendency in Japanese society to structure many group activities around notions of age appropriateness and also to organize such activities within the context of formal age grade associations. As noted in chapter 5, segregation of individuals into different age categories for the purpose of participation in group social activities and specific work responsibilities within the hamlet is structurally built in to hamlet administrative functions.

In general, only members of the Old Persons Club can participate on the gateball team, although exceptions are made for practices and some tournaments. Sometimes rules about age-grade association membership are bent in order to satisfy the interests of people who desire to participate in a certain activity. The member of the Women's Association mentioned earlier is one example and my own participation as a researcher is another. In my own case, the rules were bent to allow me to participate in one tournament. After the one tournament in which I participated, however, the head of my gateball team was told by higher-level officials that I should not be allowed to participate in tournament play unless it was limited to the relatively informal tournaments that are held among teams located in the immediate area of Jōnai and that have no connection to the formal gateball tournament association that operates at the prefectural level. Although exceptions exist, the normal pattern is that people begin playing gateball around the time they join the Old Persons Club.

The association of gateball with older people is not only part of the age-grading system, but reflects the image of the game as being appropriate only for the old. When asked if they play gateball, people below the age of sixty-five often respond similarly to one 59–year-old woman who stated rather emphatically, and perhaps even a bit irritatedly, "Me? I'm still too young for gateball; that's a game old people (rōjin) play." Another woman I asked if she was interested in playing gateball, and who was thirty-seven at the time, laughed and said, "No, no, no, that would be embarrassing (hazukashii)." Indeed, while observing a gateball match in a neighboring town, I asked a man who was awaiting his turn if I could play, too, and he told me, "No, no, gateball is a game for the elderly (toshiyori), young people don't play gateball. Young people like games that are fast, gateball is too slow for them." When I asked him if young people ever play gateball, he answered rather directly, "No," and reiterated his comments about the pace of the game being too slow for young people (I was thirty-two at the time).

Membership in the Old Persons Club, of course, does not necessarily mean one plays gateball. In fact, the gateball team only includes a small group of the older residents of Jōnai. There are seventy-eight members of the Old Persons Club in Jōnai, of which only fifteen belong to the gateball team. Several reasons for nonparticipation have been mentioned by members of the Old Persons Club. Lack of time or a feeling that gateball is a waste of time that could be better spent in other group activities, gardening, or farming is one of the major reasons people do not participate. Another reason mentioned by several informants is a feeling that the gateball team is a closed group whose members can include only those who have been playing for a long time and who are skilled at the game (although the gateball team would deny this and is, in fact, attempting to recruit new members). In connection with this, some who view the group as exclusive frequently comment that the manner of social interaction during play, which tends to be quite blunt and often includes orders from the team captain, is not to their liking—the game is sometimes referred to as an *ijime* game or a game that includes bullying behavior. One informant went as far as to state that she does not like the people who are on the gateball team because she associates them with what she sees as a bullying type of behavior.

Within the gateball team, physical and psychological factors play a role in determining the degree and manner in which one participates in gateball-related activities. For example, two players in Jōnai, Mr. Abe and Mrs. Morinaga, participate in practices on a regular basis, but generally opt out of participation in tournaments. Typically, they attend tournaments and cheer on the other team members, but they only enter tournament play as alternates in certain situations when one of the regular players is not playing well (for example, if a player is having trouble getting past the first gate, one of the alternates may be substituted for that match). Both of these players have gradually withdrawn from tournament play, citing their advanced age (Morinaga-san is 83 and Abe-san is 80) as the main reason for reducing participation. Abe-san stated that he finds the tournament situation too stressful, because there are too many people telling him what he should do and he becomes confused by all of the suggestions. He said that he enjoys playing gateball to spend time with friends and to get some fresh air and exercise, but prefers to avoid the more competitive aspects of the game. Morinaga-san stated that she avoids tournament play because it requires her to spend too much time standing. She had hip-replacement surgery five years prior to our conversation and finds it tiring to stand for long periods of time. During practices, she can sit down and rest when she feels tired, but during tournament play (tournaments usually last from about 8:30 a.m. to 4:00 p.m.) it is difficult for her to take a break whenever she feels uncomfortable.

It is important that physical or mental decline does not generate a situation in which participants are in any way pushed out of playing in tournaments. The president of the gateball team in Jōnai is very hard of hearing. Players lament the fact that increasingly he does not hear the directions of the team captain and, thus, makes mistakes in his choices about ball placement; however, no one has ever suggested that he withdraw from play. He is a valued member of the team whom people respect because of his dedication to the team and his very personable manner.

ORGANIZATION AND OPERATION OF THE TEAM

Organization of the team is fairly informal. Officers for the team include a president, vice-president, and treasurer. The president is responsible for communications with higher-level gateball authorities—particularly those related to tournaments. He receives information from the head of the Old Persons Club about club-related tournaments and also information from tournament officials for the larger townwide and regional tournaments. He then distributes this information to members of the team. In all gateball teams that I have encountered, this office is occupied by a man. This includes an all-woman gateball team in Kanegasaki. The husband of one of the women on the team, who is also the team instructor, is the captain and president and directs both practices and tournament play for the team.

The treasurer is responsible for most day-to-day operations of the team, including purchasing of tea and snacks and collection of monthly dues. On the Jōnai team, a female player is the treasurer, which is due to the fact that she has banking experience. Interestingly, this pattern follows tendencies in Japanese households to delegate responsibilities for money to women. In this case, the woman's husband also has experience in banking (in fact, he has many more years experience than his wife), so he could just as easily have taken this responsibility. Other teams also delegate money matters to women. The vice-president has no specific responsibilities other than to fill in for the president when necessary.

The annual budget for the Jōnai team generally runs around ¥150,000 per year. Appendix A shows a typical budget sheet for annual expenses of the gateball team in Jōnai. This expense sheet was passed out to all members of the gateball team at an overnight outing at a local hot spring (*onsen*), following which the team members relaxed and socialized over food and drink. Monthly dues are the primary source of income, but the team also receives small sums from organizations such as the Agricultural Cooperative. Income goes to support the purchase of equipment and some travel needs of the team as well as the regular supplies of tea and snacks for practices and tournaments. At the end of the year, if there have been no unusual expenses, such as the purchase of new equipment, the monthly dues are returned to the members of the team.

Packaged foods brought to each practice are purchased by the team treasurer using the team's money. However, these snack purchases are usually supplemented with homemade pickles or cakes that people bring to each practice and to tournaments. Also, if someone takes a trip, they normally bring back souvenir foods to share with the group. Overnight trips are paid for on an individual basis and typically amount to about ¥15,000 per person, which includes hotel, bus, and food.

SOCIAL RELATIONS ON THE GATEBALL COURT

Wider patterns of male-female interaction in Japanese society, which tend to delegate domestic responsibilities to women and nondomestic to men, are reproduced within the framework of gateball (Imamura 1987; Lebra 1976; Lebra 1984; Lock 1992). In all cases I have observed, woman are solely responsible for making sure that tea and snacks are brought to every practice and an appropriate picnic lunch is prepared for tournaments, although in some cases men will bring their own lunches to tournaments (prepared by women in their families or bought at a store). Formal positions within the gateball group that are endowed with some degree of symbolic capital, understood in Bourdieu's sense of the term as the ability to impose one's own ideas upon others, are predominately occupied by men, although there is no formal restriction prohibiting women from holding such positions (Bourdieu 1977). These positions include the directorships of local, townwide, and regional gateball groups and organizations, team captains, and officials at gateball tournaments (at one tournament in which I participated the officials—twenty in all—were entirely male). Planning for local gateball tournaments is handled by the heads of each hamlet Old Persons Club, all of whom are male.

In addition to holding most official positions throughout local and regional gateball organizations, men often control many of the decision-making activities on the gateball court during both tournament and practice play when it comes to strategizing and in relation to decisions about penalty infractions. In one tournament in which I participated, for example, of twenty teams, all but one of the team captains were men (the lone woman captain was also a playing member of a team that consisted entirely of women). There is, of course, variation in these patterns. For example, social interactions on the Jōnai team show a less clearly defined division along gender lines in terms of strategizing. During both practices and tournaments members of the group, which consists of about an equal number of men and women, usually consult each other about the best shots, and one woman is often the strategist, particularly during practices and sometimes in tournaments.

This pattern of behavior was formally changed in 1994 when the players of the Jōnai team and the team in a neighboring hamlet, with which the Jōnai team holds joint practices once per week, agreed to allow everyone to participate in suggesting strategies. Prior to this change in rules, like tournaments, at practices only the team captains could offer suggestions on ball placement and strategies; the other players involved in the game were required to remain silent. As a result of complaints by players that they were not learning the strategies of the game very well, the rules were changed to allow full participation during practices.

The dominance of males in official and decision-making positions is readily evident by looking at the distribution of umpires in Kanegasaki. There are a total of 130 umpires in Kanegasaki, of which 107 (82 percent) are men and 23 (18 percent) are women. Umpires are required to take examinations, of which there are three different levels. Those qualified to umpire at the upper levels and, thus, be involved with higher-level decision making in tournaments, are also primarily men. Of fifteen people qualified at level two, only two are women (13 percent). Both of the individuals qualified at level one are male. One woman who belongs to the Jōnai team states that she is studying for the level 1 exam and hopes to become the first female in Kanegasaki to achieve level 1 status.

Although competition is important to players and at times tempers become quite heated, gateball practices and tournaments generally can be characterized as opportunities for jovial, relaxed camaraderie and friendship among age peers. Most gateball practices I have witnessed include breaks for tea and crackers, and tournaments are as much opportunities for the group to picnic together as they are to compete against other gateball teams. At practices, when there are more than ten people present (remember five are required for each team), players draw lots to determine who will play for a particular practice round. Those who are not playing watch the match and chat or gossip among themselves while eating homemade foods and drinking tea. During the colder months, people often gather branches and twigs and build a fire around which to keep warm, converse, and eat. Whether practice or tournament, the pungent smell of Japanese pickled daikon (takuan) permeates the area around these groups of people engaged in relaxed conversation as they await their turn to play.

Participants are under little or no pressure to attend practices or tournaments. Members of the gateball groups I have observed go and come to and from practices as their schedules and physical condition allow. As tournaments approach, the tone of practice becomes more serious and intense, and during the last week prior to a tournament the number of practices increases and the practices themselves often become simulations of tournament play. But there is no pressure to participate in tournament play; usually a few weeks prior to a tournament members are asked who wants to join for that tournament and those interested pay an entrance fee that is usually around ¥1,000.

There are also special tournaments for which participation requires membership in other organizations such as the Agricultural Cooperative Tournament, which is limited to people who have some sort of connection to the cooperative. In these events, team members who are not associated with the organization often go to the tournament to cheer on their team and to chat with various people they know from neighboring hamlets. In some cases, people who want to participate find ways around the rules. In one tournament I observed, a woman who was the only member of her team not connected to the agricultural cooperative managed to play along with her team by covering her head with a scarf and pulling her hat down low over her eyes to avoid being noticed.

CHAPTER 7

Boke *and the*
Disembodiment of Social Values

Why do people play gateball? Among older people, the answer to this question is usually framed within a discourse of managing functional decline that permeates how the elderly think about their own bodies. Although the English phrase "successful aging" that runs throughout the gerontological literature in the United States is not used in Japan, the Japanese discourse on a good old age shares much with its American counterpart. Themes of managing or even preventing functional decline are frequently presented to the public through government-run symposia.

In one such event sponsored by the Kanegasaki Health and Welfare Center in 1998, for example, I was asked to discuss the features of a good life and death in old age for Americans. The event was called the HBM Symposium, for *honne* (one's true motive), *byōdō* (equality), and *maemuki ni* (aimed forward, toward the future), concepts viewed as important to a good old age, although those organizing the symposium were admittedly not entirely clear about how these concepts related to aging. In any case, according to promotional fliers, the symposium concerned itself with "the fact that how one faces death is a matter of how one faces one's life." Other members of the panel included a medical doctor who designed an assisted-living facility in a distant city, and three residents of Kanegasaki who told their stories of growing older positively and actively to an audience of about a hundred people in their fifties and above.

The discourse is also evident in the seemingly endless stream of books on how to enjoy one's later years and avoid a bleak old age confined to a bed or lost in the oblivion of dementia. Much of the discourse is couched within the idea that the key to a good old age is to find a reason for being, an *ikigai*, a concept constantly promoted through books, magazines, television programs, and government publications (see Mathews 1995). I will return to a discussion of this discourse as it is expressed at the institutional level in the next chapter. In this chapter, I focus on the lived experience of activities for older people, by considering the motivations behind participation in gateball and other activities like it.

When it comes to gateball, older people in Jōnai quickly and easily articulate why they play. In an open-ended questionnaire given to members of the hamlet gateball team (N = 11), two common themes concerning reasons for playing gateball arose. First, all respondents mentioned the importance of gateball as a means for maintaining one's health, both mentally and physically. Second, all but one stated that gateball is important as a context in which they can enjoy "communication," "interaction," and "conversation" with others. Below are examples of what some informants wrote in response to the question, "why do you participate in gateball?"

> It is like a social gathering and a good opportunity for us [older people], who tend to be lonely, to talk. Also there are about ten tournaments that usually bring about three hundred people together and we can communicate with people outside of our group.

> 1. I can get together with elderly people (kōreisha). 2. Strategies are interesting and very detailed, so I can prevent myself from becoming senile. 3. It is an outdoor sport and good for your health.

> At first I joined because my Old Persons Club started playing. Now I play to keep my health in good condition.

> I live only with my husband. I have work as a housewife, but it does not satisfy me. Gateball for me is for health, friendship, reducing stress, and getting information about society. With gateball my life satisfies me.

> (Social gathering) I can hear different stories that are circulating in society. It is also for prevention of becoming senile in old age. I can play no matter how old I am.

> 1. Because it is fun. 2. To keep my health in good condition. 3. To make friends. 4. To communicate with other people. 5. To get information about what is going on in society.

In interviews and casual conversations with members of the gateball team, these same themes usually arise in discussing participation in gateball, with particular emphasis placed on social gathering and avoidance of senility (boke bōshi) and physical frailty. Concern over becoming boke (which is usually glossed in English as "senile") or bed-ridden is a major point older residents of Jōnai mention when talking about both the process of aging and reasons for activities such as gateball in which they are involved.

As I discussed briefly in chapter 1, boke is a category of mental and physical decline that has similarities with other forms of dementia expressed in Japanese biomedical discourses, but needs to be understood as distinct because there is a notion that it can to some extent be controlled. The *boke* concept bridges a rather wide range of meanings from decline in cognitive and physical abilities associated with normal aging in biomedical discourses to more extreme forms of dementia. In many respects it is seen as a part of normal aging, much as the category of "senility" in North America was commonly associated with normal aging prior to becoming a medicalized, disease-driven condition. However, *boke* also can be distinguished from normal aging in that people see it as being a condition that is potentially avoidable or at least controllable and that one should devote oneself to avoiding.

Furthermore, the concept is distinct from North American ideas about both senility and dementia in that it encompasses both physical and mental forms of decline. Thus, rather than use the English words senility or dementia here, I will use the Japanese term, because a simple translation of *boke* as "senile" or "demented" conveys a meaning much narrower than the term connotes in Japanese.

What, then, does *boke* mean? In regular conversation, when referring to characteristics associated with old age such as forgetfulness, inability to recognize faces, or, in extreme cases, becoming a danger to oneself (e. g. forgetting to turn off gas burners) people will use the term *boke* or *bokeru* (the verb form). Older people who tend to forget where they put things or cannot recall names as they once did will half-jokingly refer to themselves as having already become *boke*, but there is a belief among most older people that if one can joke about it, one has not actually become *boke*.

In addition to the dictionary translation as "senility," the term *boke* conveys a sense of being "out-of-it" (see, for instance, *Shogakukan Progressive Japanese-English Dictionary*, 2nd edition). From a medical perspective, *boke* is viewed by some as physiologically normal aging of the brain, as opposed to *chihō* and Alzheimer's disease. It also tends to be associated with minor memory loss, as opposed to more diverse loss of mental functionality connected to dementia (Ikeda 1995:23).

One doctor associated with the Japanese National Institute of Health, for example, writes that some people in Japan simply equate *boke* and *chihō* (Kikkawa 1995:188), an equation against which he argues emphatically (Kikkawa 1995:203). Although finding much in common between *boke* and *chihō*, he emphasizes the difference between the two concepts as being expressed in the more precise, technical nature of *chihō*, invoking DSM-III (*Diagnostic and Statistical Manual of Mental Disorders, Third Edition*) as an expression of how *chihō* is clinically defined. *Boke*, Kikkawa argues, is considerably more imprecise in meaning than *chihō*. He offers his own definition of *boke*, in which he states that a person's perception becomes dull or vague. For Kikkawa, the *boke* person has entered into dotage (*mōroku*) and may come to be in a dream state in which he or she forgets himself (*muchū ni naru, ware o wasureru*). While this may sound much like aspects of AD as understood in North American biomedical discourses, there is no sense of disease here. In fact, Kikkawa (1995:213–214) differentiates *boke* from *chihō* on the basis that *chihō* is precisely defined as a "blockage of intellectual abilities" that is attributed to some form of disease and that is irreversible. Indeed, in writing about *chihō* Kikkawa presents it as a clinical concept, whereas he does not do so when referring to *boke*.

In fact, what the term seems to convey most is a degree of disorientation that, although often associated with old age, is not necessarily limited to old age. For example, jet lag in Japanese is *jisa boke*, which literally translates as "difference in time (*jisa*) disorientation (*boke*)." One author, Hayakawa Kazuteru, writing on the subject of *boke*, rather emphatically argues that, "There are phrases like 'Old person *boke*,' 'the dotage of old age'; to say that only old people become *boke*—that's offensive!" (Hayakawa 1992:204). The author goes on to discuss other forms of *boke*, including "infant *boke*" in which an infant lies in bed and has no control over bowel movements, or "playing *boke*" such as when one is using a personal computer with friends and forgets the time. He believes that even the feeling of waiting and waiting for a friend with whom one has made an appointment, but who is late, can be a kind of *boke*. Interestingly, Hayakawa, in an attempt to show that *boke* can occur at any point in life and not simply in old age, cites examples of behavior that he categorizes as "childhood *boke*" (*kodomo boke*), "boyhood *boke*" (*shōnen boke*), "young adulthood *boke*" (*seinen boke*), "prime of life (male) *boke*" (*sōnen boke*), and "old person *boke*" (*rōjin boke*) (Hayakawa 1992:202–207).

The ambiguity in defining *boke* is particularly evident when comparing the works of Hayakawa and Kikkawa. Hayakawa, on the one hand, emphatically states that *boke* is not to be described as dotage, whereas Kikkawa, on the other, uses the Japanese term for dotage when defining *boke*. Both, however, agree that whatever *boke* is, it is very diffuse in meaning. Furthermore, these books, as do many others focused on *boke*, while expressing a certain degree of fatalism about *chihō* and AD, present *boke* as something that may be preventable, delayed, or may even respond to rehabilitation. The prescription for successfully coping with or combating *boke* is invariably being active physically and mentally, particularly in hobbies and games that involve social interaction.

While doctors may debate the meaning of the term, for the lay public *boke* has come to be associated with a state of mind and body that most likely arises in old age, rather than a particular feeling such as jet lag. Heightened awareness of *boke* in old age originated with the publication of Ariyoshi Sawako's highly successful novel *Kōkotsu no hito* (published as *The Twilight Years* in English) first published in 1972 (Ariyoshi 1984). Following Ariyoshi's work, several novels and personal stories related to older parents have been published, and these often become widely read. The most recent example is Sae Shūichi's *Kōraku*, a personalized account in which the narrator deals with the difficulties caused by aging parents who are beginning to become *boke* (Sae 1995). These fictional or fictionalized accounts of caring for a *boke* parent have contributed to generating considerable fear among older and middle-aged Japanese about its potential onset.

As noted above, the condition of *boke* can become manifest in changes of both mental and physical characteristics. In the book *Why Do People Go* Boke? *Causes and Care of* Boke, the author presents a list of several characteristics that indicate when one is beginning to become *boke* (Kikkawa 1995:13–15). Both graphics and text are used to describe the signs of *boke*. Below is a translation of the text.

Bodily Indications

1. Walking becomes difficult. Falling becomes easy.
2. Walking speed slows down. You begin to take short steps. It becomes difficult to move quickly.
3. When beginning to walk you are awkward or clumsy. You stumble easily with a small height difference.
4. You stagger. It is difficult to hold your balance.
5. Words do not come out easily. Your words become entangled.
6. Hands become stiff; you cannot make small movements.
7. Lack of muscle strength, thus urination and defecation become difficult.
8. You cannot wait or control urination and defecation.
9. You change food likings; greater or less appetite.
10. Skin sensitivity decreases; you easily get sunburned.

Kokoro Indications

1. Forgetfulness; cannot remember something that you should remember.
2. You can't produce people's names or the names of places.
3. You frequently do not know the "when," where," "who" of things. You come not to know things clearly.
4. You cannot think why and what to do.
5. You cannot organize ideas or behaviors.
6. You tend to cry and get angry more easily.
7. You lose patience. You can no longer persevere (*gaman dekinakunaru*).

8. You lose emotions or express emotions [extremely].

9. You do not want to meet with people. Things that seem vague or dim become common.

10. You become laconic.

Social Indications

1. You lack the energy (*ki*) to do things. You only do something when you are told to.

2. Your interests and concerns fade. You have no challenges.

3. You doubt other people; you tend to feel that you are a victim.

4. You annoy others without feeling bad about it.

5. You make no distinctions.

6. You become excessively aggressive and mean.

7. You are jealous.

8. You do not want to take or cannot take responsibility.

9. You do not or cannot have a role [in society, family, etc.].

10. You become extremely dependent. You are confused, perplexed.

Interestingly, all but one of the cartoon characters that accompany this text are men. This underscores a gendered component to the conceptualization of *boke* in that many believe men are at much greater risk for becoming *boke* because upon leaving work they have nothing to do. As noted in the magazine *Look Japan*, retirement is often a difficult transition for men:

> Having dedicated heart and soul to work, after retirement [men] are at a loss for purpose. Some of these men are called "nureochiba," "wet dead leaves," since they stick to their wives when they go out. (Seo 1991:12; Kaplan et al. 1998:29)

The abrupt change in life men experience after retiring from work often means that postretirement is the first time in their lives they have spent a great deal of time at home and during which most of their time was not occupied with work-related activities. As a result, many view men as being susceptible to becoming *boke* because they do not know how to occupy their time. Women, in contrast, rarely work until mandatory retirement, either leaving work at marriage, birth of one's first child, or in some cases in one's fifties as a matter of choice. As one woman (59) explained, "I left my job in the town hall when I was fifty, because I wanted to have more time to pursue my own interests and hobbies." Indeed, women are usually actively involved in some sort of hobby activity from much earlier in life than men. There is no clear age at which women begin to participate in activities such as flower arranging or tea ceremony. They may gradually shift from one domain of activity to another more age-appropriate domain as they grown older, but the basis for keeping active in some kind of non-work-related activity is established earlier in life. Thus, women are perceived as being at lower risk of becoming *boke* than men.

Although perceptions about risk factors for men and women may differ, for both the defining features of *boke* are expressed in three areas of experience: body, *kokoro*, and social interactions. The indications related specifically to the body (*karada*) are largely related to problems of stiffness, balance, muscle control, and coordination. In fact, informants frequently state that one of the best ways to avoid becoming *boke* is to make use of one's hands in activities that require dexterity, such as sewing, paper folding, or even making paper dolls from spent cigarette cartons. Also, inability to carry out basic bodily functions, such as urination and defecation, is an indication that one is becoming *boke*.

Symptoms that one is becoming *boke* can also be expressed in emotions, ways of thinking, and one's desire to socialize with others. In the above list, the emotion, thinking, and memory-related indications of *boke* are connected to the idea of *kokoro*, a rather diffuse concept that is difficult to translate directly into English.

In general, the term is translated as meaning center or heart. Lebra describes *kokoro* as being at the center one's "inner self." It stands for spirit, will, mind, emotion, and in contrast to the outer self, which is "socially circumscribed," *kokoro* is able to be free and spontaneous (Lebra 1992:112). *Kokoro* as inner self is, for Lebra, the locus of self-awareness (Lebra 1992). It can be dissociated from the outer self, that which is presented and adjusted to contexts of social interaction, and "may be directed as an asocial obsession with self-expression or self-actualization through work or sheer perseverance" (Bachnik 1992:154; Lebra 1992:113).

When discussing the relationship between *kokoro* and body, some people use a computer metaphor stating that *kokoro* is like software and the body (*karada* or *shintai*) is like hardware. Others describe the relationship in terms of more generally evident cultural ideas of inside (*uchi*) and outside (*soto*) that juxtapose the internal and private with the external and public (Lebra 1976:112). These ideas refer at once to physical space such as the inside and outside of one's house and conceptual spaces related to varying degrees of intimacy and social distance. In relation to one's family as *uchi*, one's community may be *soto*. But in relation to a neighboring community, one's own community may be *uchi* and the neighboring one *soto*.

These terms are organized into concentric circles of intimacy and social distance that form permeable spheres of "I/we" and "they" (Smith

1983:94). The spheres are permeable in the sense that, for example, a person whom one meets for the first time will be *soto* but may become *uchi* if a friendship forms. New members of a group, such as a company, gain some level of *uchi* status upon entrance into the group and this will strengthen over time.

There is a great deal of variation in what people term *kokoro*, and the behaviors and elements of self associated with the concept can be vast. Table 7.1, for example, is a free list one informant wrote in response to the question "What goes to make up *kokoro*?" Although this was by far the longest list, other informants included many of the same terms and also some others, such as ancestors (*senzo*), *hotoke* (Buddha), brightness, pity, sympathy, blueness (being down), a refreshing mood, and spirit (*seishin*). Evident immediately in the list is the close connection between the physical body and *kokoro*; for instance, the first three entries in table 7.1 express emotional states in terms of the physical chest, *mune*, and the fourth (anger) in terms of the stomach. Indeed, rather than representing a distinct mind, in the Cartesian sense of the concept, *kokoro* represents a broad category of psychosomatic unity (Rholen 1986:329). Expressions like one's "chest is full" or something "comes into one's head" indicate the intersection of psychological and somatic aspects of the person expressed in the concept of *kokoro*.

On way to interpret the meaning of *kokoro* is as the internal, embodied aspect of self that animates a body. It is *uchi* to the physical body's *soto*. The body (*karada*) is the sociocentric part of the person presented to the outside world. The inner, *uchi*, *kokoro* contains the intimate elements of the person, which are only exposed in limited ways usually at the discretion of the individual. As one informant put the relationship between body and *kokoro*:

> *Kokoro* is something that comes about from birth. The things that make up *kokoro* are not innate, but come about after birth. They come from the body. You see these *mikan* [Japanese oranges] in the middle of the table? *Kokoro* is like the inside of the *mikan* and the skin is more like the body in that it is on the outside. *Kokoro* is an inner thing.

Of course, the pulp and the peel of an orange are part of the same fruit, but they can also be differentiated on the basis of that which can be seen (outer, skin) and that which is to some degree intimate and hidden from view (inner, pulp). The term used to holistically describe the person is *shinshin* 心身, which incorporates the Chinese characters for *kokoro* and body, but there is no single term that describes the whole person without at least indexing this sort of duality between the two. This is not to say that these ideas should be viewed in terms of a duality of mind and body of the Cartesian variety.

TABLE 7.1
Free list on the components of *Kokoro*

Japanese	Romanization	English translation
胸がつぶれる	mune ga tsubureru	heart (chest) is crushed (a broken heart)
胸がいっぱい	mune ga ippai	heart (chest) is full
胸がはりさける	mune ga harisakeru	heart (chest) is torn out
腹をたてる	hara o tateru	get angry
頭に来る	atama ni kuru	comes to one's head
言葉もでない	kotoba mo denai	words do not come out
あきれる	akireru	be amazed and disgusted
夢ごこち	yume gokochi	ecstasy, trance
天にものぼろ思い	ten ni mo noboru omoi	feels like you are going up to heaven (on top of the world)
目の前が真っ暗になる	me no mae ga makkura ni naru	before one's eyes becomes dead darkness
恐縮	kyōshuku	be grateful or ashamed
心配	shinpai	worry
気苦労	kigurō	worry
敬服	keifuku	admiration
心痛	shintsū	anguish, heartache
悲哀	hiai	sorrow
希望	kibō	hope
遠慮	enryo	reserve
恋しい	koishii	long for, miss
感謝	kansha	thanks
感激	kangeki	deeply moved
安心	anshin	peace of mind
心苦しい	kokoro gurushii	regrettable, sorry
休心	kyūshin	peace of mind
情熱	jyōnetsu	passion
機嫌	kigen	temper, mood
心浮き立つ	kokoro ukitatsu	mind dancing with happiness

(*continued on next page*)

TABLE 7.1 (*continued*)

Japanese	Romanization	English translation
感動	kandō	deeply moved, touched
歓喜	kanki	delight
感傷	kanshō	sentiment
感情	kanjyō	emotion
感心	kanshin	be deeply impressed
満足	manzoku	satisfaction
関心	kanshin	concern, interest
感性	kansei	susceptibility, sensitivity
愛情	aijyō	love
嬉しい	ureshii	happy
悲しい	kanashii	sorrowful
気がめいる	ki ga meiru	be depressed
楽しい	tanoshii	fun
覚悟	kakugo	readiness
感慨	kangai	deep emotion
決意	ketsui	resolution
察する	sassuru	guess, sense
熟しん	jyukushin	mature heart
満喫	mankitsu	enjoy fully
羨望	senbō	envy
想像	sōzō	imagination
期待	kitai	expectation
信念	shinnen	belief
懸念	kenen	concern
不安	fuan	uneasiness
気がかり	kigakari	concern
執念	shūnen	deep tenacity of purpose
感奮	kanpun	being deeply moved, and rouse up
感銘	kanmei	impression
願望	ganbō	desire

(*continued on next page*)

TABLE 7.1 (*continued*)

Japanese	Romanization	English translation
感想	kansō	thoughts, impression
感慨無量	kangai muryō	be filled with deep emotion
驚喜	kyōki	being delighted and surprised
興醒める	kyōzameru	be spoiled
遺憾	ikan	regrettable
残念	zannen	regret
驚く	odoroku	be surprised
羞恥	shūchi	shyness, bashfulness
望む	nozomu	hope
許す	yurusu	permit
心が重い	kokoro ga omoi	*kokoro* is heavy
悩む	nayamu	worry
勇気	yūki	courage
勘繰る	kanguru	suspect
疑う	utagau	doubt
恐怖	kyōfu	fear
懐疑	kaigi	suspicion
畏怖	ifu	fear
意志	ishi	will, volition
心中	shinjyū	lover's suicide
興味津々	kyōmi-shinshin	full of interest, very interesting
心情	shinjyō	feeling
心証	shinshō	impression
心情	shinjyō	feeling*
仁心	jinshin	benevolence
心酔	shinsui	fascination
真心	magokoro	sincerity

*This term is repeated in the free list.

As a unified entity, the person in Japan can be characterized as consisting of fluid categories of intimacy and sociality; the physical aspects of the person being more associated with the realm of the social, and the ephemeral or intangible being more associated with the realm of the intimate. *Boke*, as a state or condition of the person, is a characteristic that transcends both of these categories, for it affects both the intimate and the social aspects of the person. The inner realm of thoughts, emotions, and memories (which are, of course, expressed outwardly at times) and the outer realm of physicality, in the form of movement and bodily control, both can exhibit changes that indicate the onset of the *boke* condition. The inability to carry out one's responsibilities, to take roles in society, a lack of interests and energy to do things, and a tendency to act in negative ways vis-à-vis others (jealousy, aggressiveness, meanness) and without remorse for those behaviors, are also indications that one has become or is becoming *boke*.

Boke is a global phenomenon that can be expressed at the level of the most intimate aspects of the person, *kokoro*, to the most social, in the form of extreme dependency and inability to interact easily with others. In other words, *boke* is a matter of both the individual and the social person. It is a loss of the ability to control both inner and outer aspects of the person. The "prescription" for the prevention of *boke* involves attempting to exercise control over or manage changes that occur as a person ages at both the intimate and social levels.

MENTAL AND PHYSICAL HEALTH AS SOCIAL RESPONSIBILITY

Unlike Alzheimer's Disease or senile dementia, *boke* is seen as something over which people have at least some degree of control. For Hayakawa and many other authors of popular literature, the *boke* condition is associated with inactivity. These authors suggest that the means to avoid becoming *boke* is to be active. That is, one should be engaged in some form of activity, preferably group activity, that exercises both body and brain. I use brain here because when people discuss what it is that they are exercising, rather than saying that they exercise their mind, as is usually the case in North America, they exercise their *nō* (the brain) or *atama* (the head). The implication is that thinking exercises the brain. This does not imply a purely physicalistic conceptualization of what is being exercised, because, as noted in discussing the concept of *kokoro* Japanese emphasize the importance of mind-body harmony.

In the list cited above, withdrawal from social settings or inability to interact normally with others is a major indication that one is becoming *boke*. In the case of older people living in Jōnai, group participation necessarily means activity with members of the elder age grade, in other words, the Old Persons Club or other group activities that are formally or informally limited to older people.

It has been suggested that in Japan activity represents a role commitment that forms a basis for self-identity (Lebra 1976; Lock 1993). Confidence that one is socially useful is a source of self-worth; one should do things that contribute to the good of the social whole and avoid doing things that detract from that good (Lebra 1976:84). Becoming *boke* puts one's sense of self-worth at risk. Because self-worth is tied to social utility, avoidance of becoming *boke* becomes a matter not simply of individual health, but one of social responsibility. Failure to make significant efforts aimed at carrying out that responsibility can be a source of embarrassment to one's family and can create considerable burden on family members who must care for an inactive (*boke*) person or require some form of institutionalized care or assistance from government sources.[1]

One informant, a seventy-five-year-old man, summed this point up quite clearly in talking about his own attempts to ward off the onset of *boke*:

> There are ways to avoid becoming *boke* or to fight it and if you do not, that is embarrassing because you were too lazy to have avoided it. Being *boke* is something that I think about and am trying hard to prevent. For me, participation in the hamlet ground golf team, reading out loud for at least thirty minutes a day, and working in my garden and rice fields are ways I am trying to avoid becoming *boke*.

This informant stated that by reading aloud he gives his brain more exercise than by reading to himself silently, because he is more conscious of the content of what he reads when he reads aloud. Ground golf provides a way to exercise his mind through social interaction, and gardening and farming help him to keep physically healthy.

As noted above, fear of becoming *boke* or dealing with a *boke* parent or in-law is widespread in Japan. Why is the onset of *boke* such a source of fear or anxiety to older people? This question may appear trivial, because it seems quite natural for people not to want to lose control over mind and body as they grow older, but it is an important question to ask because it leads to the cultural assumptions that underlie that fear. In Jōnai, while people are concerned about functional decline, pain, and loss of control, there exists another and perhaps even more powerful reason they wish to avoid the onset of *boke*. The issue of not becoming a burden, particularly on family members, is a central worry people have about growing older and is one of the primary reasons they fear the onset of *boke*. In the course of more than fifty semistructured interviews conducted with people over the age of sixty living in Jōnai, concern over becoming a burden on family members was one of the most frequently cited worries of old age. This was particularly evident with individuals who lived alone or only with a spouse and was usually uttered along with concerns about the onset of *boke*.

In one such interview, Yoneyama-san (69) told me of her own experiences caring for a *boke* mother-in-law, experiences that have greatly shaped the way she thinks about her own old age. Yoneyama-san lives alone and runs one of the small grocerette-type stores in the hamlet. She lives in a section of the hamlet in which five of her immediate neighbors are women in their sixties or seventies who have lost their husbands and who now live alone. Yoneyama-san has three living daughters, all of whom live in the Tokyo area. When asked why they did not bring in an adopted son into the family, she stated that because they were poor, no-one wanted to enter their household. Although she lives alone, during the summer of 1996 her daughter and son-in-law paid for the construction of a new house on Yoneyama-san's property. They intend to eventually occupy the house with her after the son-in-law's retirement, although the timing of coresidence remains ambiguous.

Yoneyama-san described most of her life as being involved with farmwork and she called her house a *nōka* or farmhouse, but she has also been tending her store for close to fifty years, since the time they moved to the hamlet. Yoneyama-san makes a small profit, mostly from the children who come to play the arcade game machines set up in the front of the store. The remainder of her income is from the national old-age pension (*kokumin nenkin*) and also her (deceased) husband's employment pension (*kōsei nenkin*).

Living alone is not a concern for Yoneyama-san, at least as long as she has her health. As with many other older people living in Jōnai, she is concerned over maintaining her health until death, because she does not expect to be able to depend upon her children if she develops a long-term illness. Yoneyama-san and one of her widowed neighbors, Morita-san, talked about their lives as widows and their thoughts about dying.

JWT: What worries you most as you grow older?

YONEYAMA-SAN: I worry about living too long and becoming sick. If I live too long, then what will I do if I get sick? If you live too long, you might become bed-ridden or *boke*; I don't want that because that is a very unhappy and lonely life (*sabishii*).

JWT: How would you describe the characteristics of being *boke*?

YONEYAMA-SAN: The characteristics of *boke* are things like forgetting where you put things or what you did with something. It's not only forgetting things, however. Also, *boke* is doing things like accusing someone of taking something that is yours when it is actually right next to you. You tend to invent things that are not real. It is completely different from senile dementia (*chihō*). You are more able to talk when *boke* than when in a state of senile dementia.

My mother-in-law was *boke*. It was really quite embarrassing. Once she told us that the police had come to take her and they wanted her bureau (*tansu*), so she brought all of the drawers of the bureau to the entryway of the house. She said that she needed to go with a futon and rice, so I made them up for her. Grandma put them on her back, but then said it was too heavy so she didn't need them. Grandma would also sometimes say that we needed to get rice when we had lots of rice around the house.

Another time, I went to get the phone and I thought that Grandma was in her room and was o.k. While I was talking on the phone, I noticed that Grandma was not in the room. I hung up and went into the kitchen where I found all of Grandma's clothing, including her underwear, on top of the stove, which, fortunately, was turned off. The door was open so I ran out and found Grandma half way to the tobacco store across from the park—stark naked. This sort of thing went on for ten or eleven years.

The concern I have is that I do not want to become a burden to my children (*meiwaku kaketakunai*). I would rather die before that. The best way to die is to die suddenly (*pokkuri*). You do not want to be a burden.

MORITA-SAN: That way of dying is best. I would rather just go suddenly. The ideal death is to have had tea with a friend the previous day and spent time laughing together. The next day my friend comes to the house and finds me dead. That's the best way to go. I want to die while I am still able to enjoy life. I don't want to be burden on my children. They are working.

For Yoneyama-san, her mother-in-law's condition of *boke* was a serious burden. She talked about having to be constantly concerned and pay attention to what her mother-in-law did so as to prevent her from injuring herself or embarrassing the family. The example of her mother-in-law is not one that she wishes to repeat as she grows older. Rather than becoming a burden on her children, other family members, neighbors, or social services, Yoneyama-san and Morita-san stated that they would both rather die.

When people discuss the ideal way to die, they often comment that a sudden (*pokkuri*) death is preferred because it will not burden anyone else. In fact, throughout Japan there are Buddhist temples that are associated with prayer for a swift death. Wöss notes that in a recent survey on *pokkuri-dera* more than 90 percent of worshipers indicated they come because of desires to avoid becoming bed-ridden and, thus, a burden to others (Wöss 1993:195). Physical or mental decline, particularly such that it leads to prolonged convalescence or the need for constant attention is not only feared for the associated loss of functionality, but also for the fact that these conditions entail becoming dependent and, thus, a burden upon others who are most likely to be family members.

A temple known as Dōsen-ji in Kitakami, to the north of Kane-gasaki, actually set up a statue of a Buddhist saint (Kannon) at the request of the head of the local Old Persons Club so that people could come there to pray for a swift death (the individual who lead the request to have the statue installed, ironically and sadly, experienced a pro-tracted illness before he died). As a result, the temple has become known as a "Sudden Death Temple" (*pokkuri-dera*) by people living in the area. Another more well-known sudden death temple near the city of Fukushima, about two hours by car from Kanegasaki, has been a desti-nation for tours of older people leaving from Kanegasaki on several occasions.

Although a sudden death is desired by many, other informants describe the ideal death as being something that occurs at home, with family around. But even in this sort of death, avoidance of becoming a burden is a central theme.

> WAKIDA-SAN: The only worry I have is about my health. I do not want to become dependent upon my family. I don't want to become bed-ridden so I am concerned about watching my health. I hope that I will not become *boke* and that I can continue doing the things I like such as *tanka* (a form of poetry).
>
> JWT: What does *boke* mean?
>
> WAKIDA-SAN: Well, in Japan there are a lot of meanings, aren't there. It's certainly different from Alzhiemer's disease. The first thing that occurs is that you begin to forget things about yourself and in general. Also, you tend to have hallucinations (you experience things that are not there). There are various things. The problem [with becoming ill in old age] is that it takes a great deal of money. There are a lot of services such as the day-service [a government-run daycare program for the elderly], but if the family does not take advantage of those, then there are problems. In the old days, if the old person entered a nursing home, it looked bad in terms of the *yome* [co-res-ident son's wife, who usually has primary responsibility for care of his par-ents] and family. It is important to protect the human rights of bed-ridden people and also of the family. But it is good if you can return to your home rather than be in a nursing home.
>
> Living alone or as an elderly couple is not so good, it's best to live with family. It is also important to have a hobby. If you do not have a hobby or interest, well if you have a hobby, you will not grow old. I often say that youth is not limited to the young. If you have a young way of thinking, that is youth as well. Elderly people often say that it is not good to behave or feel like you are young. The purpose of hobbies is to have contact with other people and to make friends to go out into society. For example, with my poetry writing, there are people who send their books all around the

country without knowing the other people and they get to know each other. Travel is like this. You go out with people and become friends. It allows you to enter into society. By participating in hobbies, your experience of society becomes wider. Also, it is important not to develop a feeling of just staying in the house and not going anywhere. After I was sick [Wakida-san had kidney disease], I thought "I have to get well quickly so that I can go out and do things again." I do not want to feel that I am old and cannot do anything. When you get old it is really important to have some sort of interest. You have to have something that makes you think and use your head. Definitely, in order to avoid becoming *boke*, you have to have an interest and you have to be doing something.

Sometimes I tell other old people they are very energetic (*genki*) and they respond, "Well I haven't been taken away (*omukae*) yet," meaning that they have not died yet. If you say that in front of young people who are helping you, it's rude. If you are tired of living, then don't go to the doctor complaining of your ears being bad, your eyes being bad, your back hurting, your feet hurting. It's really impolite to say that in front of young people who are going to all of the trouble to help you. If you are tired of life, then you shouldn't eat food and take medicine. If you go to the doctor complaining, then you really want to live. When I was in the hospital people said about themselves, "Still living, it's a problem, isn't it" (*mada ikiteiru nā, komatta nā*). A man said that it was a problem (*komaru koto*) to be still living. I said to him, "Being alive is a problem?" I don't think that way. That's rude to say that sort of thing in front of the people who are cheering you on. Young people are not thinking that it would be good if the old people die. People are nursing and taking care of you with all their effort, so you shouldn't say that sort of thing.

I don't want to be a burden to my family, but I really do not want to die in a hospital. Maybe the best way to go is to be at home and sick in bed for a week or ten days and die with your family around you. Nowadays death does not come (*omukae ga konai*) [she implies that death does not really come at the right time, because people live much longer]. As for me, it's o.k. if I go to the hospital for a week or a month, but I don't want it to become long. I want to die naturally, I want to live normally without becoming *boke*, and then die. Dying suddenly is o.k., but it is a bit lonely because you will not have your family around you. I would like to take about a week to be with family before I go.

Wakida-san's account of what constitutes an ideal and natural death is typical of the ideas expressed by many older Japanese, and corresponds with comments expressed to Susan Long in her research on death and dying in Japan (Long 1997). For Wakida-san, the idea of a death at home is a natural death, and the idea of a protracted illness in a hospital or at home, burdening family and depending upon social services, seems unnatural. For her, it is as though the person has lived too long. In other words, the person who reaches this point in life has, in a sense, outlived his or her usefulness. Some informants actually view the idea of becoming a burden on family members as going beyond the level of embarrassment and actually view it as shameful. Nakano-san, a woman in her late seventies, indicated that living too long can be a source of shame to one's family. In the course of our conversation, we discussed the story *Ubasuteyama* (also written *Obasuteyama*).

The story recounts a fictional time in Japan's past when a person was taken to the top of a mountain to die, variously at the ages of sixty or seventy, depending upon the version of the story. There are many different tellings of *Ubasuteyama*, including plays for the *nō* theater, children's stories, and two motion pictures (Keene 1970:115–128; Ōki 1991 [1956]). In Iwate Prefecture alone there are at least five versions of the story (Inada and Ozawa 1985:159–165). As the story is recounted by older people living in Jōnai, at some time in the distant past, a ruler decreed that when a person reached the age of seventy, he or she was to be brought to the top of a nearby mountain and left to die. As one informant said, "it was a time of food shortages, and old people could not contribute work to the community and were, thus, a burden."

When her time came, one man concealed his mother under the floorboards of the house, rather than taking her to the mountain. Embroiled in political problems with a neighboring locale, war seemed immanent and the ruler lacked ideas to resolve tensions. When he visited the ruler, the mother's son suggested a plan for avoiding war. After the plan succeeded, the son told his ruler that his sixty-year-old mother, secreted away to avoid death, had actually devised the solution. Hearing this, the ruler rescinded the law, having recognized the wisdom that older people hold.

While many in Jōnai recount the story with positive imagery of wisdom in old age, they are also well aware of coexisting versions (particularly the movie versions) in which the mother is left to die, abandoned atop the mountain. In recent years, the name of the story has come to be associated with nursing homes in Japan, symbolically representing a sense that to be in a nursing home is to have been discarded by family members (Bethel 1992). However, the symbolic meanings associated with the abandonment version of story are not always negative. Indeed, in the movie versions, the mother has to convince her son to take her because it is her time to die and it is wrong to live too long. In both the 1958 and 1984 film versions (directed by Kinoshita Keisuke and Imamura Shohei, respectively), the mother knocks her teeth out with a rock because they are still strong and, she thinks, an old person should not have good teeth. She wants to look appropriate for her age when she goes to the mountain.

On informant, Nakano-san, reflected on this story in the following way:

If you live too long, it is something to be ashamed of (*nagaiki wa haji no moto nari*). It is embarrassing if you live too long. Those who live long, well, if there is no problem, it's o.k., but in the worst case your eldest son dies. If that happens, it is not a time for an old person to be living. It is better to go to the mountain [*Ubasuteyama*] before you become an embarrassment, a shame, or a burden to your family. A bed-ridden old person is an embarrassment and shameful and lonely.

As noted in chapter 1, old age in Japan is often characterized as a time when parents can depend upon their children, particularly eldest sons, for co-residence, financial support, and health care. Elderly people, having accumulated social and symbolic capital on the basis of contributions made to family and society over the life course, are seen as a group that can legitimately expect protection and to some degree depend upon others in the later years of life (Hashimoto 1996). Legitimized dependency is formally expressed specifically within the content of the father-son relationship in kinship ideologies that define obligations within the family in terms of parent-child succession and inheritance that reciprocally obligates the successor to care for his or her parents. Although it has been argued that social and economic changes have eroded the capacity of Japanese families to care for the elderly (Ogawa and Rutherford 1997:59), Nakane's (1967:5) contention that among rural populations in Japan, the household forms "a distinctive enterprise with insurance for old members" based upon the obligation successors have to feed and care for their predecessors in old age, continues to obtain even if co-residence is not necessarily practiced between parents and the eldest son or another child.

Dependency in Japanese society should not be viewed as either a wholly positive nor negative concept. Lebra argues that dependence or indulgence (*amae*) and the behavior that accepts indulgence (*amayakasu*) form a complementary relationship in which one person is the recipient of indulgence and the other the supporter or provider of that indulgence. Being able to play the role of dependent is an important skill of Japanese social interactions (Lebra 1976a:55). Those who can play this role are usually readily responded to by another willing to take on the role of supporter. There are often mutual benefits of this *interdependent* relationship in that both the depender and supporter can manipulate the other by either engaging or withdrawing from the interdependence. But when taken too far, a person who becomes self-indulgent and overly dependent upon another will be viewed with disapproval as having a lack of discipline (Lebra 1976a:55).

Dependent behavior in old age in Japan can take a variety of forms. Growing old often entails a gradual shift away from being a producing member of the family to entering a category in which one has undiminished and possibly even enhanced rights of consumption (Dore 1958:130). The time when this transition occurs varies greatly, and for individuals without children living nearby may never occur. In Jōnai, elderly people will usually continue to be involved in farming and gardening as long as they are physically able. This is particularly true for those whose children are neither co-resident nor living nearby, thus being unable to provide assistance in agricultural labor.

However, this is not to say that no dependent relationship exists between elderly parent and child even across considerable distance. In the case of Yoneyama-san, her daughter and son-in-law living in Tokyo offered to build her a new house to replace her current one, which was more than fifty years old and in need of regular repair. The new house not only would provide a better situation for the mother, but a more comfortable living space for the daughter's regular visits and when she and her husband eventually retired and returned to Jōnai permanently. Although the mother was hesitant to receive such a "large gift," the offer was accepted. This was due, in part, to the fact that she could provide reciprocal assistance to her daughter and son-in-law in the form of caring for the house until they were ready to move home on a permanent basis (but also contribute to the household beyond that time). Children (or grandchildren) of older people living in Jōnai also provide assistance in the form of buying groceries (there are no grocery stores within easy walking distance of Jōnai), giving rides for doctor visits, and performing household chores even if they do not co-reside.

Although older people appreciate such help, they also to some extent expect it. Indeed, one seventy-five-year-old woman indicated, "Since I am old, I think it would be good if my daughter did more around here" because she thought her age entitled her to do less housework and gardening. Even while indicating that she would like to get more help from her daughter, she also showed a desire to function independently: "Although I keep the amount secret from my daughter, I get a little more than ¥200,000 per month from my husband's pension. I have enough that I can give some money to my daughter for food. I also can give some money to my grandchildren." The secretive nature of the amount she receives suggests the importance of maintaining some degree of independence from other members of the household and of having a means by which to contribute to the household. In this sense, older people desire and may be able to reciprocate the support they receive. This pattern reflects Japanese cultural ideas in which dependency is complementary; it does not depend on unidirectional passive reliance upon another without some form of reciprocal exchange (Lebra 1976:50). Instead, dependency entails reciprocation either materially or through making concessions (for example, decreased decision-making influence).

The desire to avoid becoming a burden to others (*meiwaku kake-takunai*) or causing a *meiwaku*—a concept that translates as nuisance, trouble, inconvenience, or burden—is a social norm that permeates many facets of Japanese life. In relation to old age, Kinoshita and Kiefer (1992:177) found in their study of a Japanese retirement community that "the need to avoid imposing on others' comfort and freedom" was by far the most important behavioral norm for its residents. Kinoshita and Kiefer's work focuses on a group of people who do not have well-established affective and social bonds. As such, they argue, there is only limited tolerance of behaviors that may cause *meiwaku* to others, there are times at which one cannot avoid causing *meiwaku*, and those instances require calculation as to whether a relationship is sufficiently close or strong to allow for behavior that burdens another. The authors suggest that this is a unique consequence of the retirement community environment in which people lack secure social bonds.

Indeed, given the Japanese emphasis on the family as one context in which individuals (particularly the elderly and children) can legitimately indulge in dependent behavior (*amae*), one expects that the ability to depend upon and potentially burden others would be greatly limited in contexts that lack well-established social bonds (Doi 1973; Johnson 1993). However, even within the family there are limits on how much a member can cause a burden and on how much one is willing to be a burden to others.

As Smith, citing DeVos, notes, the process of socialization in Japan, "produces a self that is not independent of the attitudes and expectations of others" (DeVos and Wagatsuma 1973; Smith 1983:71). One can easily overstate the tendency in Japanese society toward emphasizing belongingness and collectivism, but there is a sense in which individuals are encouraged to identify with the collective goal of any group to which they belong, including household and community (Lebra 1976:25).

The *boke* person cannot identify with the group; he or she acts highly independently and in a way that shows little consideration for the attitudes and expectations of others. In short, the *boke* person does not follow the pattern of interdependent reciprocity that frames Japanese social behavior; he or she does things that do not take others into account (acts independently), but is not autonomous. Instead, he is highly dependent upon others because the *boke* person is a danger to himself. As such, he becomes burdensome and embarrassing to the most immediate group to which he belongs—the household. But, according to informants, the fully *boke* person him or herself is removed from the embarrassment because the *boke* condition means that the person does not care, or is not is aware of what he is doing.

The emphasis on reciprocity and interdependence characteristic of Japanese behavior and social organization helps to clarify why *boke* is feared by many Japanese. In the above narratives, Yoneyama-san and Wakida-san express their concern about not becoming *boke* directly in terms of the importance of not burdening their children. The ability to legitimately depend upon children for social support in old age is tempered by Japanese social norms against burdening others (Traphagan 1998a). A tension arises when the dependent relationship is perceived as becoming burdensome; a situation that is seen as developing in conjunction with the onset of physical and mental decline. Although such incapacitation involves an expectation that the elderly individual will be able to rely on a child for economic and social support, the social costs involved with not being able to reciprocate that support, and of placing a burden on those who must provide help, limit the desire to draw on the well of social and symbolic capital associated with elder status.

To become *boke* has particularly powerful consequences, because it represents a permanent, unrepayable debt incurred by the recipient and thus makes the burden of care seem all the more extreme. This tension between legitimized dependency and avoidance of burdensome behavior is at the basis of why *boke* is feared. To become *boke* means to place undue burden on family members. More importantly, in spite of the fact that people go to great lengths to avoid or delay *boke*, there is considerable uncertainty and even a degree of fatalism about whether, having started down the slope to becoming *boke*, one might ever improve. Hence, the onset of *boke* carries the moral implication of burdening family members without the possibility of being able to reciprocate the care one receives.

To become *boke* is at a fundamental level to disengage from the interdependencies that characterize human nature and society and, thus, to become depersonalized because it is these interdependencies that fundamentally define one as human in the Japanese context (Plath 1980:217). *Boke* means one has started a process of entering into a relationship of increasingly unilateral dependency with a care provider and, thus, disengagement from the relationships of reciprocal interdependency that are considered to be socially normative. To become *boke* is to fall into a position where one's behavior is at odds with the needs of the group—specifically, one's family. While the person experiencing any of the three categories of senility faces the potentiality of this form of dissociation, the causal link to disease that defines AD and *chihō* mitigates the sense that one might have been able to do something to prevent these conditions and, thus, mitigates the moral implications of contracting the conditions. The moral weight of *boke* arises because, unlike unambiguously pathological forms of dementia, individuals may have some degree of agency in terms of preventing or delaying its onset.

In other words, the *boke* person disembodies basic Japanese notions of how people should interact. No longer operating in the framework of reciprocal interdependencies, the *boke* person behaves in a highly independent way, failing to contribute to the communal good. The *boke* person requires care, but has little or no sense that he must function in a way that is socially useful. The *boke* person is seen as ego-centered rather than other-centered. Although self-oriented behavior is perfectly normal in Japan, self-oriented behavior at the expense of others and without consideration for the needs of others falls outside the realm of acceptability.

To return to the question at the beginning of this chapter, people participate in gateball and other activities like it as a means of staving off or, hopefully, even preventing the disembodiment of those social values that define one as a moral being in the Japanese context. The continued embodiment of social values, however, is not merely a matter of individual concern; it is also a matter of concern to the community as a whole.

CHAPTER 8

Taming Oblivion:
Power, Collectivity,
and the Body Politic

The *boke* old person is physically and mentally disoriented; that disorientation being associated with a state of inactivity that draws people out of contexts of social interaction. Inactivity or idleness as opposed to activity is at the root of understanding the role that group activities like gateball play in managing the aging process. Ideas about managing the aging process follow very closely to what Lock found in relation to what she terms the "tempering of bodies" among middle-aged women with respect to participation in various activities (Lock 1993).

Lock states that while telling the stories of their lives, the majority of middle-aged women she interviewed indicated that they invest considerable import in various hobby activities such as flower arranging, calligraphy, or tea ceremony (Lock 1993:205). Lock argues that these activities are closely tied to ideas drawn from Zen and Confucian philosophies in which people

> build their inner strength and discipline to the point where, ideally, they no longer need or desire worldly things. The process of self-cultivation is lifelong and based on an understanding of human perfectibility over time, a state that transcends the inevitable decline of the physical body. (Lock 1993:205)

When one enters into something, whether it be a hobby, a job, or a marriage, one must do so enthusiastically and committedly. Endurance, perseverance, and sticking to a task to the end are emphasized, even if this involves considerable personal hardship. The ability to endure strengthens one's *kokoro* and makes one a better person. As Kondo notes, "throwing one's all into a task is . . . considered intrinsically good" (Kondo 1990:109).

This emphasis on commitment and endurance is a moral concept. Kondo's ethnographic study of a company ethics retreat presents a good picture of how group activities are often aimed at challenging participants to persevere (Kondo 1987; Kondo 1990). In any task, one ought to *gambaru* (persevere) until the task is completed (Singleton 1993). Contests, such as the gateball or ground golf tournaments mentioned in the previous chapters, focus not on winning or losing, but on giving one's all. To be sure, the teams that lose are disappointed and those that win are pleased, but from an organizational perspective the most important aspect of the competition is enthusiastic and committed participation itself. Virtually everyone or every team walks away with some sort of prize. The winners, of course, receive large trophies and medals, but there is usually some sort of consolation prize, such as boxes of tissue paper given out at the end of the tournament, for everyone involved. Having persevered is to have done well, regardless of where one has placed in a contest. To finish last having given it one's best is superior to finishing first without trying one's hardest (Kondo 1990:100).

The notion of perseverance (*gambaru*) is fundamentally a normative (moral) construct. One *ought* to always do one's best. Good and moral persons enthusiastically throw themselves into whatever they are doing, regardless of the hardship involved or the effort required. The person who is unwilling to do this is a person who does not have a sufficiently disciplined *kokoro* (Kondo 1990). In other words, the physical and mental doing of something, and the way in which it is done, is considered an index of one's inner self, one's *kokoro*.

One way to interpret these ideas in relation to activities of old age is to suggest that life itself is a kind of normative task that requires such commitment and endurance. One must *gambaru* to the end—until death. From the perspective of older people, failure to give one's all in the goal of preventing, or at least delaying, the onset of *boke* is a failure to carry out one's responsibility to continually labor to "develop [one's] capacities to the fullest" (Smith 1983:136). The consequence of entrance into this condition entails, ultimately, becoming a burden, at least to family members and possibly to society as a whole if dependence upon social services becomes necessary. Kondo argues that "selves are produced through specific disciplines"; the activities in which people invest their energies are forms of discipline that help to produce, and I would add for older people, *maintain* selves or maintain a person's sense of self-identity as a functioning social entity. For older people the point at which one stops investing energies in building inner strength is the point at which one risks decline into *boke*, the *boke* state being one of having disembodied those values associated with activity that allow one to function as a social entity.

Although persevering at being active is a matter of individual effort, the individual person is both mentally and physically embedded in a social whole. The bodily self is not only an individual body, but also a social body, whose level of activity is an index to the inner condition of its *kokoro*, and to the outer, or extended, condition of the community of which it is a part. As Lock argues, the individual body forms an analog for an anthropomorphized social order:

> Personal responsibility coupled with care and discipline of the body in order that it may function well as a social entity are central to this ideology. An idle body (such as that of a leisured housewife [or, in this context, a *boke* old person]) is anathema, not so much because it does not contribute to the economy but because it fails (not necessarily by choice) to participate actively in what is taken to be a just political order in which activities for the public good take precedence over individual aspirations. (Lock 1993:230–231)

While Lock's work focuses on the ordering of the body in relation to menopause, her analysis is equally applicable to the issue of becoming *boke* in old age. A *boke* person who does not have some other mitigating situation, such as the medical condition of Alzheimer's disease, is a person who has to some degree failed in his or her personal and social responsibility to care for or discipline mind and body.

This brings to mind Mary Douglas's observation that perceptions of the body are constrained by social categories that define the body as a social entity (Douglas 1966). In the case of *boke*, there are two broad categories that shape people's response to or fear of the condition: the inactive body versus the active body. The inactive body is associated with the condition of being *boke* or disoriented. This body is socially constructed as having failed to have sufficiently labored to prevent his or her condition of inactivity/disorientation, failed to embody cultural ideals that emphasize activity and continual self-cultivation. The active body is one that embodies the condition of being oriented toward the realm of social interactions, of carrying out one's social responsibilities to continually work to maintain the ability to function as a social entity.

By focusing attention on the body here, I do not mean to privilege the physical body over *kokoro* as an aspect of the person in Japan. Instead, by body, I follow Strathern's formulation of the "mindful body" as meaning that there is a "mental component to all bodily states and, conversely, a physical component in all mental states" (Strathern 1996:4, see also Scheper-Hughes and Lock 1987). Strathern uses this theoretical formulation in part to avoid the pitfalls of a Cartesian dichotomy that can artificially privilege either the mental or physical aspects of the person. In the Japanese case, recalling the discussion of *kokoro* in the previous chapter, the notion of a mindful body seems particularly appropriate. Viewed as operating in harmony, *kokoro* and *karada* are both implicated in the condition of the person as a psychosomatic whole at any given time. Thus, as I use the term "body" throughout the remainder of this book, I intend for the reader to imagine the notion of a mindful body, a body as the locus of social symbolism and cognitive memory (cultural knowledge) (Strathern 1996:29).

As noted in the previous chapter, a person who has Alzheimer's disease might be described as being *boke*, but this description would not necessarily come with the moral weight that is associated with the less medicalized condition of *boke*. Having been diagnosed as diseased, the Alzheimer's patient would be viewed as having a much more limited ability to manage decline without the assistance of another (e.g., doctors, nurses, family members). The person who has simply allowed him or herself to go *boke* through inactivity, without the intervening action of an external force such as a disease, is different. If otherwise healthy, he or she had some level of control and may have failed to sufficiently make efforts to prevent him/herself from going *boke*. This type of failure is moral.

In the category of *boke*, the individual body (the phenomenologically experienced self) and the social body (the symbolically constructed self), to use Scheper-Hughes and Lock's heuristic terms, can be seen as intersecting. The disoriented individual, the *boke* old person, is both symbolically and socially marginalized from society as a result of having failed to enact his or her own person as a social entity. Inactivity is a metonym for, in the case of the *boke* person, moral failure or a *kokoro* that is in some way defective because it is not aimed toward the social good. Activity is a metonym for a person who is enacting or embodying social values of self-cultivation within the context of social groups. By embodying these values, such a person is automatically working for the social good.

To this point in the book, I have only examined the issue of activity and *boke* from the perspective of what the individual should do in the effort to prevent or control its onset. This, however, should not be viewed as only something generated at the level of the individual. The control of aging bodies is a matter of collective concern and, hence, can also be analyzed at the level of the "body politic" (Scheper-Hughes and Lock 1987).

MANAGING OLD BODIES

As we saw in chapter 3, in the absence of family, many older people depend largely upon the assistance of their neighbors when in times of need or even for daily activities such as shopping, vegetable gardening, or snow shoveling. The other alternative is for people to turn to social services provided by the town government. These services range from the fairly informal, volunteer "Snow Busters" group that walks around after a storm and clears paths for older people, to institutionalized social service programs. There is a common characteristic to town-provided services. With the exception of the town's nursing home, services emphasize in-home assistance to independently living older people or to family members who are caring for older relatives in their homes. Town-provided services available to older people include the following.

Yuaien Nursing Home

The nursing home in town, known as *Yūaien* (incorporating the characters for "friend" 友 and "love" 愛), is the only long-term care facility for older people in Kanegasaki. Yūaien is a long-term care facility that caters to people who have chronic conditions that cannot be handled at home. Most of the people in Yūaien have difficulty walking or are completely unable to walk.

Yūaien has a total of fifty beds, well short of the need in Kanegasaki. In fact, administrators in the home concede, with a considerable degree of frustration, that the wait for entrance into Yūaien is at least two years, and if someone can be cared for at home (even if it is quite difficult) the wait may be much longer. At the time fieldwork was conducted, there were eighteen people on the waiting list for Yūaien. As a result of the long wait, the town hospital serves as an overflow for the nursing home. Older people who need long-term care spend as much as three months in the hospital, return home after recovering to some degree, and then return to the hospital when it is necessary. This creates something of a revolving system in which older people in need of long-term care move back-and-forth between home and hospital until they either succumb or a spot opens in Yūaien. The situation in Kanegasaki follows patterns throughout Japan in which the number of sixty-five and over population accommodated in hospitals for extended stays is three or four times the number accommodated in nursing homes (Campbell 1992:17).

There is, at times, a defensive atmosphere among some Yūaien administrators concerning the fact that few older people are willing to live at a nursing home. During a speech to several older people who had come to visit the facility during its annual open house, the director pointed this hesitation out and also stated that Yūaien should not be viewed like a hospital. It is, he said, intended to be a place to live that people can come and go from just like home, unlike a hospital that requires the permission of the doctor before you can go home. Yūaien, according to the rather idealized views of this administrator, is for people who cannot live entirely on their own, who need some help, but it is

not intended as a hospital environment. The director rather emphatically indicated that Yūaien should not be seen as a last stop prior death.

For the most part, older people do not wish to enter a nursing home
if they become frail. However, the reality of out-migration (chapter 2)
of younger people means that many older people accept eventual residence in a nursing home with a sense of resigned inevitability. As
Watanabe-san (65) explained,

> If I become sick or have problems with my health or come to not live
> with my son [who lives at home] and I have to go to a *rōjin* home, that
> sort of thing is a worry. There is a real problem with Yūaien because
> it is too small, but it is o.k. to go to a nursing home if that is necessary.
> My wife and I often talk about this and we have told our son that we
> do not want to give him worries, so it is o.k. to go to a nursing home.
> Our idea is that if I become sick, my wife will look after me and if my
> wife becomes sick, I will look after her. If it becomes too much, at the
> very end, it is o.k. to go to a nursing home. The current facility
> (Yūaien) is only for the very end of life at the worst situation. Yūaien
> seems like Ubasuteyama, but I wouldn't say that all nursing homes are
> like that.

The director of Yūaien stated that when people show interest in the
home, but there is no space, he often counsels them to go to one of the
homes in neighboring towns of Kitakami or Isawa where there is space.
However, "people are not interested in going to these places," he
explained, "because they feel that they should live in the same community or town where they have resided throughout their adult lives. They
don't want to go to another town to spend the remainder of their lives
far from family and friends." He commented that people feel like they
are going to the mountain (*yama no hō*, an allusion to the story *Ubasuteyama*) when they go to a nursing home in another town. Thus, they
would rather wait, even if there is an opening in another town, for an
opening in the nursing home in their own town.

Activities for the prevention of *boke* at the nursing home include
games that require physical coordination, low-impact physical exercises,
and handicrafts like origami. A favorite game in several nursing homes
I have visited is one that makes use of bean bags that people throw into
low basketball hoops. This game can be played from a sitting position,
thus those confined to wheelchairs can participate.

Day Service Center

The Day Service Center is an important locale where a variety of activities are used to help people avoid the onset of *boke*. Activities such as
the bean bag and hoop game or origami are designed for the purpose of

using one's hands and eyes. There is a great deal of coordination involved. More physically demanding activities begin with stretching exercises in which participants put out their hands in front of their chests (straight arm) and clasp them open and closed. Following this, they do leg lifts while sitting down and stretching their arms over their heads. Each does the best that he or she can and staff members encourage them to work hard at the stretching. The same is true for the games. Staff members encourage everyone to clap when someone succeeds.

The center can only handle about thirty people a day, but they do not have a long list of people waiting to participate. The very nature of this sort of institutionalized setting, which draws from fairly large segments of the town, tends to mitigate against it. During an open house for the Day Service Center, people were encouraged to take advantage of the facility, but there was hesitance. In a casual conversation, one woman indicated,

> The day-service center is good but it's difficult to be a part of because you are always with people who are not really friends. There are a lot of strangers.

During this conversation, one of the women said that because she is old, she will probably make use of it. She said "*osewa ni narimasu*," "I will become a recipient of help," which implies that she is being in some way dependent. She said this with a tone that implied that it wasn't really right to do that, but that given her age, she thought she would go ahead and do so.

Other Services

Other services available to older people in Kanegasaki include the Yūaien Short Stay Program, which allows older people to stay for a week or ten-days at Yūaien, giving in-home caregivers (family members) a break and allowing the older person to get close medical attention if needed, and a meal delivery service in which lunches are delivered to older people at their homes for a fee of ¥400. The town will provide visiting nursing, physical rehabilitation, and health counseling.

Finally, the town provides a Home Helper and Bath Truck program. Through this program, older people living alone can have "home helpers" come once or twice a week to do cleaning, cooking, and to assist in taking a bath. This is particularly helpful for people with a bedridden person in the home. The bath truck provides a portable bath that can be given to a person who is unable to handle the deep Japanese bathtubs on his or her own.

All of these services are administered by the town and funded through a combination of local, prefectural, and national government sources (support is 25 percent local, 25 percent prefectural, and 50 percent national). In addition to town-provided services, the Agricultural Cooperative (JA) also provides Home Helper Services to members of the Co-operative and members of the Cooperative's Women's Association also volunteer to help with the needs of older members.

Although such programs are available, there is some resistance to use. Administrators often comment that they have a difficult time convincing people that it is acceptable, and not an embarrassment, to make use of town-provided services. Indeed, residents of Jōnai rarely make use of these services. Of 93 people over the age of sixty-five surveyed in the hamlet, 83 stated that they had never made use of any of the in-home services available to them, and 78 stated that they had not made use of health counseling or other similar services provided by the town. Of course, many do not need these services, but when in need there is a preference to rely on family members rather than government services.

Perhaps the most interesting, and for this study most important, point about these services is that they virtually all share one thing in common. All of the services provided by the town, with the exception of Yūaien, are intended to support or augment in-home care of frail older people provided by family members—normally the daughter-in-law.

It has been often noted that institutionalization of older people "violates the traditional ideal of co-residence" between parents and, usually, their eldest son and his family (Bethel 1992:110). As of 1985, for instance, 65 percent of Japanese over the age of sixty-five lived with children, as compared to 77 percent in 1970—a trend that has continued into the present (see chapter 1). In areas like Kanegasaki, rural to urban migration of younger people has, of course, had a significant influence on this process, contributing to a situation, as noted in chapter 3 (figure 3.1), where 30 percent of the households in Jōnai consist of older widows/widowers or conjugal pairs.

Services that emphasize in-home care and self-help (counseling services) reinforce the ideological emphasis on focusing health care within the home. By the types of services offered, the town focuses its attention on those who lack family members to care for them. In fact, although town officials would not confirm this, some informants indicated that for those who want help, it is very difficult to get it if there is a female family member who can provide care, even if this requires her to quit her job. Preference will be given to people without a co-resident female who is not earning the household's primary income, even if it means the care provider must quit her job.

Emphasizing the responsibility of families to care for older people who are in need suggests that primary responsibility for maintaining health of mind and body lies in the household and with the individuals who live in the household. But these are not viewed as being independent of the social order. This responsibility has been institutionalized in Kanegasaki, not only in the form of services that encourage in-home care of frail elderly, but also in the form of government-run contexts for group activities that emphasize maintenance of mental and physical health among those older people who have not become frail or *boke*.

TOWN MAKING

The basic ideational theme under which activities for older people (and people of all ages) are institutionally structured in Kanegasaki is a concept known as *machizukuri*, which is part of a community development drive encouraged and, in part, financially supported by the national government (Knight 1994b; Robertson 1991; Kaplan et al. 1998:56–57). In Kanegasaki, the concept of *machizukuri*—which translates literally as "town making"—is an ideology bureaucrats employ to "foster a sense of community and citizenship appropriate to a modern, democratic society" (Bestor 1988:430). The concept is very broadly defined and incorporates an enormous range of activities, events, and building projects that symbolically represent the community.

The most immediately obvious symbols of community that have been constructed through *machizukuri* are a range of new facilities such as a public sewage system to replace the pit toilets common in most houses, the Health and Welfare Center (where, for example, rehabilitation and health counseling for people of all ages is conducted), a public golf course, and a large sports complex including a baseball stadium (capacity over 3,000), track, Olympic swimming pool, squash and racketball courts, and exercise rooms, and the new town hall.

At the center of much of this construction has been a system of facilities called the Shōgai Kyōiku Sentā or Center for Lifelong Education (hereafter referred to as the Center, see Kaplan et al. 1998:51–53 for a discussion of this program at the national level). The Center forms the primary framework for practicing *machizukuri*, because it is here that individuals can engage in the cultivating, or what Kondo would refer to as "crafting," of self-identity that is viewed as part of a larger process of building and maintaining community (Kondo 1990).

In developing the Center, the town used several preexisting *kōminkan*[1] (community halls) as facilities, each of which being situated within one of the six school districts of the town. These facilities became satellite centers and primary points of contact for residents to make use of the facilities and services of the Center for Lifelong Education as a whole. In addition, the town built the sports complex mentioned above, brought the preexisting public library and the culture center (*bunka kaikan*, which is in essence a large meeting hall) administratively into the scope of the Center for Lifelong Education, and built a large new building, the Chūō Shōgai Kyōiku Sentā, (which I will refer to as the Central SKS), which is the main office of the entire system (see figure 8.1.). The Central SKS handles various kinds of activities that are either too expensive or require too much space for the smaller, satellite centers and coordinates activities among the different centers and other facilities in the system.

All of the facilities known specifically as Centers for Lifelong Education (this includes the satellites and the Central SKS; the library, culture center, and sports complex are not referred to as lifelong learning centers, although the sports complex is often called the "Lifelong Sports Center" by public employees) are designed in essentially the same way. They include conference/class rooms, large *tatami* mat rooms in which lectures and various ceremonies are held, a well-equipped kitchen, a gymnasium, and an athletic field. The newest building, which opened in April of 1995, also has a room for aerobic exercise. The Central SKS is larger than the other buildings and includes a 200–seat auditorium, an all-purpose room with a stage for theater productions (in addition to the auditorium), a computer training room (equipped with older eight-bit computers), and several classrooms. In addition to these facilities, the sports complex and public library also have been organizationally placed under the direction of the Center. The Center operates as a separate branch of the government that comes under the direction of both the board of education and the mayor's office. In addition to the actual facilities, the center also is the coordinating vehicle for a variety of committees, such as the Social Education Committee, the Physical Education Committee, and so on (see figure 8.1).

Activities pursued at the centers are very diverse. Sports or games for older people such as gateball, *go*, and ground golf are among the most common activities connected, at least indirectly, to the Center via the Old Persons Club, whose administrative hierarchy makes use of Center facilities for meetings. Exercise classes, group calligraphy lessons, and group instruction in traditional Japanese musical instruments such as *shamisen* and more recently developed instruments such as Taishō *koto*—an electrified string instrument aptly described by an instructor as a cross between a traditional Japanese *koto* and an accordion that was developed in the Taishō period (1912–1925)—are also mainstays of the Center curriculum. At some of the facilities women get together weekly to participate in group sewing meetings or the women's chorus. Local townspeople can make use of conference rooms for meetings and an annual activity of early spring that occurs in several of the centers is

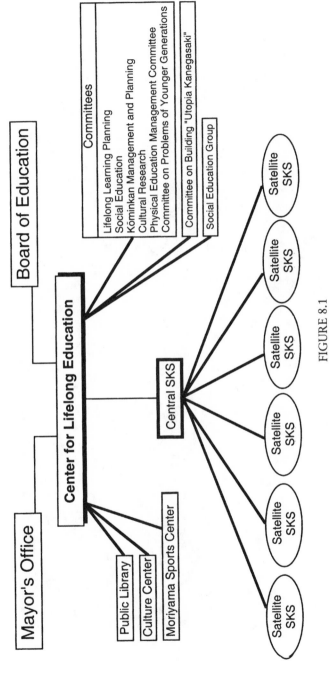

FIGURE 8.1
Organizational structure of Center for Lifelong Education.

FIGURE 8.2

Older women participate in a Taishō Koto class at one of Kanegasaki's Centers for Lifelong Education.

the use of the kitchen facilities by local farmers to make *miso* using soy beans and rice they have grown (*miso* is a paste used as a soup stock).

In addition to the above activities, there are regular lectures and discussions on a wide range of subjects, particularly those of interest to older people. The HBM symposium mentioned in chapter 7, was held at one of the centers. At the Central SKS, there is an annual Senior Citizens' College (*kōreisha daigaku*) that lasted for one week and in 1996 offered classes in dancing, calligraphy, magic, and karaoke. There are also regular club activities such as the Trivia Club and the Town History Club, both of which attract older members of the community, and there are sporting activities for younger people at the sports center, as well as activities such as Taikwando, and English and Chinese conversation classes.

Satellite centers are also frequently used by town bureaucrats to disseminate information related to the political aims of the town government; special public meetings are held occasionally to allow residents to voice their opinions on important topics related to governing and future directions for town planning (these often turn into gripe sessions about specific problems troubling residents). There are also lectures held at the Central SKS on subjects such as maintaining good health in old age. Finally, the Center also holds regular meetings of town officials and important members of the community to discuss future plans and to identify needs and problems related to the promulgation and development of the Center itself. One such meeting I attended was intended to strengthen ties between the Center and the school system in order to get children more involved in the activities of the Center. This was sponsored by the Center and was to be attended by the principals of the kindergarten, elementary, middle, and high schools as well as the corresponding heads of the PTA, although few school officials actually attended.

There are no fixed criteria stipulating what can be done in the Center, but the emphasis is clearly on group or collective activities rather than individual activities. Any group of individuals in the town interested in a particular subject can form a club and use the facilities of the Center. If there are more than ten people who wish to pursue a particular activity, the town will provide money that the group can use to pay an instructor. The range of activities is sometimes surprising. For instance, on one Sunday morning at the Central SKS, a performance held by the *seinenkai* or Young Persons' Association included a man wearing a "naked woman suit"—a flesh-colored cloth suit with a black patch representing pubic hair sewn into the crotch and cloth breasts sewn onto the front—underneath a winter coat. The performer did a somewhat embarrassed stripper act, at which the ten members of the audience, both men and women, laughed heartily.

Certain activities, particularly exercise and sports, are strongly promoted by the town. Under the auspices of the Center, the town sponsors a marathon and various athletic meets for people of different age groups, such as baseball tournaments and volleyball tournaments. For older people, there are a wide range of activities sponsored by the Center, including gateball tournaments, athletic tournaments, dance classes, music classes, the above-mentioned Senior Citizens' College, and so on. During the initial introductions by town leaders (aisatsu), such events are invariably placed into the framework of lifelong education, and one can frequently see townspeople at these events wearing shirts with the slogan "Health Pioneer Town Kanegasaki" on the back (in English). Many public, town-sponsored events begin with group stretching exercises and the town encourages residents of all ages and physical condition to participate in Center exercise classes either at the satellite facilities or the sports center, and to obtain physical workups that show their actual ages as compared to their physical ages—a service provided by the sports center.

INDIVIDUAL AND SOCIAL SELVES

Indeed, it is at the locus of individual selves where machizukuri is enacted. The central ideational theme upon which machizukuri is based—a theme explicitly stated by town officials—is that by improving individuals, the entire town will become a better community in which to live. As the story of the Center's foundation is repeated by current officials of the system, when the previous mayor embarked upon the plan to develop lifelong education and build the Center, he wanted to make a "town of culture" and improve its general living conditions. This was to be done by improving each person. According to the former director of the Central SKS, who went on to become the head of the sports complex, "the idea of lifelong education is connected to the notion that by pursuing learning over the life course, people will continue to better themselves and this will be reflected in the children of the community. If parents better themselves, children will also become better people. If everyone studies [study includes exercise of both mind and body] it will bring in experiences and ideas to the town, improving the community as a whole."

It is here that the collective idea of machizukuri is directly linked to individual selves through a second concept—hitozukuri, which translates literally as "person making." When taken together, these two ideas, as they are employed in Kanegasaki, imply a notion of self-improvement of individuals that generates an improvement of the town as a whole (Kanegasaki Board of Education 1988). In other words, it is through these two concepts that the individual body is connected to the body politic—the collective whole that forms a community and expresses a communal self-identity.

The means to accomplish *hitozukuri* and, thus, *machizukuri* is by encouraging and providing contexts in which individuals in the town can structure their self-identities around the notion of *shōgai kyōiku*, a concept that is difficult to define, even for those involved with the dissemination and promulgation of the ideology. Like *hitozukuri* and *machizukuri*, *shōgai kyōiku* is part of a larger, national discourse that is promoted by the national government and is directly linked to the notion of community building (Hatano 1972; Nanri 1993; Sasaki 1993; Senuma 1993).

In Kanegasaki, as one informant told me, if you ask 100 people, "What is *shōgai kyōiku*?", you will get 100 different answers to the question—photography, sports, music, or even making paper dolls from spent cigarette cartons can qualify as *shōgai kyōiku*. Although the term translates literally as "lifelong education," this translation does not sufficiently convey the meaning as it is reified as an ideational construct. This particular informant suggested that *shōgai kyōiku* is linked to the idea of *ikigai* or one's raison d'être; it is the thing that makes one's life meaningful (Mathews 1995).

Although related to learning and education, rather than emphasizing edification for its own sake, the pedagogical concept of *shōgai kyōiku* emphasizes activity (Thompson 1998). It stresses doing. Other than encouraging physical and mental fitness in general terms, there is little or no direction given from the Center on what should be considered *shōgai kyōiku*. In interviews, this point was repeated frequently by officials involved with the Center. For example, in an open-ended questionnaire given to all employees of the Center (N = 16), the director of one of the satellite centers responded to the question "How would you define *shōgai kyōiku*?" in the following way:

> [*Shōgai kyōiku* is] creating opportunities to learn freely in one's own way and creating opportunities to utilize what one has learned for other people, for the purpose of making one's life meaningful.

In terms of learning, this emphasis on being able to follow whatever path one desires indicates the pedagogical nature of *shōgai kyōiku* and helps us to understand the wide range of activities—from sports to photography to comedy skits with men dressed in naked-women suits—that come under the framework of the Center. Being active, particularly in something that is oriented toward group participation, is an indicator of a healthy self. In the case of *shōgai kyōiku*, the content of the activity in which one engages is not important, rather what matters is that one *is* active—specifically in the activity of self-cultivation, improving or, at least maintaining, mental and physical health. Activity is the point where ideational constructs of *hitozukuri* and *machizukuri* are united in practice through the doing of *shōgai kyōiku*. At the level of the individual, activity indexes a healthy body. At the social level, healthy, active, individual bodies index a healthy communal whole. The symbolic equation here does not appear to indicate that the body is a metaphoric representation of society. Rather, the body is at once a social and individual entity. Society is the symbolic abstraction of the individuals who live within a given geographical and social space, or, to use Bourdieu's terminology, the body is a carrier of a set of dispositions—the individual habitus or form of life—"which are themselves the conduits of interests within the habitus or life-world of the actors" (Bourdieu 1977; Turner 1992:91). The habitus of the individual body/mind is intersubjectively linked to the habitus of the community as a whole. Rather than being a metaphor for the communal whole, the bodies/selves of individuals are the collective source from which the communal whole is abstracted.

The moral weight of this pedagogical ideal focuses not on the self as a discrete, inviolable thing, but on a notion that disciplined, moral bodies are constructed in the context of social activities. This process of constructing disciplined bodies needs to be interpreted within the framework of power relations. *Machizukuri, hitozukuri,* and *shōgai kyōiku* can be understood in part as a broadly conceived strategy through which power is exercised through the control of individual bodies. In other words, these ideological constructs reflect a form of what Foucault calls a "political technology of the body" in that they represent a context for the generation of a kind of knowledge of the body related to the mastering of its forces (Foucault 1977:26).

> The body is directly involved in a political field; power relations have an immediate hold upon it; they invest it, mark it, train it, torture it, force it to carry out tasks, to perform ceremonies, to emit signs. This political investment of the body is bound up, in accordance with complex reciprocal relations, with its economic use; it is largely as a force of production that the body is invested with relations of power and domination. (Foucault 1977:25–26)

Foucault's basic insight that the body is reified or socially constructed within the field of political interactions, or power relations, is important for understanding the construction of self-identity and the managing of aging bodies in Kanegasaki. The Center for Lifelong Education forms an institutionalized framework through which older people can engage in the ongoing project of crafting or maintaining disciplined, moral bodies and, thus manage changes in self-identity associated with old age. This context is politically encouraged, financially supported, and operated by the local government (with assistance from prefectural and national governments, as well).

However, the use of power differs from Foucault's unidirectional imprinting upon the body through forces of domination. In one respect the bodies of those who participate in the Center are, as Foucault would have it, embedded in power relations of dominance, the external discourses of power, that determine what is a moral body. The active body at this level is disciplined and molded by the public discourse that associates the good with the active, and the inactive aging body with antisocial behavior (Turner 1994:38). But to stop at this theoretical juncture would miss the fact that people willingly engage this discourse.

Individuals not only are molded by this discourse, they are active agents who participate in a collective construction of the discourse and exercising of its associated power. There is not a unidirectional power hierarchy operating, rather the Center forms both a context for people to manage their identities through collective activities and a context through which leaders manage the development of the social whole by encouraging self-cultivation (Smith 1983). Since actors are willing participants in this process, dominance relationships should not be taken as superseding the collective exercise of power by both users and promoters of the Center.

Sangren, in a critique of Foucault's use of the concept of power, argues that the exercise of power can operate through "the production of ideologized consciousness" or the "production of cultural selves" (Sangren 1995:21). Power is neither solely "the property of individual subjects nor of intersubjective discourses or practices; rather, it manifests itself in the activities in which both subjects and collective institutions are produced." Power, in the sense that Sangren uses the concept, means control over production, not only in the material sense of the concept, but also in terms of the production and reproduction of social institutions and socialized bodies (Sangren 1995:20). For Sangren, classically Marxian materialist conceptualizations of power as control over material production can be extended to include control over the production of forms of social organization and consciousness (Sangren 1995:26).

In Kanegasaki, the body is not simply the product of discursive activities, shaped and disciplined by discourses of dominance (Turner 1994:38). While people are influenced and encouraged to regulate their bodies through participation in the Center's activities, they are also driven by internal forces that recognize the potential loss of control over social and symbolic capital that arises when a person becomes *boke* and disembodies the values that make one a viable social entity.

The *boke* person is in a situation in which he or she is spending social capital and accessing symbolic capital by the very fact that he or she is receiving care from family members. But control over that capital is in the hands of those providing care. They become the decision-makers. Feelings of love and affection for the *boke* individual form a well of social capital. Nonetheless, in cases where family members feel burdened, the ability of the *boke* person to access such social capital can become weakened and symbolic capital associated with one's position in the household may lose value. The *boke* person, having reduced capacity to function, has diminished ability to make use of accrued capital and capital associated with his or her position in the household, because he or she is not able to exercise it at will (the *boke* person is dependent upon those giving the care). Finally, there is little ability of the *boke* person to replenish spent social capital or recoup loss in value of symbolic capital, because the release from *boke* is death.

In short, the desire to participate in these activities comes both from external and internal forces. Normative values that stress self-cultivation throughout one's life take on particular urgency when one's status as a social entity is threatened by conditions such as *boke*. The bodies are not bodies, in the Foucaultian sense, that are merely "subjected to forces over which they have no control" (Lyon and Barbalet 1994:49). Rather, they are bodies engaged in the production of embodiment itself. That is, they are doing the value of activity and in so doing, embodying that basic value of Japanese culture. It is this doing, itself, that generates the social and symbolic capital associated with being a good, active person.

Social and symbolic capital are not only a property of the individual, but are collectively constructed and reflected in the context of the community, and the Center is an institutionalized framework for collectively generating symbolic and social capital. In short, active selves are healthy selves, healthy selves are disciplined selves that retain embodied social values as they grow older, and healthy selves make a healthy community.

Officials involved in the Center hierarchy clearly use the notion of *shōgai kyōiku* in a manner that is explicitly linked to the extending of individual identities to the level of the body politic. As Takanabe-san, a retired math teacher and a town leader who was involved in the formation of the Center, told me when I asked him about what *shōgai kyōiku* means to him,

> The notion of *shōgai kyōiku* is involved with building a town together by building individuals. This is not simply something that is done alone, but something that is done with other people. The Center allows for many different ideas about what *shōgai kyōiku* is to be followed. It

serves as a central point through which people can follow different ideas about what they want to learn, thus making themselves better and improving the town at the same time.

Furthermore, in the above-mentioned open-ended questionnaire responses to the question "How would you define *shōgai kyōiku?*" all reflected this kind of relationship between the individual and the social whole. Two responses were particularly clear in this:

Assistant Director of the Central SKS:

Making people (*hitozukuri*)—It is difficult to lead a "rich life" and deal with the rapid changes occurring in modern times with only a school education. Social education in a broad sense involves educational activities for living in society, such as job-training. About 90 percent of people want to learn something. They really need to continue to learn for their whole lives. With this situation, there are efforts to organize an environment where people can learn voluntarily and to provide appropriate learning opportunities in public education.

Making the town (*machizukuri*)—By learning we would like to enrich our knowledge and wisdom and create a foundation for constructing a "bright, rich, and comfortable town," together, through various activities in communities, and through construction of an image of the town and through enhancing volunteer spirit.

A means to realize lives with *ikigai*—We want to construct places for conversation and communication and inform more people of the pleasure of communication and learning and stimulate "town lives," "family lives," and "community lives," as well as to assist the formation of groups, such as voluntary learning groups, as necessary.

Assistant Director of a different satellite center:

It is destined that people will change (progress) over their lifetimes. Therefore, they cannot stay with one thing (place) or one way of thinking and, thus, individuals as well as the whole (across races and nations) need to make efforts not to hold back evolution and development in both physical and mental terms. Individual learning and group and community learning are necessary in that framework. And I think other forms of learning are necessary, as well. Public organizations (such as the Center) provide opportunities for those types of learning. It is important that we make daily efforts to avoid providing opportunities in the wrong directions and instead provide opportunities with global vision.

Although both reflect the public discourse that emphasizes the embedding of the individual in the social whole, the first response, in particular, puts this directly into the ideational framework of *machizukuri* and *hitozukuri*. In both cases, there is a clear relationship between the activities of individual selves and the improvement or cultivation of the broader community in which those individuals live.

What these examples point to is an ideational framework in which the body politic is not a metaphor for, but an expression of, the individuals who inhabit it. *Hitozukuri* and *machizukuri* represent the homogenization in ideology of egocentric and sociocentric modes of production and control of minds and bodies, and through those minds and bodies, the social whole. This homogenization process is structured around those activities associated with *shōgai kyōiku*—itself the "homogenization of dispositions and interests," or what Wittgenstein would call a "form of life" (Bourdieu 1990:192; Wittgenstein 1953). The Center represents a context through which individuals in the community can structure their sense of self-identity around a predefined form of life—active and lifelong self-cultivation, the pursuit of *shōgai kyōiku*.

Although leaders in the town are particularly prone to place various public events and activities into the context of *machizukuri* and *shōgai kyōiku*, regular townspeople also often use these notions when referring to their own activities. Particularly when talking to older individuals, who represent the bulk of those who use the Center, *shōgai kyōiku* is an important theme they bring up when talking about themselves in relation to the activities in which they participate. Lifelong education is a discipline many people, not simply town leaders, see as an important facet of their own self-identities and frequently note that activities in which they are engaged, even those that have no connection to the Center, are *shōgai kyōiku*. When discussing *shōgai kyōiku* during a conversation one informant went so far as to define *shōgai kyōiku* as his *ikigai*. He said that it is his fundamental source of meaning in life and is directly connected to his efforts to avoid becoming *boke*. The source of meaning in life for him is the very fact of doing—being active, and, thus, preventing a disorientation from the context of social interaction that comes with inactivity.

The Center is an institution designed for the purpose of generating an ideologized consciousness. Individuals who are involved in the Center participate in the collective exercise of "productive power" as they participate in activities associated with and that further *hitozukuri* and, through that, *machizukuri* (Sangren 1995:21). This productive power is used by those who access the facility to control changes in body/mind that occur with aging. It helps them to maintain healthy, active, and moral minds and bodies. As a result, it provides them with a tool to continually work toward maintaining the embodied social values that define a person as a moral entity.

Institutional frameworks in which self-cultivation, or discipline of one's body, is encouraged and developed "serve as intermediaries between individual intentions to aid the greater society and the actual realization" of the social good (Rohlen 1986:309). Discipline of the body is a means through which social morality is defended, interpreted, and maintained. An orderly society is generated from the level of the individual; through the continual embodiment of those values associated with individual character and personal fulfillment—the cultivation of the individual—an orderly and good social whole is generated. Individuals have a social responsibility to ensure that they continually embody those characteristics associated with a good and moral life and, thus, a good and moral society.

Embodiment, then, is a matter of collective concern and collective exercise of power, not simply in the Foucaultian sense of power as the instrument of dominance, but as the phenomenological ground of the production of persons who embody social values associated with both individual and collective good. Just as embodiment is a matter of collective concern, so is disembodiment. The potential loss of these embodied values is equally the concern of all. As such, institutional frameworks such as the Center become the means through which continued maintenance of the ability to function as a social entity (to embody social values) is, if not ensured, at least encouraged.

CHAPTER 9

Conclusion:
In the Shadow of Obasuteyama

Awakening, at night,
My eyelids are wet with tears:
There was a child who said
"May you live long, without becoming *boke.*"[1]

—Haiku written by Wakida-san (Chapter 7)

In contrast to older Japanese living in institutional settings—who often experience alienation and social distancing from their age peers (Bethel 1992; Kinoshita and Kiefer 1992)—older people living in Jōnai experience little or no social distancing or alienation from people within their own age group. They participate in group activities, attend parties, and visit on a daily basis with their age peers. There are close bonds among neighbors of the same age group within the hamlet, and older people experience a sense camaraderie with their consociates—those with whom they have related across time and experienced varying degrees of intimacy throughout much of their adult lives (Plath 1980). While on the surface, one might take this as painting a rosy picture of aging in rural Japan, older people in Jōnai, like their compatriots elsewhere in Japan, are by no means insulated from stresses of alienation and social distancing from others in their community.

Bethel suggests that because older Japanese continue to maintain expectations of family care, even in the face of economic and social changes that have occurred in Japanese society over the past fifty years, there is a feeling of bitterness among some elderly living in institutions who feel they have been abandoned by their children (Bethel 1992). To some extent, this holds true in Jōnai, as well. Although bitterness may be an overly strong description of how older people feel, there is a definite sense of lamenting by many that their children have left and are unlikely to return to provide care and take over the household.

Although not abandoned in the sense suggested by contemporary symbolic meanings of the Obasuteyama legend, there is a clear feeling among older people that they live in the shadow of Obasuteyama. Any serious decline in health will likely require institutionalization, stimulate a move to live with children in a distant place, or force a child to return to provide care. In such an environment, interdependency often takes on a horizontal character in which people rely upon neighbors and friends of the same age group—their age peers and members of their own age grade—in times of need, rather than a vertical orientation in which they rely on children or grandchildren.

Even those older people who are living in multigeneration families experience alienation from younger family members. There may be only limited interaction among members of the household, and older people often express feelings that their family does not operate in a way that they like. As one eighty-two-year-old woman explained:

> Here in our household everyone has a television in their own room and we all eat at different times. It is rare for all three generations to eat together. It is as though we are three separate families living in the same house.

The system of age grading that operates in the hamlet contributes to the segregation of older people from younger people in daily life. The formal age-grade associations limit social interactions among different age groups because most hamlet-oriented activities are conducted on the basis of age-grade association membership and are, thus, limited to one's age peers. In short, while older people experience integration within the confines of their own age group, they experience segregation and alienation in relation to other age groups. This should not be taken as suggesting that older people would have things differently. Although they do often lament the lack of communication within their families, older people in Jōnai show little interest in socializing with people of other age groups outside of the family unit. For most older people, the social world is limited by preference to people of their own age group—the circle of consociates with whom they have experienced much of their lives.

Smith has suggested, as noted in the previous chapter, that for Japanese one's accomplishment in life is directly related to the extent to which one has labored to develop one's abilities and potentialities. Groups of age peers like the gateball team and institutions such as the Center for Lifelong Education offer support in this endeavor and function as contexts in which public discourses about managing the aging process are promulgated, engaged, and contested. But the individual, as an autonomous entity, is ultimately the primary locus of responsibility for success or failure, because the individual is the one who chooses or fails to be active (Smith 1983:136).

One of the interesting features of the data presented here is that when thinking about how to manage and control the aging process, it is to this value of self-cultivation that people in Japan turn. This helps us to understand the nature of activities, such as games and sports, that play such an important role in the behavior of older people. In many societies where aging has become a major feature of the social landscape, filling the "leisure" time that comes with a period of as much as thirty years (or more) in retirement has become a concern for many older people. There is a sense that older people need to find a lifestyle that is satisfying and find leisure activities that are meaningful in order to fill otherwise empty time (Lawton 1993; Mannell 1993).

This is certainly part of the motivation behind participation in games like gateball. And to some extent this can be seen as an outgrowth of what Cohen eloquently argues is the tendency in gerontology to assume the universal applicability of theories of aging with little or no attention to the role of culture in how people experience and react to the aging process (Cohen 1998:98). In Japan, as in the United States, gerontology has grown as a major field of study, and gerontologists and medical doctors have developed a discourse delineating how to successfully negotiate the later years of life. The enormous push from governmental offices in Japan to keep older people active is part of this discourse and is informed by the writings of the gerontological establishment.

But this is only part of the story. The activities that are directed at helping older people manage and maintain control over embodied values and, thus, prevent or delay the onset of *boke*, are not simply leisure activities, they are a form of work. As such, they are part of the logic of doing that forms the basis for what it is to be human in Japanese culture. In chapter 5, I noted that all of the age-grade associations in the hamlet, with the exception of the Old Persons Club, have clearly assigned work responsibilities in the hamlet. This differs somewhat from Old Persons Clubs in some neighboring towns, which often are responsible for activities like planting flowers in the local park.

While community work assignments of Old Persons Clubs vary from town to town or hamlet to hamlet, they all carry out another, perhaps more important, form of work. Although not administratively formalized as an assigned duty of the Old Persons Club, keeping mentally and physically healthy is the work of the Old Persons Club and of older people in general. In the annual booklet produced by the Jōnai Old Persons Club, the first page of text includes a list of "Our Beliefs" (*watashitachi no shinjō*), the first of which states: "Let us, for the purpose of promoting the maintenance of the health of our bodies (*shintai*), continue to advance on a daily basis bright work and exercise." The list goes on to emphasize being socially involved as important for both mental and physical health. It also emphasizes maintenance of social utility, particularly in the form of visiting bed-ridden elderly at the Yūaien

Nursing Home. The object is to keep active and, thus, healthy both mentally and physically. This contributes to the community because it keeps people doing something in social settings, and as I have stressed earlier, doing is fundamentally important for being a moral person.

David Plath eloquently makes this point in talking about how Japanese people view human relationships when he notes:

> What is special about homo sapiens is its capacity for sentience and spontaneity, for tears and laughter. What is special about an individual is not that he uniquely "has" these capacities but what he "does" with them. (Plath 1980:217)

Humans spend their lives working to carry out their responsibilities to others and to continually improve themselves, in part, through interaction with others. As Plath notes, the "cultural nightmare" of Japan is to be excluded from the realm of social interactions (Plath 1980:217). In order to be a fully realized, mature individual, one must be *in* society as an active player. The *boke* condition is one in which a person has *allowed* himself or herself to drop out of the game. The work of older people is to stay in the game as long as possible.

This is what makes *boke* ultimately a moral construct. Japanese moral values emphasize self-cultivation, social utility, and a sociocentric orientation on the part of persons.[2] To become *boke* is to have failed in one's responsibility to care for oneself and, thus, to remain a member of the social world. The defining feature is activity—inactivity is the route to experiencing the cultural nightmare of which Plath writes.

From an ethnological perspective, this suggests that in contrast to Bourdieu's notion of a durable habitus, the reification of those abstract values that shape and regulate behavior and contribute to the formation of self-identity is tenuous and exists in relation to the condition of the body of that person. *Boke* indexes an inability, or worse unwillingness, to enact agency. It is a loss of the embodied cognitive memory, the cultural knowledge, that makes one a good person. This, in turn, recasts one as dependent, burdensome and, ultimately, antisocial. While diagnosed diseases such as Alzheimer's may put the individual in the same physical and dependent condition, because the *boke* condition is viewed as controllable, or as something one should make every effort to control, it becomes a symbol of moral failure.

To this point, I have investigated the cultural construction of *boke*, but have not considered the function the concept serves in Japanese society. In one sense it seems odd that a concept with such negative moral connotations would become a primary concept that forms one of the central themes through which people think about old age. If *boke* has such negative connotations in Japanese culture, and if the biomedically defined forms of dementia do not carry the same moral weight, one may ask, "Why does the concept *boke* persist?"

Throughout the later chapters of this book, I have explored *boke* as a pattern of meaning in Japanese culture. My analysis has suggested that *boke* is a cultural construct that is ambiguous, polysemous, and sometimes conflicting in the meanings it represents. The condition is distinguished from diseases like Alzheimer's, but it also overlaps with the pathological forms of dementia from which it is more generally set apart on the basis of agency.

In order to explicate this point, it is helpful to employ Horacio Fabrega's ethnomedical approach in which he draws a distinction between illness and disease. Illness, according to Fabrega, is a category that refers to socioculturally defined departures from normal health. Disease, by contrast, is a category defined by members of the biomedical community (Fabrega 1975). Employing this distinction in the Japanese context, it becomes clear that from an ethnomedical perspective *boke* for the most part is perceived as an illness, while *chihō* and AD clearly fall into the category of diseases.

The differentiation between *boke qua* illness and dementia *qua* disease lies in attitudes toward human agency in relation to the onset and progression of the two conditions. To put it rather simply, the term *boke* implies a potential for individual agency. The limits of personal or human control come at the point where the condition becomes unambiguously linked to a disease (Long 1997), where there is a biomedically defined cause; at this point there is no or little potential for agency on the part of the individual. This should not be taken as suggesting that people do not take steps to avoid the onset of the biomedical conditions. They do. The activities aimed at avoiding or delaying *boke* are seen as being generally good for maintaining health, thus other conditions are not necessarily excluded from the purview of their influence. It is at the point where ambiguity dissolves to clarity, at the point of a diagnosis, that older people shift to a sense of resignation—*shō ga nai*—that as a disease, rather than as an illness, senility is beyond a person's ability to direct or control and, thus, not so clearly identified with moral implications (Ohnuki-Tierney 1984).

This point helps in understanding the cultural work that *boke* does in the Japanese context. Unlike unambiguously pathological forms of dementia, with *boke* its very ambiguity allows for the possibility that one may be able to make efforts to prevent or delay its onset.

Boke as a symbol of decline in old age mediates the gap between cultural, moral norms emphasizing the idea that one *should* always be making efforts to be a good individual and, thus, contribute to the social whole, and the fatalistic reality that decline and entrance into the oblivion of seniliy may rob one of the agency needed to do so. The idea that *boke* may respond to actions aimed at preventing it, unlike pathological forms of dementia, allows people to respond to functional decline in old age through the lens of familiar cultural themes that effort and doing are what matter most in life. *Boke* functions to maintain congruity between the cultural framework of meaning and the concrete realities of functional decline that variably take their toll as people grow old (Geertz 1973:169). In short, *boke* persists because in a society that places great emphasis on individual effort and responsibility to others, it provides a category of decline that meshes with the logical frame of Japanese culture that emphasizes a close link between morality and doing.

But the very mediative qualities of the concept make its onset all the more painful. For the *boke* condition is associated with a loss of self-identity and entrance into a form of life outside that of normative social tendencies. It is its negation of agency that forms the basis for it to intersect with a cultural framework that privileges agency as fundamental to humanness. *Boke* is the end of social life and the beginning of a potentially extended period of social dissociation; a social death from which one is released only in physical death.

As I discussed in chapter 7, people hope for a good death, meaning a death that is not preceded by a period of burdensomeness and one-way dependence upon others (as antisocial behavior). The concern or fear older people have about the aging process is not so much with death per se, but with loss of social identity. Indeed, death in Japan does not necessarily mean loss of social identity. As both Smith and Plath have argued, the ancestors are thought to be involved in the realm of the living. They are concerned with the continuity and fortunes of the household and they retain membership in the household after death (Hamabata 1990; Plath 1964:312; Smith 1974:36). The living care for the ancestors by making offerings of food, informing the dead of family news, and caring for the family grave. In return, the ancestors watch over and protect the household of the living. In contrast to *boke*, death does not mean a disembodiment of social values related to reciprocal interactions with others, nor does it mean a loss of social utility. It is, instead, a change in form of these relationships. But the dead remain involved in the realm of the living and continue to have utility as protectors of the household.

By contrast, *boke* places the person into a situation of being physically alive, but socially dead. As such, the *boke* condition represents a depersonalized, liminal state between life and death. Indeed, it is a fate worse than physical death because it dislodges the person from the context of reciprocal obligations and social interactions that define what it is to be human. I do not want to suggest that others, such as family members, necessarily see the *boke* person in this way. As Jenike suggests, for many the personal salience of filial piety appears to be "a natural, affectionate role of helping one's own parents" (Jenike 1997: 233). Providing care often is not so much a burden, but something that many children do with affection, sometimes fulfillment, and a sense that it is part of a natural intergenerational exchange. But for older people, *boke* means unidirectional dependence and social death.

Examination of *boke* as a cultural construct is important for our understanding of Japan, but also raises questions of a more general nature for our understanding of senility, not as a medical condition, but as a culturally constructed feature of human experience. In North America, the medicalization of decline due to aging (whether mental or physical) has lead us to focus on senility as a disease to be conquered without fully understanding the nature of senility as a culturally shaped form of lived experience for those who care for the senile person, those who are growing older and see themselves at risk of becoming senile, and those who become senile themselves. Attempts by the medical establishment, whether in North America or Japan, to universalize the category of senility as a discrete and unambiguous form of pathology present problems of a conceptual nature, because they mask over the dynamic of senility as an attribution of difference to an individual old person or to the elderly as a class of people in a society (Cohen 1995:317). Our understanding of senlity/Alzheimer's/senile dementia/*boke* needs to be placed within the framework of the cultural patterns that shape ways in which people who experience such conditions are classified as social entities.

The definition of *boke* transcends the purely mind/brain approach that characterizes Alzheimer's disease or other forms of senile dementia as they are constructed within medical establishments in Japan or in North America. Indeed, *boke* affects the whole person, as a mental, physical, and social entity. Furthermore, as a matter of collective concern, *boke qua* illness is recontextualized as not simply a personal, but also a social experience and responsibility. The personal space of the body becomes a locale that, in its own disorder, indexes the potential for social disorder, whereas through being active it indexes social order (Becker 1995:113). Clearly, such a specter lying on the horizon of old age gives a culturally bounded meaning to the onset of one's later years and the potential of functional decline that is a powerful influence on how old age is experienced.

By interpreting the experience of senility as it intersects with public discourses on aging, I have attempted to show that people are not only affected by those discourses, but use them to negotiate their movement through the later years of life. The elements of public discourse that are resisted prior to entrance into old age can become the instruments of agency as older people engage in age-appropriate behaviors in an attempt to prevent or delay the onset of functional decline. Just as a person may resist playing gateball when sixty-five, at seventy-five he or she may well be a devoted player in an effort to stave off the onset of *boke*. Indeed, it is the effort of fighting decline that at once keeps older people engaged as social entities and, ultimately, engaged as active agents in the public discourses that define old age and help to shape the experience and meaning of aging in Japan.

The meaning and experience of senility in Japan, as in any society, is not simply a matter of biological or psychological changes that occur as the result of a pathological condition. It is equally a matter of human identities as they change and are negotiated between and among people over their lives. The identity of the senile person is an identity as much integrated into the fabric of meaning, the cultural milieu, as any other person. Thus, understanding the meaning of senility—the ways in which the concept, rather than the condition, of senility is intertwined with the context of social and cultural meanings—begins with understanding the manner in which senility is reified as a category of the person and the cultural factors that contribute to how people respond to its potential onset.

APPENDIX

Report on Accounting of Gateball Club, December 1994–1995

Income	Amount (¥)	Remarks
Brought forward	1,956	
Membership dues	130,000	$12,000 \times 9 = 108,000$ Watanabe-san = 11,000 Suzuki-san = 9,000 Anthropologist = 2,000
Miscellaneous revenue	33,882	
Items	1,691	Remainder of stick fee from last year
	12,000	From Ueno, snack money
	7,191	Snack money from Aki; Nagaoka Onsen Cup
	1,000	From Suzuki
	2,000	From Agricultural Cooperative
	4,000	From Association for Participation in Prefectural Sport and Recreation (APSR)
	3,000	From Director of APSR
Interest (bank)	674	
Total	166,512	

(continued on next page)

Report on Accounting of Gateball Club, December 1994–1995 *(continued)*

Expenses	Amount (¥)	Remarks
Transportation	3,870	Nagaoka Onsen Cup taxi
Study meeting expenses	8,940	4/30 gateball rules study meeting and wild flower watching
Participation fee	2,600	10/29 Prefectural Sport Recreation (1,600), 10/30 Sanpia Kanegasaki Cup (1,000)
Tea and snacks	13,416	
Membership fee return	130,000	
Total	147,826	
Carry forward	7,686	
Total	166,512	

Special accounting:
30,606 – 6,000 (expense for indoor balls) – 10,000 (line tape) = 14,906

NOTES

CHAPTER 1. INTRODUCTION

1. Giddens has also discussed the notion of disembodiment in relation to the schizoid personality (Giddens 1991:59–60).

2. It has been noted on several occasions that the rapid increase in elderly population is a function of a decline in both birth and death rates (Kumagai 1984:191; Bethel 1992:109)

CHAPTER 2. *INAKA*

1. Given the regularly changing dollar/yen exchange rate, when discussing currency, I will use only yen throughout this book. In 1995–96, the exchange rate hovered around ¥100 = $1. Thus, ¥50,000 was about $500.

2. *Enka* is a form of music reminiscent of country music in the United States. It is quite popular among older people.

3. Japanese ideologies related to kinship stipulate the eldest son as successor, however, in practice other children often do succeed. Sometimes younger sons or daughters, depending upon circumstances such as the competence of the eldest son or the lack of male heirs, will also succeed to the household headship. See Hamabata 1990, particularly chapter 5, for a good discussion of variations in descent patterns in Japan. Also, see Brown 1966 and 1968.

CHAPTER 3. HISTORY AND CONTINUITY

1. The terms *inegari* and *inegoki* are dialect for the standard Japanese terms *inekari* and *inekoki.*

2. The phrase translates as "name of Amida Buddha." In the Jōdo sect of Buddhism, faith centers around the belief that sincere vocalization of the name of Amida Buddha is the means by which one can gain entrance into the Pure Land or Buddhist heaven (Bloom 1965).

CHAPTER 4. TALKING ABOUT AGE

1. In the case of twins, the one who is born first is older brother/sister and the one who is born second is younger brother/sister. In some cases, twins may simply refer to each other by name.

2. Another possible translation for the name of the *rōjin kurabu* is Senior Citizens' Club. I have chosen to translate the term literally because it better conveys the connotation of the term *rōjin* to older people living in Jōnai.

CHAPTER 5. AGE GRADING AROUND JŌNAI

1. Although the *seinenbu* literally translates as "Youth Association" I will follow the convention of translating this as Young Men's Association because it is more descriptive of the actual nature of the association (Norbeck 1953).

2. The Old Persons Club is the last age grade that people in Jōnai enter. Hendry observed that in the village in Kyushu she studied there was a further age grade for those over the age of seventy-five called the *keirōkai* (Hendry 1981).

3. The mean age for members in the OPC is 76.99 (σ = 7.26), and for the population of people over the age of sixty in Jōnai the mean is 71.03 (σ = 8.43). In order to determine whether or not the variation in means is statistically significant, a two-sample, one-tailed t-test (H_0: $\mu1$ = $\mu2$, H1: $\mu1$ > $\mu2$) was run using the hypothesis (H_1) that people are likely to delay entrance into the OPC (H_0 = variation in age distributions between club and hamlet is random relative to the age at which one joins the club). Assuming a level of statistical significance of p < .01, the hypothesis is strongly supported with p $\leq$ 0.0001 (difference between means = 5.95, t-statistic = 5.25 with 159 degrees of freedom). These data are also discussed in Traphagan 1998a.

CHAPTER 6. BEING A *RŌJIN*

1. Ground golf is a game that has become popular among older people in Iwate Prefecture in recent years. It follows the rules of golf, but uses a large, wooden club and large, plastic balls that are hit into a circular area at the bottom of the flag for each "hole." The flags/holes can be easily placed in any open space, so there is no need to have a golf course for play. Usually, ground golf groups have their own flags/holes which they set up in parks or playgrounds two or three times a month.

CHAPTER 7. *BOKE* AND THE DISEMBODIMENT OF SOCIAL VALUES

1. This connection between morality and functional decline in old age as a reflection on the character of a family is not unique to Japan. Cohen notes that in India dementia in old age can be stigmatized: "Crazy old people do not belong in old-age homes; they invoke the bad family and challenge the institution's benevolent self-construction" (Cohen 1995:329).

CHAPTER 8. TAMING OBLIVION

1. The term *kōminkan* is still used in reference to some of these facilities, although the town prefers the use of *shōgai kyōiku sentā*. The attempt at con-

verting the *kōminkan* into lifelong learning centers has been so total that many residents are unaware that the centers were ever *kōminkan*—even though some of the buildings retain their original signs over the entrances stating that they are *kōminkan*.

CHAPTER 9. CONCLUSION

1. Many thanks to J. Thomas Rimer who assisted greatly in translating this haiku from the original Japanese. The original Japanese is:

呆けないで生き永らへと言ら子いて覚ぬいる夜の瞼を濡らす

2. By sociocentric, I do not mean collectivist, as has often been attributed to Japanese society in the past. Japanese people assume a basic orientation of the individual toward others. One should be concerned with the interests and needs of others, and anticipate them if possible. In contrast, at least in the ideal, one should not dwell deeply upon one's own interests or needs, particularly if they are at the expense of others.

BIBLIOGRAPHY

Anderson, Nels. 1962. "The Urban Way of Life." *International Journal of Comparative Sociology* 3:175–188.

Ariyoshi, Sawako. 1984. *The Twilight Years*. Mildred Tahara, transl. New York: Kodansha International.

Atchley, Robert C. 1989. "A Continuity Theory of Normal Aging." *The Gerontologist* 29:183–190.

————. 1993. "Continuity Theory and the Evolution of Activity in Later Adulthood." In *Activity and Aging*. J. R. Kelly, ed. Pp. 5–16. Newbury Park, Calif.: Sage.

Bachnik, Jane. 1992. "*Kejime*: Defining a Shifting Self in Multiple Organizational Modes." In *Japanese Sense of Self*. N. R. Rosenberger, ed. Pp. 152–172. New York: Cambridge University Press.

Barth, Fredrik. 1975. *Ritual and Knowledge among the Baktaman of New Guinea*. New Haven: Yale University Press.

Baumann, Gerd. 1996. *Contesting Culture: Discourses of Identity in Multi-Ethnic London*. Cambridge: Cambridge University Press.

Beall, Colleen S. et al. 1996. "Normal versus Pathological Aging: Knowledge of Family Practice Residents." *The Gerontologist* 36(1):113–117.

Beardsley, Richard K., John W. Hall, and Robert E. Ward. 1959. *Village Japan*. Chicago: University of Chicago Press.

Becker, Anne E. 1995. *Body, Self, and Society: The View from Fiji*. Philadelphia: University of Pennsylvania Press.

Befu, Harumi. 1963. "Patrilineal Descent and Personal Kindred in Japan." *American Anthropologist* 95(6):1328–1341.

Bestor, Theodore C. 1988. "Traditionalism and Identity in a Tokyo Neighborhood." In *Urban Life: Readings in Urban Anthropology*. G. Gmelch and W. P. Zenner, eds. Pp. 424–434. Prospect Heights, Ill.: Waveland Press.

Bethel, Diana Lynn. 1992. "Life on Obasuteyama, or, Inside a Japanese Institution for the Elderly." In *Japanese Social Organization*. T. S. Lebra, ed. Pp. 109–134. Honolulu: University of Hawaii Press.

Bloom, Alfred. 1965. *Shinran's Gospel of Pure Grace*. Tucson: University of Arizona Press.

Boddy, Janice. 1989. *Wombs and Alien Spirits: Women, Men and the Zar Cult in Northern Sudan*. Madison: University of Wisconsin Press.

Bourdieu, Pierre. 1977. *Outline of a Theory of Practice*. New York: Cambridge University Press.

————. 1990. *The Logic of Practice*. Richard Nice, transl. Stanford: Stanford University Press.

Bourguignon, Erika, ed. 1973. *Religion, Altered States of Consciousness, and Social Change*. Columbus: Ohio State University Press.

———. 1976. *Possession*. San Francisco: Chandler & Sharp Publishers.

Brinton, Mary C. 1992. "Christmas Cakes and Wedding Cakes: The Social Organization of Japanese Women's Life Course." In *Japanese Social Organization*. T. S. Lebra, ed. Pp. 79–107. Honolulu: University of Hawaii Press.

Brown, Keith. 1966. "Dōzoku and Descent Ideology in Japan." *American Anthropologist* 68:1129–1151.

———. 1968. "The Content of Dōzoku Relationships in Japan." *Ethnology* 7(2):113–138.

———. 1998. "Family History and the Ancestors." Paper presented at the 97th Annual Meetings of the American Anthropological Association, Philadelphia, December 5.

Brown, L. Keith, trans. 1979. *Shinjō: The Chronicle of a Japanese Village*. Pittsburgh: University Center for International Studies, University of Pittsburgh.

Brown, Naomi C. 1998. "Housing the Elderly: The Effects of Current and Projected Demographic Movements on the Composition of Private Family Homes in Contemporary Japan." Paper presented at the 97th Annual Meeting of the American Anthropological Association. Philadelphia, December 5.

Campbell, John Crieghton. 1992. *How Policies Change: The Japanese Government and the Aging Society*. Princeton: Princeton University Press.

Cardona, Ramiro, and Alan Simmons. 1975. "Toward a Model of Migration in Latin America." In *Migration and Urbanization: Models and Adaptive Strategies*. B. M. D. Toit and H. I. Safa, eds. Pp. 19–48. The Hague: Mouton Publishers.

Clark, Scott. 1994. *Japan: A View from the Bath*. Honolulu: University of Hawaii Press.

Creighton, Millie. 1997. "Consuming Rural Japan: The Marketing of Tradition and Nostalgia in the Japanese Travel Industry." *Ethnology* 36(3):239–254.

Cohen, Lawrence. 1995. "Toward an Anthropology of Senility: Anger, Weakness, and Alzheimer's in Banaras, India." *Medical Anthropology Quarterly* 9(3):314–334.

———. 1998. *No Aging in India: Alzheimer's, the Bad Family, and Other Modern Things*. Berkeley: University of California Press.

Comaroff, Jean. 1985. *Body of Power, Spirit of Resistance: A Culture and History of a South African People*. Chicago: University of Chicago Press.

Counts, Dorothy Ayers, and David R. Counts, eds. 1985a. *Aging and Its Transformations: Moving toward Death in Pacific Societies*. Pittsburgh: University of Pittsburgh Press.

———. 1985b. "I'm Not Dead Yet! Aging and Death: Process and Experience in Kaliai." In *Aging and Its Transformations: Moving toward Death in Pacific Societies*. D. A. Counts and D. R. Counts, eds. Pp. 131–156. Pittsburgh: University of Pittsburgh Press.

Coupland, Nikolas et al. 1988. "Accommodating the Elderly: Invoking and Extending a Theory." *Language in Society* 17:1–41.

Cummings, Jeffrey L. 1995. "Dementia: The Failing Brain." *The Lancet* (North American Edition) 345:1481–1484.

DeVos, George A., and Hiroshi Wagatsuma. 1973. *Socialization for Achievement: Essays on the Cultural Psychology of the Japanese.* Berkeley: University of California Press.

Doi, Takeo. 1973. *The Anatomy of Dependence.* New York: Kodansha.

Dore, Ronald P. 1952. "The Ethics of the New Japan." *Pacific Affairs* 25(2): 147–159.

———. 1958. *City Life in Japan.* Berkeley: University of California Press.

———. 1978. *Shinohata: A Portrait of a Japanese Village.* New York: Pantheon Books.

Douglas, Mary. 1966. *Purity and Danger: An Analysis of the Concepts of Pollution and Taboo.* New York: Routledge.

Edwards, Walter. 1989. *Modern Japan through Its Weddings: Gender, Person, and Society in Ritual Portrayal.* Stanford: Stanford University Press.

Embree, John F. 1939. *Suye Mura: A Japanese Village.* Chicago: University of Chicago Press.

Emori, Itsuo. 1976. *Nihon sonraku shakai no kōzō* [The Structure of Japanese Village Society]. Tokyo: Kōbundō.

Endō, Taiyoshi. 1997. *Gēto bōru nyūkin* [A Private School in Gateball]. Tokyo: Gotō Shoin.

Evans-Pritchard, E. E. 1940. *The Nuer.* New York: Oxford University Press.

Fabrega, Horacio. 1975. "The Need for an Ethnomedical Science." *Science* 189:969–975.

Featherman, David L., L. Kevin Selbee, and Karl Ulrich Mayer. 1989. "Social Class and the Structuring of the Life Course in Norway and West Germany." In *Age Structuring in Comparative Perspective.* David I. Kertzer and K. Warner Schaie, eds. Pp. 55–94. Hillsdale, N.J.: Lawrence Erlbaum Associates.

Fortes, Meyer. 1984. "Age, Generation, and Social Structure." In *Age and Anthropological Theory.* David I. Kertzer and Jennie Keith, eds. Pp. 99–122. Ithaca: Cornell University Press.

Foner, Nancy. 1984. *Ages in Conflict.* New York: Columbia University Press.

Foucault, Michel. 1977. *Discipline and Punish: The Birth of the Prison.* Alan Sheridan, transl. New York: Vintage Books.

Frerichs, F., and G. Naegele. 1997. "Discrimination of Older Workers in Germany: Obstacles and Options for the Integration into Employment." *Journal of Aging & Social Policy* 9(1):89–101.

Fukuda, Ajio. 1982. *Nihon sonraku no minzokuteki kōzō* [The Structure of Japanese Village Folk Customs]. Tokyo: Kōbundō.

Fukurai, Hiroshi. 1991. "Japanese Migration in Contemporary Japan: Economic Segmentation and Interprefectural Migration." *Social Biology* 38(1–2):28–50.

Geertz, Clifford. 1973. *The Interpretation of Cultures.* New York: Harper-Collins.

Giddens, Anthony. 1991. *Modernity and Self-Identity: Self and Society in the Late Modern Age.* Stanford: Stanford University Press.

Gmelch, George, and Walter P. Zenner. 1988. "Introduction." In *Urban Life: Readings in Urban Anthropology.* G. Gmelch and W. P. Zenner, eds. Pp. 1–7. Prospect Heights, Ill.: Waveland Press.

Good, Byron J. 1994. *Medicine, Rationality, and Experience: An Anthropological Perspective.* New York: Cambridge University Press.

Hamabata, Matthews Masayuki. 1990. *Crested Kimono: Power and Love in the Japanese Business Family.* Ithaca: Cornell University Press.

Hanley, Susan B., and Kozo Yamamura. 1977. *Economic and Demographic Change in Preindustrial Japan.* Princeton: Princeton University Press.

Hashimoto, Akiko. 1996. *The Gift of Generations: Japanese and American Perspectives on Aging and the Social Contract.* New York: Cambridge University Press.

Hatano, Kanji. 1972. *Shōgai kyōiku ron* [Lifelong Learning Theory]. Tokyo: Shōgakkan.

Hayakawa, Kazuteru. 1992. *Boke nai hanashi, rōke nai hanashi* [Talking about Not Being Senile, Not Being Old]. Tokyo: Shōgakkan.

Hendry, Joy. 1981. "Tomodachi Kō: Age-Mate Groups in Northern Kyushu." *Proceedings of the British Association of Japanese Studies* 6(2):44–56.

Herskovits, Elizabeth. 1995. "Struggling over Subjectivity: Debates about the 'Self' and Alzheimer's Disease." *Medical Anthropology Quarterly* 9(2):146–164.

Henderson, J. N. 1997. "Dementia in Cultural Context: Development and Decline of a Caregiver Support Group in a Latin Population." In *The Cultural Context of Aging: Worldwide Perspectives,* 2nd ed. J. Sokolovsky, ed. Pp. 425–442. Westport, Conn.: Bergin & Garvey.

Henderson, J. N., and M. Gutierrez-Mayka. 1992. "Ethnocultural Themes in Caregiving to Alzheimer's Patients in Hispanic Families." *Clinical Gerontologist* 11:59–74.

Higuchi, Teizo, and Tamotsu Kawamura. 1987. "On the Characteristics of Saving Behavior and Debt Problems in Japanese Farm Households." *Journal of the Faculty of Agriculture, Iwate University* 18(2):99–124.

Ikeda, Hisao. 1995. *Rōnenki chihō wa ranō no korin de fusegeru ka?* [Does Choline from Egg Yolks Protect against Senile Dementia?] Tokyo. Kōdansha.

Imamura, Anne E. 1987. *Urban Japanese Housewives.* Hawaii: University of Hawaii Press.

Inada, Kōji, and Toshio Ozawa. 1985. *Nihon no mukashi banashi tsūkan* [A General Survey of Japanese Folk Stories]. Volume 3: Iwate. Tokyo: Tosho Insatsu Dōhōsha.

Ineichen, Bernard. 1969. "Senile Dementia in Japan: Prevalence and Response." *Social Science & Medicine* 42(2):169–172.

Iwate Prefecture. 1995. *Iwate-ken jinko idō hōkoku nenpō* [Iwate Prefecture Population Movement Annual Report]. Morioka, Japan: Iwate Prefecture Statistics Association.

Jenike, Brenda Robb. 1997. "Gender and Duty in Japan's Aged Society: The Experience of Family Caregivers." In *The Cultural Context of Aging: Worldwide Perspectives.* J. Sokolovsky, ed. Pp. 218–238. Westport Conn.: Bergin & Garvey.

Johnson, Frank A. 1993. *Dependency and Japanese Socialization: Psychoanalytic and Anthropological Investigations into Amae*. New York: New York University Press.

Jussaume, Raymond Adelard. 1991. *Japanese Part-Time Farming: Evolution and Impacts*. Ames: Iowa State University Press.

Kalab, K. A. 1992. "Playing Gateball: A Game of the Japanese Elderly." *Journal of Aging Studies* 6:23–40.

Kanegasaki Town Board of Education. 1988. *Machizukuri o motomete 15 nen* [Desire for Town and People over the Next 15 Years]. Kanegasaki, Japan: Kanegasaki Town Government.

Khachaturian, Zaven S., and Teresa S. Radebaugh. 1996. "Synthesis of Critical Topics in Alzheimer's Disease." In *Alzheimer's Disease: Cause(s), Diagnosis, Treatment, and Care*. Z. S. Khachaturian and T. S. Radebaugh, eds. Pp. 3–12. New York: CRC Press.

Kawano, Satsuki. 1996. "Gender, Liminality and Ritual in Japan: Divination among Single Tokyo Women." *Journal of Ritual Studies* 9(2):65–91.

Kaplan, Matthew et al. 1998. *Intergenerational Programs: Support for Children, Youth, and Elders in Japan*. Albany: State University of New York Press.

Keene, Donald, ed. 1970. *Twenty Plays of the Nō Theatre*. New York: Columbia University Press.

Keith, Jennie et al. 1994. *The Aging Experience: Diversity and Commonality across Cultures*. Thousand Oaks, Calif.: Sage.

Keith, Jennie. 1989. "Cultural Commentary and the Culture of Gerontology." In *Age Structuring in Comparative Perspective*. David I. Kertzer and K. Warner Schaie, eds. Pp. 47–54. Hillsdale, N.J.: Lawrence Erlbaum Associates.

Kertzer, David I., and K. Warner Schaie, eds. 1989. *Age Structuring in Comparative Perspective*. Hillsdale, N.J.: Lawrence Erlbaum Associates.

Kikkawa, Takehiko. 1995. *Hito wa naze bokeru no ka: boke no genin to keā* [Why Do People Become Senile? The Causes and Care of Senility]. Tokyo: Shinseidehansha.

Kinoshita, Yasuhito, and Christie W. Kiefer. 1992. *Refuge of the Honored: Social Organization in a Japanese Retirement Community*. Berkeley: University of California Press.

Knight, John. 1994a. "Rural Revitalization in Japan: Spirit of the Village and Taste of the Country." *Asian Survey* 34:634–646.

———. 1994b. "Town-making in Rural Japan: An Example from Wakayama." *Journal of Rural Studies* 10(3):249–261.

Kondo, Dorinne K. 1987. "Creating an Ideal Self: Theories of Selfhood and Pedagogy at a Japanese Ethics Retreat." *Ethos* 15(3):241–272.

———. 1990. *Crafting Selves: Power, Gender, and Discourses of Identity in a Japanese Workplace*. Chicago: University of Chicago Press.

Kumagai, Fumie. 1984. "The Life Cycle of the Japanese Family." *Journal of Marriage and the Family* 46(1):191–204.

Kurosu, Satomi. 1991. "Suicide in Rural Areas: The Case of Japan 1960–1980." *Rural Sociology* 56(4):603–618.

Kurusawa, Susumu, and Ritsuo Akimoto. 1990. *Chōnaikai to chiiki shūdan* [Neighborhood Associations and Regional Groups]. Tokyo: Mineruvā Shobō.

Lawton, M. Powell. 1993. "Meanings of Activity." In *Activity and Aging.* J. R. Kelly, ed. Pp. 25–41. Newbury Park, Calif.: Sage.

Lebra, Takie Sugiyama. 1976a. "The Dilemma and Strategies of Aging among Contemporary Japanese Women." *Ethnology* 18:337–353.

———. 1976b. *Japanese Patterns of Behavior.* Honolulu: University of Hawaii Press.

———. 1984. *Japanese Women: Constraint and Fulfillment.* Honolulu: University of Hawaii Press.

———. 1992. "Self in Japanese Culture." In *Japanese Sense of Self.* N. R. Rosenberger, ed. Pp. 105–120. New York: Cambridge University Press.

———. 1993. *Above the Clouds: Status Culture of the Modern Japanese Nobility.* Berkeley: University of California Press.

Liaw, Kao-Lee. 1992. "Interprefectural Migration and Its Effects on Prefectural Populations in Japan: An Analysis Based on the 1980 Census." *The Canadian Geographer* 36(4):320–335.

Littlefield, D. 1997, June 12. "Parliament Asked to Back Anti-ageism Bill." *People Management* 3:9.

Lock, Margaret M. 1992. "The Fragile Japanese Family: Narratives about Individualism and the Postmodern State." In *Paths to Asian Medical Knowledge.* C. Leslie and A. Young, eds. Pp. 98–125. Berkeley: University of California Press.

———. 1993. *Encounters with Aging: Mythologies of Menopause in Japan and North America.* Berkeley: University of California Press.

Long, Susan Orpett. 1987. *Family Change and the Life Course in Japan.* Ithaca: East Asia Program, Cornell University.

———. 1997. "Reflections on Becoming a Cucumber: Images of the Good Death in Japan and the U.S." Unpublished Paper Presented at the Center for Japanese Studies, University of Michigan.

Lutz, Catherine, and Lila Abu-Lughod, eds. 1990. *Language and the Politics of Emotion.* Cambridge: Cambridge University Press.

Lyon, M. L., and J. M. Barbalet. 1994. "Society's Body: Emotion and the 'Somatization' of Social Theory." In *Embodiment and Experience.* T. J. Csordas, ed. Pp. 48–66. New York: Cambridge University Press.

Mannell, Roger C. 1993. "High-Investment Activity and Life Satisfaction among Older Adults." In *Activity and Aging: Staying Involved in Later Life.* J. R. Kelly, ed. Pp. 125–145. Newbury Park, Calif.: Sage.

Mathews, Gordon. 1995. *What Makes Life Worth Living? How Japanese and Americans Make Sense of Their Worlds.* Berkeley: University of California Press.

Marshall, Victor W. 1985. "Conclusions: Aging and Dying in Pacific Societies: Implications for Theory in Social Gerontology." In *Aging and Its Transformations: Moving Toward Death in Pacific Societies.* D. A. Counts and D. R. Counts, eds. Pp. 251–274. Pittsburgh: University of Pittsburgh Press.

Martin, Linda G. 1989. "The Graying of Japan." *Population Bulletin* 44(2).

Morris, John C. 1996. "Diagnosis of Alzheimer's Disease." In *Alzheimer's Disease: Cause(s), Diagnosis, Treatment, and Care*. Z. S. Khachaturian and T. S. Radebaugh, eds. Pp. 76–84. New York: CRC Press.

Mosk, C. 1983. *Patriarchy and Fertility: Japan and Sweden, 1880–1960*. New York: Academic Press.

Nakane, Chie. 1967. *Kinship and Economic Organization in Rural Japan*. New York: Humanities Press.

———. 1970. *Japanese Society*. Berkeley: University of California Press.

Nanri, Yoshifumi. 1993. *Asu e no shōgai gakushū to chiikizukuri* [Lifelong Study and Community Building for Tomorrow]. Tokyo: Kouseikan.

Nelson, John K. 1996. *A Year in the Life of a Shinto Shrine*. Seattle: University of Washington Press.

Nihon Gētobōru Rengō [Japan Gateball Union]. 1995. *Kōshiki gētobōru kyōgi kisoku 1995* [Formal Gateball Contest Rules 1995]. Tokyo: Nihon gētobōru rengō.

Noguchi, Paul H. 1983. "Shiranai Station: Not a Destination But a Journey." In *Work and Lifecourse in Japan*. D. W. Plath, ed. Pp. 74–96. Albany: State University of New York Press.

———. 1990. *Delayed Departures, Overdue Arrivals: Industrial Familialism and the Japanese National Railways*. Honolulu: University of Hawaii Press.

Norbeck, Edward. 1953. "Age-Grading in Japan." *American Anthropologist* 55:373–383.

Ochiai, Emiko. 1997. *The Japanese Family System in Transition: A Sociological Analysis of Family Change in Postwar Japan*. Tokyo: LTCB International Library Foundation.

Ogawa, N., and R. D. Retherford. 1997. "Shifting Costs of Caring for the Elderly Back to Families in Japan: Will It Work?" *Population and Development Review* 23(1):59–94.

Ohnuki-Tierney, Emiko. 1984. *Illness and Culture in Contemporary Japan: An Anthropological View*. New York: Cambridge University Press.

Ōki, Yūji. 1991 [1956]. *Nihon no mukashi banashi* [Old Stories of Japan]. Tokyo: Kaisei-sha.

Ots, Thomas. 1994. "The Silenced Body—The Expressive *Leib*: On the Dialectic of Mind and Life in Chinese Cathartic Healing." In *Embodiment and Experience*. T. J. Csordas, ed. Pp. 116–136. New York: Cambridge University Press.

Palmore, Erdman. 1975. *The Honorable Elders: A Cross-Cultural Analysis of Aging in Japan*. Durham, N.C.: Duke University Press.

Parkin, Robert. 1997. *Kinship: An Introduction to the Basic Concepts*. Malden, Mass.: Blackwell Publishers.

Plath, David W. 1964. "Where the Family of God Is the Family: The Role of the Dead in Japanese Households." *American Anthropologist* 66:300–317.

———. 1980. *Long Engagements: Maturity in Modern Japan*. Stanford, Calif.: Stanford University Press.

———. 1989. "Arc, Circle and Sphere: Schedules for Selfhood." In *Constructs for Understanding Japan*. Y. Sugimoto and R. E. Mouer, eds. Japan Studies Series. London: Kegan Paul International.

Plath, David W., ed. 1983. *Work and the Lifecourse in Japan.* Albany: State University of New York Press.

Radcliffe-Brown, A. F. 1929. "Age Organization Terminology." *Man* 29:21.

Riley, Matilda White. 1976. "Age Strata in Social Systems." In *Handbook of Aging and the Social Sciences.* R. Binstock and E. Shanas, eds. New York: Van Nostrand Reinhold.

Roberson, James E. 1995. "Becoming Shkaijin: Working-Class Reproduction in Japan." *Ethnology* 34(4):293–313.

Robertson, Jennifer. 1991. *Native and Newcomer: Making and Remaking a Japanese City.* Berkeley: University of California Press.

Rohlen, Thomas P. 1983. *Japan's High Schools.* Berkeley: University of California Press.

———. 1986. "'Spiritual Education' in a Japanese Bank." In *Japanese Culture and Behavior.* T. S. Lebra and W. P. Lebra, eds. Pp. 307–338. Honolulu: University of Hawaii Press.

Ryan, Ellen B. et al. 1986. "Psycholinguistic and Social Psychological Components of Communication by and with the Elderly." *Language and Communication* 6(1/2):1–24.

Sae, Shūichi. 1995. *Kōraku.* Tokyo: Shichōsha.

Sangree, Walter H. 1989. "Age and Power: Life-Course Trajectories and Age Structuring of Power Relations in East and West Africa." In *Age Structuring in Comparative Perspective.* D. I. Kertzer and K. W. Schaie, eds. Pp. 23–46. Hillsdale, N.J.: Lawrence Erlbaum Associates.

Sangren, P. Steven. 1995. "'Power' against Ideology: A Critique of Foucaultian Usage." *Cultural Anthropology* 10(1):3–40.

Sasaki, Minoru. 1993. *Shōgai gakushū jidai no kōminkan unnei* [Management of the Lifelong Learning Era]. Tokyo: Daiichi hōki shuppan kabushikigaisha.

Scheper-Hughes, Nancy, and Margaret M. Lock. 1987. "The Mindful Body: A Prolegomenon to Future Work in Medical Anthropology." *Medical Anthropology Quarterly* 1(1):1–36.

Senuma, Yoshiaki. 1993. *Shōgai gakushū to chiiki renasansu* [Lifelong Learning and Community Renassaince]. Tokyo: Saidan hōjin zen nihon shakai kyōiku rengōkai.

Seo, Akwi. 1991. "Generations: Retired People." *Look Japan,* April:12.

Shaw, R. Daniel. 1990. *Kandila: Samo Ceremonialism and Interpersonal Relationships.* Ann Arbor: The University of Michigan Press.

Shinohara, Norihiko. 1995. "*Yome fusoku nōka ni mo sekinin*" [Shortage of Farm-Wives Is Also Responsibility of the Farm Household]. *Kahoku Shimpo,* July 20:5.

Singleton, John. 1993. "*Gambaru*: A Japanese Cultural Theory of Learning." In *Japanese Schooling: Patterns of Socialization, Equality, and Political Control.* James J. Shields, ed. Pp. 8–15. University Park: The Pennsylvania State University Press.

Smith, Robert J. 1974. *Ancestor Worship in Contemporary Japan.* Stanford: Stanford University Press.

———. 1983. *Japanese Society: Tradition, Self, and the Social Order.* New York: Cambridge University Press.

Sōmucho (Japanese Government General Affairs Section). 1998. *Kōreika Shakai Hakusho*. Tokyo: Ōkurashō insatsu kyoku.

Stewart, Frank Henderson. 1977. *Fundamentals of Age-Group Systems*. New York: Academic Press.

Strathern, Andrew J. 1996. *Body Thoughts*. Ann Arbor: The University of Michigan Press.

Suenari, Michio. 1981a. "Tshshima nishihama no bon odori to nenrei kaiteisei (1)" [Bon Festival Dance and Age-Grade System of a Fishing Village of Tsushima Island (1)]. *Seishin joshi daigaku ronsō* [Sacred Heart Women's University Studies] 57:37–74.

——. 1981b. "Tshshima nishihama no bon odori to nenrei kaiteisei (2)" [Bon Festival Dance and Age-Grade System of a Fishing Village of Tsushima Island (2)]. *Seishin joshi daigaku ronsō* [Sacred Heart Women's University Studies] 58:136–192.

——. 1996. "Betonamu no kan ni tsuite no oboekaki" [A Note on the Giap as an Age-Grade System]. *Jinruigaku kara mita betonamu shakai no kisoteki kenkyū: Shakai Kōzō to shakai hendō no rironteki kentō* [Anthropological Research on Vietnamese Society: A Theoretical Exploration of Social Structure and Social Change]. M. Suenari, ed. Pp. 44–54. Tokyo: Tokyo University Institute for Research on Oriental Cultures.

Thomas, Keith. 1976. "Age and Authority in Early Modern England." *Proceedings of the British Academy* 42:206–248.

Thompson, Christopher S. 1998. "Anytime, Anyplace, Anybody: Lifelong Learning in a Tohoku Town." Ph.D. dissertation, University of Illinois.

Tinsley, H., T. C. Barrett, and R. A. Kass. 1977. "Leisure Activities and Need Satisfaction." *Journal of Leisure Research* 5:67–73.

Tinsley, H. E. et al. 1985. "A System of Claryfing Leisure Activities in Terms of the Psychological Benefits of Participation Reported by Older Persons." *Journal of Gerontology* 40:172–178.

Tinsley, H. 1984. "The Psychological Benefits of Leisure Participation." *Society and Leisure* 7:125–140.

Traphagan, John W. 1997. "In the Shadow of Obasuteyama: The Disembodiment of Social Values in a Japanese Town." Ph.D. dissertation, University of Pittsburgh.

——. 1998a. "Contesting the Transition to Old Age in Japan." *Ethnology* 37(4):333–350.

——. 1998b. "Localizing Senility: Illness and Agency among Older Japanese." *Journal of Cross-Cultural Gerontology* 13(1):81–98.

——. 1998c. "Reasons for Gateball Participation among Older Japanese." *Journal of Cross-Cultural Gerontology* 13(2):159–175.

Tsukamoto, T., A. Furuno, and K. Yamaji. 1985. *21 Seiki e no hitozukuri machizukuri* [Town-Making and People-Making in the Twenty-First Century]. Tokyo: Nichijyō Shuppan.

Turner, Brian S. 1992. *Regulating Bodies: Essays in Medical Sociology*. London: Routledge.

Turner, Terence. 1994. "Bodies and Anti-Bodies: Flesh and Fetish in Contemporary Social Theory." In *Embodiment and Experience*. T. J. Csordas, ed. Pp. 27–47. New York: Cambridge University Press.

Turner, Trudy R. and Mark L. Weiss. 1994. "The Genetics of Longevity in Humans." In *Biological Anthropology and Aging: Perspectives on Human Variation over the Life Span.* D. E. Crews and R. M. Garruto, eds. Pp. 76–100. New York: Oxford University Press.

Turner, Victor. 1977. *The Ritual Process.* Ithaca: Cornell University Press.

Van Gennep, Arnold. 1960. *The Rites of Passage.* M. B. Vizedom and G. L. Caffee, transl. Chicago: University of Chicago Press.

Vogel, Ezra F. 1971. *Japan's New Middle Class.* Berkeley: University of California Press.

Wittgenstein, Ludwig. 1953. *Philosophical Investigations.* G. E. M. Anscombe, transl. New York: Macmillan.

Wöss, Fleur. 1993. "Pokkuri Temples and Aging: Ritual for Approaching Death." In *Religion and Society in Modern Japan.* M. R. Mullins, S. Susumu, and P. L. Swanson, eds. Pp. 191–202. Berkeley, Calif.: Asian Humanities Press.

Zenkoku shakai fukushi kyōgikai. 1995. *Zusetsu kōreisha hakusho 1995* (Illustrated White Paper on the Elderly, 1995). Tokyo: Zenkoku shakai fukushi kyōgikai.

GLOSSARY OF JAPANESE TERMS*

aka-chan 赤ちゃん
    Baby or infant. The term is usually used from birth to the time walking begins or the time of weaning. In some cases, it is used up to three years old.

akambō 赤ん坊
    Baby or infant. The term is usually used from birth to the time walking begins or the time of weaning. In some cases, it is used up to three years old. Synonym for *aka-chan*.

amae 甘え
    A form of dependent behavior. The implication is that it is part of an interdependent relationship that includes *amayakasu* or indulgence from the person upon whom one is depending. The term has both positive and negative connotations.

arutsuhaimā アルツハイマー
    Alzheimer's disease.

atama 頭
    The head.

boke ぼけ or ボケ
    Normally translated as meaning senility or dementia. The term more accurately reflects a sense of disorientation. In the case of senility, this disorientation is from the realm of social interactions.

bokeru ぼける
    To become *boke*.

---

    * The order in this glossary follows the Roman alphabet rather than the Japanese in order to make use easier for non-Japanese readers. Romanization throughout this book follows the widely used Hepburn system.

boke bōshi ボケ防止
    To avoid becoming *boke*.

bōya/bōt-chan 坊や / 坊ちゃん
    A young boy. Generally used after the period of infancy until entrance into grade school. This term also can be used to refer to someone's son honorifically. The "-chan" ending is a diminutive.

(o)bon お盆
    The festival for the dead that occurs in mid-August.

bunke 分家
    A branch family.

bunkyōbu 文教部
    Education section of the Self-Government Association.

buraku 部落
    A hamlet. This term is used in Tōhoku, where there is no history of the undercaste known as the *burakumin* who, during the Edo period, were the lowest caste in Japanese society and who continue to experience discrimination in the present. In other areas of Japan, this term is no longer generally used. Instead the term *chiku* is used, which is also used sometimes in Kanegasaki. This can be confusing because it also is used to delineate the next level of political organization above the *buraku*.

butsudan 仏壇
    Buddhist altar on which tablets representing the ancestors are kept.

byōdō 平等
    Equality.

chihō 痴呆 (also chihō-shō 痴呆症)
    Dementia, primarily understood as a medical condition. *Rōjinsei chihō-shō* means senile dementia and refers specificially to dementia that occurs in old age.

chiku 地区
    A neighborhood that forms a specified administrative division of the town.

chōnan 長男
    The eldest son in a family.

chōrō 長老
An elder or senior, such as in the village elders or a council of elders.

chūgakusei 中学生
A middle school student.

chūnen 中年
Middle age.

dekasegi 出稼ぎ
Working away from home.

dōkyūsei 同級生
A member of one's class in school. An age-mate.

dōryō 同僚
One's colleague.

dōzoku 同族
Japanese descent units. These are usually hierarchically organized groupings of families consisting of stems and branches that are bound together through ties of mutual obligation, emotive bonds, and economic relationships (see Brown 1966).

erai 偉い
A famous person, a superior, a bigwig.

fujin 婦人
An adult woman. In its use with age-grading practices, this suggests a woman in the middle years of life.

fujinbu 婦人部
The Women's Association. Age-grade association that includes women from some time after marriage until entrance into the Old Persons Club. In some areas, this association is called the *fujinkai*.

fujinkai 婦人会
A women's association similar to the *fujinbu*, however it is organized at local, regional, and national levels. This is not to be confused with hamlet-level *fujinkai* or *fujinbu* that are not necessarily tied to any larger organizational structure.

fukushibu 福祉部
Welfare section of the Self-Government Association.

furui 古い

Old, outdated, obsolete. Older people sometimes use this term to describe both their ideas and themselves.

furusato 故郷

One's home. Can refer both to one's own home and to romanticized images of rural Japan and its associated traditional Japanese values.

gakusei 学生

A student, usually from high school through college, but sometimes also including middle school.

gaman suru 我慢する
gambaru 頑張る

These two terms indicate perseverance or giving it one's all. As moral conceptualizations, these terms are tied to notions of self-discipline and self-control that are central in Japanese culture.

genki 元気

To be energetic. To feel good.

giri 義理

An obligation that does not imply the obligated individual holds any sense of gratitude.

gyōseikai 行政会

Hamlet Administration Association. Administrative arm of the town government that disseminates information to members of individual hamlets.

han 班

The smallest level of community organization above the household. In Kanegasaki, a *han* usually consists of about twenty households. *Han* headship is on a rotating basis, such that all households are at some time the administrative head.

hazukashii 恥ずかしい

Embarrassing.

hito 人

A person. People.

hoken taiikubu 保健体育部

Physical health section of the Self-Government Association.

honke 本家
   A stem family.

honne 本音
   One's true, inner motive.

hotoke 仏
   The Buddha. Also is used to refer to a deceased person.

ie 家
   The household. This can refer to a dwelling place or to a family, including both the living and dead.

ihai 位牌
   Buddhist mortuary tablets. A posthumous name, granted by the temple priest (paid for by the family of the deceased) is written on the tablet and the tablets are kept together in a box which is placed on the family altar (*butsudan*).

ijime 苛め
   Teasing or bullying of other people.

ikigai 生きがい
   One's raison d'être or reason in life. An enormous range of activities can form one's *ikigai*, from sports, to study, to beer drinking (see Matthews 1995).

ikuseikai 育成会
   Upbringing Association. Age-grade association for children following elementary school until graduation from either high school or junior high school, depending upon the locale.

inaka 田舎
   The countryside. Associated with ruralness and traditional Japanese life and values.

inakamono 田舎者
   A person who lives in or is from a rural area.

inegari 稲刈り
   Rice reaping. Mowing of rice plants. This is dialect for *inekari*.

inegoki 稲ごき
   Rice threshing. This is dialect for *inekoki*.

jichikai 自治会
A hamlet Self-Government Association.

jidō 児童
A child or juvenile. Applies to both boys and girls.

jisaboke 時差ぼけ
Jet lag.

jitsunen 実年
A new word for women describing women in middle age. Implies a period of sincerity, kindness, and fidelity.

jō-chan 嬢ちゃん (さん)
A young girl, usually from the end of infancy until entrance into grade school. Also is an honorific term to refer to someone's daughter.

josōzai 除草剤
Chemical weed killer. Herbicide.

jukunen 熟年
A time in life when one has reached a high level of knowledge and sense of familiarity with the world. Suggests either middle age or early old age.

kami 神
A wide range of entities associated with Shinto rituals. The *kami* are connected to protection, fertility, good luck, and so on. Sometimes translated as deities or gods, although this translation is somewhat obfuscatory. (See Nelson 1996.)

kanji 漢字
Ideographic characters brought from Chinese that are used in the Japanese language.

kanreki 還暦
Ritual of passage from middle to old age. Occurs on or around one's sixtieth birthday.

karada 体
The physical human body.

kawaii かわいい
Cute or dear. The term is used in a variety of ways. Both children and old people are often referred to as being *kawaii*.

ki 気

This term is difficult to translate into English. It suggests spirit or energy. It is used in describing various states of mind such as timidity (*ki ga chisai*), impatience (*ki ga aseru*), to name only two. It is an element of the person that often has both bodily and nonbodily characteristics.

kinjo 近所

Neighborhood. Vicinity.

kodomo 子供

A child. This term is an inclusive term that applies to children of all ages.

kodomokai 子供会

Children's Association. Age-grade association for children in elementary school (grades 1 through 6).

kōhai 後輩

One's junior.

kokoro 心

Usually translated as heart, center, or mind. The term indicates a sense of nonphysical innerness, as opposed to the outerness of the physical body. It includes both emotions and logical thought.

kōkōsei 高校生

A high school student.

kokubetsu shiki 告別式

The ceremony of departing for the dead. This usually takes place at a temple (although it may also take place in the home of the deceased or a relative). It is a ceremony for sending of the dead.

kokumin nenkin 国民年金

National pension.

kōreisha 高齢者

An elderly person. This is a fairly recent term that has been used in place of other, less attractive terms.

kōsei nenkin 厚生年金

Employee pension system that covers employees in most companies and pays benefits from age sixty.

koseki 戸籍
    Family register. Includes one's birth, parentage, and history of descent.

kotatsu こたつ
    A foot warmer. A *kotatsu* consists of a low table with a warmer underneath. A quilt or blanket is placed between the table top and the frame/legs and an electric warmer is attached to the bottom of the frame. People sit around this table with their legs underneath and the quilt over their laps. In some cases, the table/quilt combination sits over a pit into which one places one's feet. In the bottom of the pit there is placed a kerosene heater that provides warmth.

ku 区
    A ward or district within a larger governmental unit such as a city or town.

kuchō 区長
    The head or chief of a ward.

kyōdai 兄弟
    Sibling. When talking about the number of siblings in a family, this term includes all children of the same generation.

kyōsai kumiai 共済組合
    Mutual assistance associations.

maemuki ni 前向きに
    Facing or aimed forward (in the example in this book it implies toward the future).

mamoru 守る
    To defend or protect.

meiwaku 迷惑
    A burden, trouble, inconvenience, or nuisance. The phrase *meiwaku kaketakunai* indicates that one does not want to impose a burden upon others.

mōroku 耄碌
    Dotage, befuddlement.

mukoyōshi 婿養子
    A man adopted into a family as husband to the daughter of that family.

mune 胸
> The chest.

myōjin 明神
> A deity (*kami*) devoted to the protection of one's household, including both the property, the inhabitants, and ancestors.

nembutsu 念仏
> A form of Buddhist prayer.

nembutsu-kō 念仏講
> A lay organization for the purpose of group prayer, normally done at the time of a funeral.

nenchōsha 年長者
> A superior in age, an elder.

nenpai 年配
> A person of many years.

nō 脳
> The brain.

nōka 農家
> A farming household.

nyūji 乳児
> An infant. The term suggests a baby who is still nursing.

(o)ba-san おばさん
> Aunt. Also identifies a woman who is middle-aged or significantly older than another person who is using the term. Can be used by nonkin as an identifier of relative age.

(o)baa-san (-chan) おばあさん（ちゃん）
> Grandmother. Also identifies a woman who is perceived as having entered old age. Can be used by nonkin as an identifier of relative age.

(o)haka お墓
> A grave site that contains the remains of all deceased household members.

(o)ji-san おじさん
> Uncle. Also identifies a man who is perceived as having entered middle age. Can be used in reference to male nonkin as an identifier of relative age.

(o)jii-san (-chan) おじいさん (ちゃん)

Grandfather. Also identifies a man who is perceived as having entered old age. Can by used in reference to male nonkin as an identifier of relative age.

(o)mairi お参り

Visiting to pray. For example, one goes to a shrine to do *omairi*.

(o)miai お見合い

Arranged marriage. An interview meeting for the purpose of introducing potential marriage partners.

(o)mukae お迎え

To be taken away. When older Japanese use this term, they often use it as part of the phrase *omukae ga konai*, which literally means "being taken away does not come" or I have yet to die. So frequently is this phrase used by the very old that case workers and others have told me that for many it is little more than *aisatsu* or a greeting. It does not necessarily indicate that one wants to die, although in many cases it does.

on 恩

A debt one is obliged to carry out and that is done with a feeling of gratitude for something previously received. A sense of moral indebtedness. See Jenike 1997:233 for a discussion of *on* as it relates to the notion of *gimu* (obligation).

(o)nee-san お姉さん

Older sister. Can also be used with nonkin as an identifier of relative age and familiarity.

(o)nii-san お兄さん

Older brother. Can also be used with nonkin as an identifier of relative age and familiarity.

otona 大人

An adult.

oya kōkō 親孝行

Filial piety. Being good to one's parents. A dutiful and obedient child will be referred to using this term. This term is also sometimes used in reference to being good to one's ancestors, as well.

pokkuri ぽっくり

Sudden, unexpected, in an instant.

pokkuri–dera ぽっくり寺
   A Buddhist temple at which people pray for a sudden death. Typically this sort of temple has a statue of Kannon, the Buddhist god associated with mercy. People request a sudden, or merciful death, devoid of long-term illness.

rajio taisō ラジオ体操
   Early morning exercise sessions that are usually held in a local park. The are accompanied an NHK broadcast of an exercise program at 6:30 a.m.

rōjin 老人
   Old person. Officially a person becomes *rōjin* at the age of sixty-five, although people sometimes use the term earlier or prefer to delay use of the term until later in life.

rōjinteki 老人的
   Like an old person. Unflatteringly implies behavior that is characteristic of the elderly.

rōjin hōmu 老人ホーム
   A nursing home. There are various types of nursing homes in Japan. For a detailed description see Campbell 1992.

rōjin kurabu 老人クラブ
   Old Persons Club. This is the age-grade association for people who are over sixty or sixty-five.

rōjinsei chihō 老人性痴呆
   Senile dementia.

rōnen 老年
   The years of old age.

rōreisha 老齢者
   A person who is old or advanced in age; from *rōrei* (老齢), meaning old age.

sabishii 寂しい
   Sad or lonely.

seijinshiki 成人式
   Ceremony for coming of age. This takes place at the turn of the new year. People at the age of twenty normally visit a shrine and women wear often extravagant kimonos.

seinen 青年
   Youth. Refers to young adulthood.

seinen 成年
   Full age. Refers to the age of twenty, at which time one is officially considered an adult.

seinenbu 青年部
   Young Men's Association. Age-grade association for men from entrance into adulthood until their early to middle forties. Men often leave this organization at the age of *yakudoshi* (42).

seinenkai 青年会
   Young person's association similar to the *seinenbu*, however it is part of local, regional, and national organizations. In some areas, hamlet-level young men's associations like the *seinenbu* in Kanegasaki's hamlets are called *seinenkai*. In this case, these are not necessarily tied to larger organizational units.

seishin 精神
   Spirit, mind, soul. Generally associated with mental or spiritual aspects of the person. There is an element of meaning in this term associated with morality. *Seishin kyōiku*, as it was used prior to the Pacific War, meant moral education and still carries a sense of creating a disciplined, thus moral, self.

seito 生徒
   A pupil, student.

senpai 先輩
   One's senior.

senzenha 戦前派
   The prewar generation. See Plath 1980:50.

shakaijin 社会人
   A public person. A person who has entered society and is functioning as an adult (e.g., holds a job).

shinshin 心身
   The mind and body as a whole.

shintai 身体
   The human body as a physical entity.

shirubā シルバー
Silver (from English). A new term used in reference to older people, such as "silver seat," a reserved space for older people on public transportation.

shōgai kyōiku 生涯教育
Lifelong education or learning.

shōgakusei 小学生
An elementary school student, grades one through six.

shō ga nai しょうがない
The phrase litterally translates as "there is no way" or there is nothing one can do. It implies a sense of resignation to an untennable situation.

shōgi 将棋
Japanese chess.

sōmubu 総務部
The general affairs section of the Self-Government Association.

sōnen 壮年
Prime of manhood. This is a period of one's forties and fifties at which one is seen as being at his peak of abilities.

sōnenbu 壮年部
Middle-Aged Men's (Prime of Manhood) Association. This age grade association does not exist in all hamlets. It includes men who have left the Young Men's Association and allows participation up to the age of around 55 or 60 (depending upon the locale).

soto 外
Outside. Can refer to physical spaces such as the outside of a house versus the inside. It also can refer to relative social distance and intimacy such as outside a group as opposed to inside (intimate).

takaki たかき
Flooding rice fields with water.

takuan 沢庵
A pickled radish (daikon) that is extremely salty and is usually either yellow or white.

tanemaki 種蒔き
Sowing rice seeds into beds prior to transplanting to fields.

tatami 畳
Straw mats placed on the floor of many rooms in most Japanese homes and also in some public meeting places.

tauchi 田打
Tilling of a paddy field.

taue 田植
Rice planting; rice transplantation.

toshiyori 年寄り
A person of upper years; an old person.

tsumetai 冷たい
Cold. In general this refers to something that is cold to the touch. However, a cold-hearted or unpleasant person can be described with this term as well.

uchi 内
Inside. Can refer to physical spaces such as the inside of a house versus the outside. It also refers to relative social spaces of distance and intimacy such as inside a group as opposed to outside.

wagamama 我がまま
Selfishness.

wakatsuma 若妻
A young married woman.

wakatsumakai 若妻会
Young Married Women's Association. This age-grade association includes newly married women who have yet to bear children.

yakudoshi 厄年
Inauspicious years. For men, yakudoshi comes at the ages of 25 and 42, for women it comes at the ages of 19 and 33. These are years in which one is more likely to encounter misfortune than other years. At the new year for the year of this birthday, people are likely to visit a shrine for good luck throughout that year.

yasashii 優しい
Gentle or kind. A person who is warm-hearted.

yōji 幼児
Childhood, the early years of life. This is sometimes used to refer to infancy and sometimes used to refer to toddler years.

yōnen　幼年
Early years of life.

zaisan 財産
An estate, fortune. One's property.

INDEX

Abu-Lughod, Lila, 10
activity
  and *boke*, 5
  domains of, 113
  Japanese concepts of self in
    relation to, 5, 157–59
  as social responsibility, 144,
    158–59
activity and inactivity, 144, 157
activities of elderly, 113–14, 157
adoption
  of blood related children, 52–57
  of husband, 52
age
  incongruity, 73, 86
  Japanese calendar and, 73–74
  reckoning, 73
age-appropriate behavior, 13–14,
  111–12
age grades, 85–107, 111, 145, 180,
  190 n
  as concept in anthropology, 85–86
age-grading practices, 9, 85–107
age identities, 106
age sets, 86
age-structuring practices, 74
age stratification, 85–86
age terms, 73–84
  periodic, 79–83
  relational, 75–79
  subjective response to, 98–102
agency, 184–86
aging
  as biological process, 8
  as cultural process, 8–9
  in England, 105
  managing, 180–81
  public discourse on, 9–10

aging bodies, 172
agricultural cooperatives, 23, 32, 114,
  128, 131
Akimoto, Ritsuo, 87
alienation, 45–46, 179–80
Alzheimer's disease, 2–3, 144, 154,
  159, 183, 185
  compared to *boke*, 136
  incidence in Japan, 11
ancestors, 52, 55–60
Anderson, Nels, 32
arranged marriage, 38
Ariyoshi, Sawako, 137
Atchley, Robert, 111, 113

Barbalet, J. M., 174
Bachnik, Jane, 139
Barth, Fredrik, 6
Baumann, Gerd, 10
Beall, Colleen, 3
Beardsley, Richard, 49, 86, 103
Becker, Ann, 185
Befu, Harumi, 50
Bestor, Theodore, 165
Bethel, Diana Lynn, 150, 164, 179,
  189 n
biomedical discourses
  in U.S., 2–3
  in Japan, 3–4
Bloom, Alfred, 189 n
body, 14, 136
  and *boke*, 137, 139, 159–60
  control over, 107, 133
  discipline of, 165, 176–77
  inactive vs. active, 159
  as index to inner condition of
    kokoro, 158–60
  and metonymy, 112

219